DOORS TO MADAME MARIE

"The heart is like an apartment."
—MADAME MARIE

DOORS TO
MADAME
MARIE

Odette Meyers

A McLellan Book
University of Washington Press
Seattle and London

This book is published with the assistance of a grant from the
McLellan Endowed Series Fund, established through the generosity of
Martha McCleary McLellan and Mary McLellan Williams.

Library of Congress Cataloging in Publication Data

Meyers, Odette.
Doors to Madame Marie / Odette Meyers.
p.   cm.
ISBN 0-295-97576-8 (alk. paper)
1. Meyers, Odette—Childhood and youth.   2. Jews—France—Biography.
3. Chotel, Marie—Biography.   4. Holocaust, Jewish (1939–1945)—
France—Personal narratives.   5. Righteous Gentiles in the Holocaust—
France.   6. Jewish children in the Holocaust—France.
7. France—Ethnic relations.   I. Title.
DS135.F9M49   1997   940.53′18′092—dc20
[B]   96-28470
CIP

The paper used in this publication is acid-free and recycled from
10 percent postconsumer and at least 50 percent pre-consumer waste.
It meets the minimum requirements of American National
Standard for Information Sciences—Permanence of Paper for
Printed Library Materials, ANSI A39.48-1984.

DEDICATED TO

all Jewish children caught in the Shoah
—those who did not survive
and those who did

and also to the memory of

my husband, lyric poet Bert Meyers
—and my close friend,
children's book illustrator Margot Zemach

PREFACE

IN MAY 1949, my family migrated from Paris, France, to Los Angeles, California, where one of my father's brothers was a union organizer in the garment trade and had found a job for him. My parents decided to move because of rumors of the imminent outbreak of World War III as a result of the siege of Berlin; they felt that they had experienced World War I in Poland, World War II in France and Germany; they simply didn't want to stay around for World War III. As for me, a fourteen-year-old in love with my native city of Paris—a love I apparently shared with the whole world—I much resented the move. But I was a minor and had no choice in the matter.

I adapted, of course, and little by little I found much to love in my new country. In time, there were friends, California wildflowers, American poetry, American folk songs, American landscape as seen through a train window or from the back of a truck, and eventually, an American lyric poet whom I married and with whom I had two children. Paris, my French childhood, the war—all this turned into distant, occasional memories neatly folded away for brief answers to questions arising from my French accent: Where had I come from? And sometimes, especially from Jews: Was I there then? and if so, what happened to me? In those days, the answer to that last question was easy: Nothing happened to me. I was lucky. In German-occupied Paris, I was saved by my self-declared godmother, Madame Marie, the concierge of our working-class-district apartment house. After that, I had lived under false identity in the remote countryside, first with a foster family, and then with my mother for the duration of the war.

I DID NOT RETURN to France until Christmas vacation of 1967. What broke the spell of my long, uninterrupted exile was a letter from Madame Marie's husband, Monsieur Henri. Madame Marie had died, and Monsieur Henri wrote: "If you want to see me again, come soon." And so I did. And we talked and talked about Madame Marie. And once back home, I continued, this time by mail, to ask him questions about my godmother who had indeed fulfilled her role, not only in shaping my soul but in saving my life and the life of my mother. A few letters from him gave me his answers. Then he, too, died.

From then on, I became obsessed with trips to Paris which I made every few years. Each time, I went first to my old neighborhood, to visit my ghosts. Standing across the street from my apartment house, I could visualise Madame Marie sitting at her sewing machine. As always, she brought me comfort, equilibrium. And then I could move on, do the other things, see the other people on my agenda.

As long as I kept Madame Marie to myself, or spoke of her simply as the good woman who had rescued me, she remained my personal icon. My difficulties began when I was asked to make public presentations, to speak of her in the larger context of my story as a Jewish child in danger during the Shoah. By then, the enormity of the Holocaust, the grief of the survivors, the incomprehensible cruelty of the persecutors and of the Third Reich, all this had been studied. What stayed a mystery was the altruistic behavior of Gentiles who had rescued Jews and others at the risk of their own lives. Madame Marie was in that category. I had been close to her. Could I explain why and how she came to do what she did? Could I explain why, as we would find out much later, she had helped not only my family but also other Jews and members of the Resistance? I didn't know if I could come up with a clear explanation. I wasn't sure. I searched my memories, those of my parents, books on rescuers. I participated in conferences, read articles, wrote some. It only got more complicated. It had been much easier simply to praise her, to have her as an icon, as my own religious medal that would protect me from harm.

In the meantime, while interest in the Shoah increased, the number of camp survivors available for public presentations decreased. Child survivors were then called upon to replace them. Occasions to speak of my childhood with Madame Marie multiplied. I spoke in classrooms of elementary schools, high schools, and colleges, in churches and temples, at scholarly conventions and survivor gatherings. And in 1984, I told her story as part of a film called *The Courage to Care: Gentile Rescuers of Jews during the Holocaust*. The film was nominated for an Academy Award, and a book of the same title was published by New York University Press. Questions, reactions, comments from all these audiences stretched my memory. It became clear to me that people of all ages liked my Madame Marie. Children wrote: "When I grow up, I hope I can be like Madame Marie and stand up for people who are persecuted." In our dangerous world, she was of great comfort. She was a gift. It was clearly up to me to take the time needed to present her in book form, so she could continue being a gift. But how to do her justice?

In his poem "The Pretty Redhead," French poet Guillaume Apollinaire says of modern poets that they seek to give color and shape to overlooked mysteries. And among such mysteries is goodness: "We would explore goodness, a vast country where everything is silent." It is hard to speak of what is silent. How then should I get to the words that would open doors to Madame Marie, to let us see her goodness and begin to understand its effects?

I FIRST CONSIDERED writing a standard kind of biography of Madame Marie. But there were so many parts of her life I didn't know; would I have to fictionalize them? While I was a resident at Yaddo Artists Colony in 1984, a novelist suggested that it would be more honest and more interesting to stick to the truth and put myself in the story: it would also give me the widest range to show Madame Marie's full impact on at least one life—mine. That was excellent advice and I followed it. It necessitated, though, confronting my own story as a Jewish child who had abruptly entered the Christian world during the war and exited it painfully after the war. I would have to sort out what had happened to my pre-war world: who had survived and who had not — and how. This further complicated what had appeared to be a very simple tale of rescue and survival.

It took me many years to complete the manuscript. The demands of work, family, and community involvement had always to be met. As I continued to write in private and to tell the story in public, I was pressed to refine my memories, to hone my storytelling, to distill and streamline the complexities.

I WROTE THIS BOOK in occasional and much-interrupted solitude, sometimes with great pleasure, sometimes with fear of not doing the subject justice. Still, it would not have reached this point without the help of many people. I want to thank first my family: My "dybbuk" husband, Bert Meyers; my daughter, Anat Meyers, and her husband, David Seifert; my son, Daniel Meyers; my sister, Anne-Marie Miller; and my parents, Bertha and George Miller. Also, thanks to my editor at the University of Washington Press, Gretchen Van Meter, whose sensitivity and clarity helped improve the completed manuscript, and to my Yaddo novelist friend, Peter Speilberg, whose advice helped formulate its structure. For sponsoring my benefit party, which gave me money to purchase a computer and time to write: Seymour Fromer, director of Judah Magnes Museum, and his assistant Paula Friedman, as well as Eda Pell and Milly Mogulof; and for hosting the party with much flair, Lynda Koolish. And my thanks, for reading my manuscript and offering comments and encouragement, to Rasa Gustaitis, Gila Bercovitch, Patricia Dacey, Rita Kuhn, Shirley Stuart, Ursula Sherman, Andrée Teperman-Schute,

David Shaddock and Toby Furash, Susan Bowie-McCoy, Gloria Orenstein, and Margo Hackett and Bob Yagura. My thanks also for other varied but vital support to Fred Rosenbaum, director of Lehraus Judaica, Janet Kransberg, Dr. Harvey Peskin, Monique Saigal, Gerda Mathan, Arnoldine and Dr. Herman Berlin, Glenn Reeder and Duane Aten, Abigail Van Allyn, Max and Estelle Novak, Sharon Gerard, Maya Narayan, Arisika Razak, Eva Maiden and Marty Primack, Glenda Raikes and Terence Bennett, Sue Flynn and Eric Houts, Yishai Hope, Leah and Jim Watson, Ruth Koeninsberg, Linda Miller, Omar Gulchin, Jessica Rosenfeld, Miri Malmquist, Paul and Kathy Vergeer, and Sid Gershgoren. Special thanks to all my adopted "cousins" in my Berkeley kinship group of child survivors, *Yaldei Hashoah*, and to all my other "relations" in the network of Holocaust survivors of the San Francisco Bay Area, *Tikvah Acharei Hashoah* (Hope After the Holocaust). Also of the Bay Area: the Holocaust Center of Northern California, with its research and education programs, and The Oral History Project, which recorded so many of our stories. And in France, to Monique and Jacques Raffin of Chavagnes-en-Paillers, Cécile Popowicz, Pérel Wilgowicz, Suzanne and Michel Sablic, Ida Kaptur, Edith Sorel, and Marlotte Reinharez of Paris.

Thanks for the comments, the advice, the encouragement, the love and friendship. Also, to all the wonderful teachers and their students—thanks for the questions. You asked for the book. Here it is. It is the truth I remember, except that some of the names are changed.

DOORS TO MADAME MARIE

ONE

M A D A M E M A R I E came into my life before I did.

W H E N M Y M O T H E R was pregnant with me, in 1934, my parents were then living in a fifth-floor loft of which they were very proud. True, there was hardly any standing room for two persons, and no window except an old skylight, through which a sudden rainfall would pour down on their mattress, and the wooden railing to the last flight of stairs had been replaced by a thick rope—but, unlike most new immigrant workers in Paris, my parents were not confined to a transient hotel room: they had their very own place! That spring, though, their American relatives, on a visit to Paris, were horrified at the condition of their housing and insisted upon giving them the required "key money"—that customary, relatively substantial rental deposit—for a better apartment; now, they could find "a decent place in which to raise a child." My parents started looking. None too soon, as my mother's pregnancy was beginning to show.

One afternoon, my mother, in a loose dress, came to a grey apartment building, old but solid, facing a pleasant town square complete with trees, benches, one statue, and one water fountain. She had heard there was a vacancy. Worried about her foreign accent, her Jewish looks, her slightly bulging belly, she crossed the lobby and saw the alert concierge open the door of her ground-floor "loge." Stern but amiable, Madame Marie listened to her inquiry, then preceded her up one flight of stairs that had a well-polished wooden railing, and immediately they faced the door of the vacant apartment.

Though it was midday, Madame Marie turned on the light. My mother could then see a small but totally furnished room, with a green sofa against one wall, and near it, against another wall, a drop-leaf table forming a half circle with its own three chairs. But that was not the end of the wonders: another door to another small room, the size of a closet, which actually had a toilet in it, a private one with a seat, instead of the usual squatting Turkish-style toilet situated on every floor to be shared by all the tenants! And to the right was a tiny kitchen. Two people would easily crowd it, but it had a sink with cold running water, a coal stove for winter and a two-burner gas stove for the rest of the year, old and shabby cupboards, shelves high up under the ceiling. My mother could hardly contain her admiration.

But there was yet one more room to see, off the dining area at the end of a brief hallway. And that room needed no artificial light: it had a full window with its own set of wooden shutters for nighttime privacy. In the afternoon daylight, you had a view of the street and the trees, the statue, the water fountain. The room also had a double bed and an armoire and a pot-bellied stove for winter heat. The whole apartment had a faded wallpaper with a memory of a green flower-print; the ceiling had many cracks; the worn furniture had been used by generations of poor people. If the American relatives had still been around to see it, they would have thought it ideal for a bachelor on a modest income, but to my mother it was a "real" apartment and she was radiant with desire. Once the key-money was paid, the rent was affordable. If only her belly would keep its secret!

"Listen, Lady," said Madame Marie. "The owners don't want to rent to children; but you don't have to hold in your stomach. I haven't noticed anything. I'm just renting to an employed couple who can afford the key money and the rent. If you want it, it's yours."

And so I got smuggled—just in time—to a safe territory.

MY FIRST MEMORIES are round.

All around my crib, the round faces of my Polish parents, their relatives, their friends. On my crib blanket, little round medals of Catholic saints, sewn on by Madame Marie to protect me at night. That way, no harm could come to me when she herself was "far away"—one flight down—in the one-room apartment she shared with her Monsieur Henri and her sewing machine, and to which, during the day, she gave me free access, a special privilege since she had no children of her own and had claimed me as her godchild.

In the upstairs-downstairs world of my early childhood, I went up and down like a yo-yo, at home in either place.

Upstairs: the half-round drop-leaf table (covered by a blue-checkered oilcloth, under which my parents had spread letters and papers as evenly as they could so the dishes wouldn't tip) held a round porcelain fruit bowl, especially beautiful when filled with grapes. Round too were my favorite toys, kept in an odd closet behind the sofa: a hoop I would guide with a stick on the sidewalk; a large, brown rubber ball and a few smaller ones; and also a small Japanese parasol, which opened up to a glory of painted flowers, but which I was not allowed to take out in the rain because it might get spoiled.

Downstairs: at the sewing machine, Madame Marie's round face bent down so you could see her long, long hair rolled and rolled into a bun. On the wall behind her, the round face of an antique wooden clock with its brass pendulum. Now and then its ringing must have held enormous meaning for her, because she would suddenly interrupt her sewing and get up to do something else.

When a customer came in for a fitting (and a long chat), Madame Marie sent me to play ball in the lobby, of which she had a clear view through the glass entrance to her loge and the glass inner doors of the lobby itself.

Eventually, my parents would come home from work, and I would go upstairs to be fussed over, and fed, and read to, and put to bed, closing my eyes and the circle of my day to the reassuring touch of the holy medals on my yellow blanket.

WHY DO WE SPEAK of the moon as round, yet not of the sun, which is never anything but round? We are always moved by the monthly roundness of the moon; soothed and pleased. As if it were a special gift. A personal caress. When you're a child and the sun is particularly bright, you're told not to stare or you might go blind. As for the moon, you get to see it only on those special occasions when you're out with your parents past your bedtime. Then, no one tells you not to stare. And if you say: "Look, look, it's round!" they immediately reply: "Not quite. The full moon is tomorrow." Grown-ups are always right. But tomorrow, it's the usual bedtime again; so you ask for nursery rhymes, poems, and stories about the full moon, and there is a bounty of those! And as you grow up, for the rest of your life, whenever you see a full moon, a special joy comes over you.

To me, Madame Marie was like the ideal moon. Always round, always full. Even when I couldn't see her, at night in my parents' home, when she stayed downstairs with the sewing machine and the clock, by the light of a lamp. Whatever could she be doing, after having served her man the soup and stew she had cooked during the day? But she was there, sure as the moon, and her holy medals on my blanket were her stars, also round but smaller . . . and I could touch them, caress them till I fell asleep.

BOTH MY PARENTS worked all day.

My mother's name was Berthe Melszpajz (or Bronsha in her Yiddish world), and she was a bobbin-winder in a shop that manufactured knitted clothing. She paced the wide range of a huge knitting machine. Quickly, she replaced near-empty bobbins with others of identical color, re-stocked the backup row of fresh bobbins. It had to be done fast, so the machines could uninterruptedly pursue their obsessively repetitive sliding motions. She was well appreciated as a worker: quick and alert, of small stature but athletic and fit. She was also very sociable, got along with everyone.

My father, on the other hand, was slow and dreamy and always carried a newspaper. His own father had been a poor Chassid, so absorbed by his relationship with the Almighty that, when he worked at his weaving loom, he had moved to the slow rhythm of soulful liturgy while his young Polish co-workers had moved along to the faster pace of popular Polish songs (and made twice as many pieces and twice as much money as he!). My father, adapting the family tradition, was so absorbed by his relationship with the working class that he moved slowly to the rhythm of his epiphanic visions of a future world free of all injustice, violence, and poverty. The better to take a most fitting place in the sacred struggle to secure such a harmonious world, he had refused to practice one of the trades traditional to his class of Polish Jews: garment work, carpentry, or shoemaking. Instead, he chose to be an unskilled "real" factory worker. And as such, he was quickly hired, quickly laid off or fired, in a variety of factories: some made cars, some made soaps, some made machine parts. He was well liked by the other workers but was always in trouble with his supervisors, to whom he was quick to point out any signs of unfair treatment of workers. And through it all, he was sustained by his faith in humanity. His name was George Melszpajz (or Yitsrok in his Yiddish world).

TO MARK THE END of the work week, both my parents had a ritual.

My father would bring me a book, some chocolates, or a wind-up toy. I knew it was a wind-up toy when he would tell me he had a surprise; I should stand by the pot-bellied stove in the bedroom and close my eyes. That was the one spot in the apartment with the greatest floor space—at least space enough for a wind-up toy to go round and round, obsessively, without bumping into the furniture or my mother preparing dinner. I could hear the grinding sound of a key being turned and turned until it came to a halt, then of a small object placed on the floor starting its noisy journey. "Now, you can open your eyes," said my father. And I did, and I would, of course, show much surprise and pure delight. Actually, I preferred books or choco-lates—or dolls—but I loved to see my father so happy: he was so fond of wind-up toys!

By then, my mother's own ritual end-of-the-week sponge cake was already cooling on top of the kitchen cupboard. She had come home earlier than usual and, as soon as she had put away her day's shopping, she had made the pale yellow dough and poured it into that special cake-making pot called a "Pales-tinian," which she then placed on the two-burner gas stovetop. It was a tall aluminum pot with a donut-like hollow inside and rows of little peepholes all around the outside, through which you could watch the progress of the cake as it rose. When that began to happen, my mother would call me to look through the holes. I felt like Alice in Wonderland watching the mush-room grow! Later, when my mother had judged the cake fully done and had carefully slipped it onto a platter, I could smell it and wait till it was cool enough to sprinkle the top with white sugar—"Not too much! Not too much!" It then stayed, waiting to crown that special supper my mother was now busily preparing on her two burners.

And I knew that, downstairs, Madame Marie was giving her sewing machine a rest, and she too was fussing over food and Monsieur Henri.

Blessings of the Sabbath on the fullness of our home.

MY ELEMENTARY SCHOOL was nearby, and it was new—the pride of the neighborhood.

On a little street of grey transient hotels with broken shutters, it stood out with its well-textured salmon-colored bricks, its pleasant curved lines, its abundance of windows.

It was designed to accommodate the recent educational reforms of the mid-thirties' "Popular Front" socialist-oriented government. A whole wing had been set aside for small girls, two years and over. There they received good care and education until they were ready for first grade, at which point they were transferred to the main section of the school, on the other side of the inner wall. The pre-school was open from seven in the morning till seven at night, so working mothers could drop off their children on the way to work, and pick them up when they finished working. At midday a well-balanced lunch was served; and snacks at midmorning, midafternoon.

The school was immaculately clean, orderly, peaceful. All the personnel, teachers and nurses, were certified by the state; all had been trained in early-childhood care and education.

When you were dropped off, you waited by the door in the

entry court. There, you were greeted and ushered in, one by one. If you had a note pinned to your clothes that said you had a cold or any other infectious illness, a nurse's aide would discreetly take you to the quarantined area, where you would be encouraged to nap, take cough medicine and aspirin, blow your nose, and drink a lot of broth. If you had no such note, you crossed the large assembly hall with its long dining tables still empty, and then you could choose to join other children in a variety of places: a quiet room with books and quiet games; a playroom with all sorts of toys, to build little towns or to play house; the nap room with its hushed atmosphere and its simple, neat cots; or the courtyard—located at the outer limit of the school building, the farthest away from the regular grade school—where you could run, jump rope, play ball.

There was so much to do—so many children, so many toys, books, teachers, so much space, so much time in the day—that I would try each room in turn and move on quickly. And best of all, I liked to stand by the glass doors, stare into the courtyard, watch the other girls run and yell, play hopscotch, catch or not catch a ball, fall, cry, get up and be hugged by a teacher. So much movement in every direction, so much noise tossed around, so many emotions aired out!—A large hand on my shoulder, a large presence by my side: "Why don't you go out with the others?" "I don't want to." "Then, what do you want to do?"—Actually, I just wanted to keep standing there, looking through the door into the courtyard, but I couldn't say that: teachers were happy only when they thought they had figured out what it was you were in the mood to do. "I know!" my well-trained teacher would say. "Right now, you don't feel like being in a group. We have a new Cinderella puzzle that no one has tried yet. I'm sure you can do it!" And so I would follow her to the quiet-games room and put together the puzzle, quite slowly, wondering who had won at hopscotch. My teacher was patient, encouraging, very pleased with herself. Soon she would leave, in search of another idle child; then I could go back to stare at the courtyard.

We were expected to grow up to be like our teachers: kind, soft-spoken, polite, pleasant French women distinguished by their discreet but cheerful presence, their gracious modesty, the rational order of their everyday lives. We were being "civilized" into French society. Whenever we strayed from the enlightened path, we were called "little savages."—"Look at yourself!" they would say. "Your pinafore is stained; your socks are falling; your face is dirty; your braid is undone; you yelled like a fishwife; you pinched your neighbor; you left the puzzle on the floor; you mixed up all the toys; you didn't say please or thank you. What a little savage you are!"

In the scheme of that enlightened society, one showed unfailing respect and obedience to grown-ups, tolerance to younger girls and admiration to the older ones. That would get you many good points. The best strategy was to rush to the courtyard bushes, retrieve a ball, and bring it back to a little crying brat. Or if you noticed an older girl walking with a book of La Fontaine's fables and muttering to herself, you could walk alongside and flatter her: "You can read that book!" "Of course!" she would say and would walk away, muttering louder. The day was long in such opportunities if you watched out for them! As a single child, I was slowly "socialized" into the complex hierarchy of the children's world.

But at times, it could get very tiresome! Then, it was nice just to stand and look out into the courtyard, not to have to do anything, say anything! Or even to lie quietly on a cot and daydream of being inside a fairy tale, or out at the beach with my parents, or in Madame Marie's loge, by her sewing machine. It was so comforting to slip inside oneself, where time flowed easily, images and feelings came and went as they pleased; there, you were totally free and needn't answer to anyone.

THE TIME I DREADED most was the weekly lice inspection.

We sat quietly in little groups, in a corner of the large assembly hall. When it was our turn, we stood in front of the nurse or her assistant, who were armed with stubby double-edged fine-tooth combs. They would undo our ribbons or hairpins for us to hold while they bent over our heads, working a comb systematically through every strand of hair. The silence would be broken only by little cries of victory: "There! There is one!" and then little crushing sounds with a fingernail. If ever that happened to you, you felt totally naked. Even if you kept your head down, you knew everyone was looking at you. Those who had already gone by—and had proven "pure"—stared at you with contempt; the others, still waiting, were holding their breaths with anxiety. The lice inspectors were too absorbed in their task to attend to any infractions of the proper code of behavior. In any case, nothing was said, polite or otherwise; all the fear, all the humiliation was exchanged in silent glances, out of the reach of the women's concentrated looks. This sorting out of lice carriers or noncarriers added yet another dimension to the bewildering array of distinctions among the children.

There were many other considerations, varying in importance from neutral to very potent in establishing one's rank in the pre-school community. Some girls were the eldest children in their family; some were the babies; some, like me, had neither brother nor sister. Really high status was to have a grown-up brother in the army, a sister in grade school who told you what it was like "on the other side," a father in civil service, an uncle who had a farm in Normandy where you spent vacations, Shirley Temple curls with no lice ever, and a mother who picked you up early. I had none of that.

Some girls were picked up soon after the four o'clock snack. Those of us who had to wait till almost closing time got to see the janitorial staff stack the tables, the empty chairs against the walls. There was more space, more freedom. We were even allowed to run indoors. Especially on the now fully uncovered, wide mosaic floor map of the whole world. We hopped and jumped, from one block of color to another—all different shapes, all different sizes. Our teachers never failed to let us know where we landed: "You're in Argentina. Now, you can jump into Brazil— it's blue!" And so we were unwittingly introduced to elementary geography.

Then, one by one, or in bunches, our mothers came. The fewer children, the more running space, the more attention for us. Teachers even had time for a brief oral report card: "Your

daughter still moves slowly and doesn't join the others in outdoor games, but she's very sweet and doesn't bother anyone; pre-
fers quiet activities; shows good imagination; obeys her teachers; is considerate of others. I wouldn't worry about her: she'll
get quicker, take more initiative in group situations. The main
thing is, she's a good-hearted girl and well-behaved."

How wonderful to hold my mother's hand, take the way
home—all two blocks of it—and once in the building: a short
stop at Madame Marie's, to get the mail and to chat; then upstairs, to wait for my father and have him read me a story.

At times, though, I had a special treat and got to go home
earlier: Madame Marie's errands would take her near my school
and she would pick me up. I didn't mind missing the mosaic
map then! I would have Madame Marie all to myself.

Unlike my teachers, Madame Marie had an old-fashioned
attitude towards children. Grown-ups told them what to do;
children did it. There were no discussions, no suggestions about
moods, wishes, desires. Most of the time, however, she told me
to do things I very much wanted to do—like using a magnet
to pick up all the pins from the floor around the sewing machine, then sticking them, one by one, into the flowered cloth
pin cushion, or sorting out remnants, or shelling peas.

Best of all, I could be in on everything that was going on.
Tenants who stopped by to chat with her would also acknowledge my presence: "Oh, you've got your little helper!" "Yes," she
would say, "and a good worker she'll make some day!" I was very
proud; I knew that I too would grow up to become a concierge,
keeping a clean, well-run house and making everyone in it com-

fortable and happy. I would also have a Singer sewing machine, and all day long, when I was not busy cleaning the halls and stairs or attending to the tenants, I would be sewing dresses for the women and girls of the neighborhood, measuring their shoulders, chest, waist, hips, and arms with a measuring tape, later trying the pinned garments on the fitting form, replacing the thread on the sewing machine. And I would wear flower-print dresses in summer, plain dark ones and a wool shawl in winter. At the end of the day I would serve supper to my huge man, who would sit quietly while I told him all the day's happenings.

I had only two problems.

I wanted to have long hair that I would roll into a bun like Madame Marie's, but my own hair, wild and curly, grew very slowly and never below my shoulders. Sometimes she let down her long hair; it was so long that she wrapped it around her arm to brush it. I was amazed to see such a volume of hair, and more amazed still to see how little space it took once she had it rolled up several times! Maybe when I got older, something would happen and my hair would start to grow and grow, like Rapunzel's.

The other difficulty I foresaw was that I wanted to have several children, and I couldn't figure out where I would fit them in the tiny loge. Maybe I'd have to wait, to put off becoming a concierge till I was a grandmother, my children all grown and away from home. But that wasn't fair! What would I do until then? What kind of worker could I be? What shop, what factory would I work in, dropping my children at school in the morning and picking them up in the evening? Why couldn't I work at home, run the house, making everything pleasant and cheerful for the tenants, and yet have beds for all my children? Maybe I would find a way: maybe I could work so hard at making dresses, and my man could work hard at whatever, and we'd rent one of the apartments, just to place the children, beds everywhere. . . .

I would find a way: I would watch and learn and grow up to be a concierge, suddenly have long hair and lots of children. . . .

TWO

AND SO, for years of months of days—mornings, afternoons, evenings—life went on with great regularity: school with the lice inspections and the mosaic map of the world; home with the bowl of fruit on the table, my box of toys underneath; Madame Marie in her loge by her sewing machine; my blanket at night with its holy medals; and occasionally, on a night out with my parents, the moon. I was a little girl with curls, well taken care of; and I had dolls who were well-dressed—handmade clothes of wool or cotton by Madame Marie, hand-knitted sweaters, caps, mittens, socks by my mother. Madame Marie was always sewing and my mother always knitting; my father read me stories every night. At home, I spent hours looking out the window; at Madame Marie's, I spent hours dressing and undressing my dolls; and at school, I spent as much time as the teachers would tolerate, looking out the glass door at the noisy courtyard.

THEN LIFE began to change.

1940: I was five. Sundays at the park or in the local woods were my favorites, for then I would be in the company of other

Jewish children, even boys. Our mothers sat and knitted, talked, while we played ball or circle games. "Drop the handkerchief" was most popular. You sat intently, staring at the vacant spot, either directly or from the corner of your eye, depending on where it was, and your back was listening for the fall of the handkerchief—no, not yet, maybe at the next round! And the circle reconstituted itself, continuously, though with a different seating arrangement; still, always, the same children, the same mothers nearby.

That wasn't true of the men in our circles of friends and relatives. Fathers, uncles, older brothers would one day wave a handkerchief from a train window—and not come back to their seats at the dining room table. Instead, photographs in soldiers' uniforms would appear on mantelpieces, bedside tables.

My father's picture showed him wearing his winter uniform—a wool coat and wool cap—and a thoughtful, slightly surprised expression. It stood on the table by my parents' bed.

My aunt Georgette (Gitl), who was my father's sister, and Cousin Sarah came to live with us, temporarily, while they figured out whether or not they should go seek shelter on the farm of their Gentile in-laws. They left the picture of my uncle, Henri (Hershl) Schwartz, standing short and proud in his uniform, on the dining room buffet of their apartment.

Our own small apartment filled up with visitors, women and children. I would pull out my box of toys from under the table, and we would set up house where we could. Our mothers talked of rationed food, news from Poland, children's illnesses, letters from their menfolk. They were anxious and irritable and would tell us to hush, even when we thought we were being quiet. Then they were sorry and would give us biscuits.

ONE LATE AFTERNOON, when I was playing ball by myself against the walls of the lobby, waiting for my cousin to come back from school, I overheard two neighbors—spinster sisters who lived together on the third floor—coming in from shopping. One was saying: "Imagine that. You can't get coffee anymore!" I worried: what would we do for breakfast? So I asked: "Why? Why can't we get coffee anymore?" "Because of the war," the other sister answered. I ran upstairs. Only my aunt was home, ironing. "Auntie, Auntie," I cried. "You can't get coffee anymore because of the war! What are we going to do for breakfast?" My aunt calmed me down: "We'll just drink tea like the English."

So that was war: men waved their handkerchiefs and then became photographs of soldiers, and we would all drink tea like the English!

MY AUNT AND COUSIN left. They had decided, after all, to go to the country. I suddenly felt lonely.

On the way to school, one grey morning, a Jewish boy I knew approached me: "Do you really feel like going to school today?" "No," I answered, wondering what else one could do on a schoolday. "Me neither," he said. "I just got some new toys from my cousin who left Paris. Why don't you come back with me to my apartment and we'll play with them. My mother's at work, so no one's home." It sounded better than school; I was eager to see a boy's toys, so we went to his apartment.

We had to be very quiet and not turn on any lights so the neighbors wouldn't hear, wouldn't tell his mother.

He pulled out his box of toys: it was full of trucks and tanks and airplanes, and lead soldiers in various uniforms. He started arranging them on the floor. Some of the soldiers were German, some were French, though I couldn't figure out how he knew which were which. They all looked stiffly British to me; they bore no resemblance to the photograph of his father on the mantelpiece, wearing the same uniform my father wore in our photograph, trying out the same vague smile.

Did I want to be the Germans or the French? he gallantly asked. I'd be the French, though I didn't know what to do. He tried to tell me; I tried to understand but couldn't, and apparently I made all the wrong moves. "The French wouldn't fight so stupidly!" he complained. I felt ashamed: I was sure they wouldn't fight stupidly, not with my father, my uncle, and so many friends' fathers, brothers, uncles who had all joined the French Army to "fight fascism and protect us from the enemy!" I represented them so badly! "Maybe I should play the Germans," I suggested. "That way, the French would win!" "No," he cried. "That wouldn't be right: wars take longer than that! You have to have generals who give orders to brave soldiers and planes that go fast and clever strategies and all that. If you were a boy, you'd understand; girls are no fun!"

I didn't think boys were any fun, either, and I began to wish I were back in my school, playing house with other girls, or singing songs, playing circle games, or just standing by the courtyard door and watching the others at play. But it was too late to go to school. So, now I would have to stay at the boy's apart-

ment till the usual afternoon hour for me to go back home to
Madame Marie—such a long time still to wait! I asked my friend
if he would carry on his war game by himself and let me do
some puzzles or look at picture books. He mumbled something
about how he should have known better than to ask a girl to play
with him, but he pulled out another box for me, repeating his
warning to keep quiet or else I'd get him into trouble. I crouched
by the window that overlooked the courtyard, just to get a little
more light to see the pictures. "Be careful that no one sees you!"

It was strange not being able to look out the window, re-
stricted instead to moving about or whispering softly in the
semidarkness of the unlit apartment! Strange, too, that there was
no adult around, no mother with an apron making noise in the
kitchen! I was ill at ease, alone in the room with a cranky boy
venting his rage and disappointment on the Germans—or the
French—I still couldn't tell, now that he was playing both sides at
once. I was glad girls didn't grow up to become soldiers, or generals, or airplane pilots: I would never have to learn any of that!

Time was passing and his war was going on and on. I had
looked at all the books; some had fewer pictures than mine because he was older. I liked pictures; I didn't want to get older. I
was getting bored and hungry. At school, we would have had a
snack, but here no grown-up would offer something to eat and
drink. My friend was so absorbed by his war, and surely still
so mad at me, that I didn't dare interrupt him. I stayed hungry
and bored and secretly wished that his mother, an aunt, a neighbor—someone—would suddenly appear, full of kindly concern:

"Poor child, why are you sitting there in the dark? What would you like? How about cookies and a cup of hot chocolate?" And she would scold my friend: "What's the matter with you? Don't you know how to treat your guests?" But no, that wouldn't work, because we were both supposed to be in school and we'd both be scolded and punished.

I was stuck there, maybe forever, in that dim room. I wondered how many hours had passed. I began to sing silently to myself every song I knew; then when I couldn't think of another song, I started going through all the fairy tales I knew, very slowly, with all the details. By the time I couldn't remember another one, I was so tired and hungry I was near tears—but the war was still on, the room littered with fallen soldiers, overthrown tanks and trucks; the boy kneeling, arms outstretched, a plane in each hand; the planes chasing each other in one direction, then suddenly colliding, one of them falling on a cushioned chair. Maybe the war was ending and then he'd play dominoes with me? But to my surprise, he began to pick up most of the fallen soldiers and line them up neatly. "What's happening?" I whispered. "Reinforcements, dummy!"

How I wished I were at Madame Marie's. She never called me dummy. If only I were there now. She'd let me get the pop-up picture book my father had sent me for my fifth birthday, Walt Disney's *Snow White and the Seven Dwarfs*, and I'd open it to the page with the tab to pull that made Snow White sweep her cheerful little cottage in the forest, far away from harm; or I'd get the porcelain doll she had given me, and she would cut some remnants to make a shawl, or an apron I could pin on her dress. Maybe school was over by now, and I could leave and go to Madame Marie as I always did, and she would think I had spent the day at school, and all would be back to normal. So much time had passed, so slowly, slowly, that surely I could now be free from this quiet boredom, this endless dim nothingness of a day spent with a boy playing war! I put all the books, the puzzles, the domino set back in the box and announced I was leaving. "Where are you going?" "It's time for me to go to Madame Marie." "Oh, all right," he said, picking up a fallen airplane. "Just remember to close the door quietly."

I had escaped the war! I was free! I hurried home through the daylight streets, rushed through the lobby of my house, opened the door—and there was Madame Marie at her sewing machine, looking up at me through the loge window. She seemed astonished and turned her head to check the time on her wall clock: I froze like someone playing "Take a giant step." To my left was the staircase, and I wished I could run up to my apartment, but she was staring at me so sternly that I knew I had no choice but to start walking again, straight ahead to her loge to face judgment.

As soon as I walked in, Madame Marie stood up. She placed a high stool against the window by her front door. "Sit there," she ordered. "Face the wall. Don't look back." I did as I was told, and waited for the next development. She went back to her machine and kept ominously silent. I sat and sat and stared resentfully at the clock, which continued its regular loud ticking as if nothing unusual had happened. After a long while, Madame Marie, having finished a sleeve, asked me softly: "What did I tell you the heart is like?" I wished it were nighttime and I, tucked away safely in bed under her yellow blanket with its quiet medals, but I answered obediently: "You told me the heart is like an apartment, Madame Marie. If it's clean and cheerful, if there are flowers on the table, and food and drink for guests, then people want to come in and stay; but if it's messy and gloomy, and there is nothing to offer guests, people stay away. If it's extra nice, though, God Himself comes in and does something to make it even nicer."

Madame Marie was still not satisfied: "And how often do you have to dust and clean and sweep and put everything away in its right place?"

"Every day, Madame Marie. Every day."

"Dust is a funny thing," she mused. "It doesn't announce itself: you can't see it coming in; you can't see it settle on the floor, the furniture; but it gets there, as sure as Tuesday follows Monday. And if you don't look, if you forget it, it gets thicker, takes over everything." She was silent again for a while and took up the other sleeve. She started lining it up under the needle, but then, without looking up, she stopped for a moment and said: "I surely wouldn't enter your apartment today: it's a disaster! You'd better stay still on this stool. Take a good long look inside and see what needs doing. Take up your broom and dustcloth and mop and start working. Clear all the mess. Check the cupboards. See what you have to offer visitors. When all is clean and pleasant again, then put some flowers on the table. When I can smell them, you can get off the stool. Until then, get your housework done, and be sure it's thorough."

I was mortified but I didn't waste a moment. I entered

my heart, which looked exactly like my apartment upstairs. I stumbled on toys scattered on the floor, noticed that the oilcloth on the table was all askew. Papers and documents had fallen onto the chairs, together with the photo of my father in his soldier's uniform which really belonged on my parents' bedside table. It was terrible. I had to work hard and fast to put it all back together properly—sweep, dust, clean. It would be a long time before I got to put flowers on the table! I had never had a day with so many long hours, yet there was no choice but to get to work immediately and keep working as hard and fast as I could. It was too lonely there, in all that mess. I couldn't bear the thought that no one would want to come in and visit!

Too ashamed to look at Madame Marie, I held my head down. I was so used to her incessant chatter that her silence was awesome. There was only the sound of the sewing maching and the regular ticking of the wall clock that must have doubled the usual amount of hours it took to get through a normal after-noon. Madame Marie kept sewing, the clock kept ticking, and I kept scrubbing and mopping and dusting and putting away.

I knew I would never ditch school again.

THREE

I AM NOW in grade school. The courtyard is much larger;
you can see it from the classroom window when you walk back
to your desk. You spend a lot of time practicing your letters in
your lined notebook. There are no toys; no mosaic maps of the
world on the floor of the assembly hall. Instead, on the classroom wall, there is a map of France, and you have to learn to
name the rivers, the mountain ranges, the major cities, the prov-
inces. Teachers don't ask you what you are in the mood to do;
they tell you what they expect you to do, how well, how neatly,
and in how much time.

The school day proceeds in a very orderly manner. Even
lunchtime has its rituals. We straighten our desks, line up to
wash our hands, line up to enter the dining room, stand by our
assigned seats, turn to face the large portrait of Marshal Pétain
overshadowing the plaster bust of young Marianne—that old
symbol of the French Republic—and listen to our principal. She
tells us how lucky we are that Marshal Pétain, the good father of
the French, is so concerned with us, the children of France, her
future glory, that he makes sure every schoolchild has a nour-

ishing lunch; even in hard times such as ours when food is so scarce, our good father, full of loving kindness, still manages to see to it that we remain well fed; we should be grateful. In return, we should work hard at school, respect our parents and teachers, and always be what our country expects of us: well-behaved French children. When she finishes saying grace to our provider, we are allowed to sit down. The food appears, is passed around: lentil soup, or puree of rutabaga, or kidney bean casserole with an occasional piece of lard. As soon as I know the dish of the day, I look up at Marianne; I really prefer her: she is young, fresh, bold, proud—though of course she isn't the one who has put lunch on our table. Marshal Pétain looks nice enough, like a French grandfather on a large estate, talking to his gardener—everything will work out for the best, as long as everyone remembers his place and does his duty.

TODAY IS DIFFERENT from all other days. There is a special announcement at lunchtime. Marshal Pétain, our good father, explains the principal, is so proud of his brave French soldiers who have had the misfortune to be taken prisoner, that he wants to show his fatherly love to the children of those prisoners by allocating an orange to each of them. There will be a distribution center in each neighborhood. School-age sons and daughters of prisoners can come there accompanied by their mothers, who will have to show the proper documents to prove their eligibility. Then, each child will be given an orange, a beautiful orange that comes from the colonies.

This time when we sit down, I hardly notice which dish we are being served. I can't wait for the day to be over, for my mother to come home, for me to tell her what a good father Marshal Pétain is, what a treat he has for us. I look at Marianne, so bold and proud—but she doesn't offer us oranges. Now, I definitely prefer Marshal Pétain. I imagine walking behind the gardener on the large estate. The Marshal notices me: "Ah, little girl, you are a daughter of one of my brave soldiers who has been taken prisoner. I am proud of your father, and I will take care of you in his absence. First, I want you to have a beautiful orange from the colonies. Later, I may have other surprises for you. And, since you are like a daughter to me, feel free to walk around my gardens as if they were your own father's gardens; and you can choose three roses that the gardener will cut for you. Go now, my child, and remember: you are the hope and the future glory of France; you must study hard, be obedient and well-behaved."

THAT NIGHT, when my mother came home looking tired and worried as usual, I was glad I could cheer her up with the story of my forthcoming orange—we hadn't seen one for a long time! But to my surprise, she mumbled something about Marshal Pétain being a traitor to the French Army, selling out his soldiers for oranges. I couldn't understand. It was always so complicated when your teachers said one thing and your parents another. For me the point was: would I get my orange? Yes, of course, my mother said. You might as well have it! Your father has surely earned it for you!

My mother and I walked up the stairs of an old building to get my orange. She had taken time off from work and hoped we wouldn't be too long. We entered a room as crowded as a clinic.

At a desk, someone was checking papers. We waited our turn. On the right-hand side of the desk, two women surrounded by crates of oranges handed out the fruits, one at a time, to each child whose mother's papers had been verified by the clerk. I stood by my mother, who had managed to get a seat and was talking to her neighbor. So, I too would hold out my right hand, and a woman by a crate would place an orange in it! All my attention was focused on that spot in the room. As time went on, a couple of crates were emptied. I worried that they would run out of oranges before our turn had come, but then somebody took away the empty crates and replaced them with full ones. How could I have doubted that our good father Marshal Pétain would not honor his promise to all the children of prisoners of war! I calmed down. Finally my mother stood up, we went to the desk, she showed her papers, the clerk nodded approval, I went to the crate, put out my right hand, and a woman placed an orange in it. I walked quickly behind my mother, who rushed out down the stairs into the street, kissed me good-bye, and went back to work.

WALKING CAREFULLY, I carried my orange through the grey streets of my neighborhood, eager to get it home safely. At a small plaza, a Gypsy was showing off his trained goat who, on command, was slowly climbing the rungs of a high wooden stool. I stopped to look. The goat reached the narrow circle of the seat. I knew what would happen next. The goat, precariously balanced, would patiently wait while the Gypsy boys would pass a hat through the crowd. I had nothing to put in it except my orange, so I left quickly before the conclusion of the performance. From there on, the only street entertainer was the blind accordionist at the entrance of the subway station; but his music was sad and the people passed him by as if they too were blind.

The town square by my house had only old people on the benches, and babies in carriages wheeled by their mothers. The girls from the convent school weren't there to recite the dangers of being a pagan. Maybe they were praying for their salvation to God the Father, the one who created the world in seven days, or to God the Son, the one who ended up on a cross, or to the Virgin Mary, who was young and shy, not young and bold like our Marianne.

I crossed the lobby of our house and went to Madame Marie to show her my orange. "From the colonies!" I said. "Oh my!" she cried. "What a splendid fruit! Take it upstairs, and mind you don't eat it till your mother comes home. She'll be so glad to see you eat!"

I ran up. I didn't even turn the light on in the front room but went straight to our bedroom window and placed the orange on a lace doily in the very center of the round wooden table facing the window. It was our best piece of furniture, our special pride: its three curved legs held down the floor tightly with its three lion's paws—like tables in fancy shop windows.

I looked at the orange: it was so naked in the full daylight that I untied the thin beige curtains and let them hang down loosely like the curtains on a closed cinema stage before the show.

Now we could start.

First, I made sure the orange was in the exact center of the round lace doily. There! Then, I stood in front of it, in respectful admiration: my own orange, from far, far away in the colonies where the sun was always bright, where camels wandered in the desert and occasionally rested by a clear blue pond under tall palm trees—just like the postcard illustrations of the geography text book. Somehow, it had come all the way to Paris in a crate, and now it was alone with me, on my table by the window! When my mother would come home, she would peel the orange, and underneath would be a glorious fruit, to eat slice by slice, full of sweet juice—but then it would no longer be on the table, shining in the afternoon light, full of its secret, half-remembered taste.

In the meantime, I wanted the orange to feel good here, and so I laid my hands softly on it and waited. Soon, I could feel it grow bold against my fingers, grow larger and larger till it was as big as a beach ball, looming large in the middle of the sky, floating towards my father standing in the sand with open hands. My father, oh my father, far away, smiling, waiting to catch the ball—but it floated more and more slowly, rising higher toward the sun—rising and rising until it stopped in midair, transformed into an orange balloon without a string. Magnificently alone, complete unto itself, it stayed poised in the quiet sky; I shrank like Alice in Wonderland. My father on the sand, the long beach between us, even the sun had disappeared. Instead, the distant golden sphere, glowing like a Christmas star in a dream. . . . I froze in adoration.

But as I stared at it in full devotion, it slowly, slowly descended, getting gradually, gradually smaller . . . smaller, till it rolled back into my hands on the altar by the window. I let go of it, stepped back and waited.

Nothing happened. The room was growing dim. Where was I? I had stood still so long that I was numb. I made myself circle around the table several times, looking down at my feet, counting my steps out loud—six, seven . . . when I got to ten, maybe my mother would come. Oh, that was it: I was back at my daily evening ritual, waiting at the window for my mother to come home from work! But I couldn't see out the window. I lifted one of the curtains and tied it up again at its side; then I did the same thing to the other. Now, the window looked like a lighted stage when the show is on. My show was the street, with all the minor actors passing by on their way to somewhere, till at last, the long-awaited lead actress would make her grand entrance—the star of the show, my own mother who always looked up at the window and smiled at me. Sometimes, I had to count, very slowly, many series of one to ten, with a long pause in between. And with each pause, I would get lonelier and my longing to see my mother appear would grow stronger in hope and anxiety.

Now I looked at my orange, still sitting in the middle of the lace doily: it seemed lonely too, abandoned, sad, like a ball left behind on a beach after an outing.

IN THOSE DAYS, food—or the lack of it, or the difficulty of locating certain items, or the time it took to stand in line hoping they wouldn't run out of stock before you reached the counter—was more of a conversation subject than the weather. It seemed to be on every grown-up's mind. Not on mine, though. To my mother's dismay, I had become a finicky eater. To trick me into eating, she would spontaneously invent mealtime stories. It became a ritual: "You eat and I'll tell you a story." I was so hungry for a story that I ate, without interest in the food, but I ate. If I slowed down, she slowed down; if I stopped, she stopped, even in the middle of an exciting part.

One night I asked her if there really were a God who was sometimes Father, sometimes Son, as the convent girls across the street insisted. "No," she said. "Then who made the world?" I asked. "How long did it take? What was there at the very, very beginning?" And my mother, anxious to have me eat, quickly said: "At the beginning, there was a beautiful meadow. In the meadow was a cow, the Original Cow. She had lots of milk. There were no grown-ups yet—just two babies, a boy and a girl. The babies drank the cow's milk and grew strong and healthy. When they were all grown up, they married and had children. Their children had children. And those children grew up, got married, and had their own children until, all over the world, there were lots of people. And finally, your father and I got married, and we had you. And if you eat well, you'll grow up strong and healthy and get married and have children."

And so I ate. I also developed a lifelong attachment to cows. As for my mother, she continued her obsession with food.

Once, when I had spotted her about to enter the house, I ran down to meet her as usual. She was crossing the lobby, clutching a string shopping bag filled to bursting capacity, with onions and potatoes most in evidence. It looked like a fishing net holding a good catch. But just as my mother opened the inner lobby door, there was Madame Marie, coming in from the courtyard, staring at her bag in astonishment, then blocking my mother from going any farther. "Open that bag!" she ordered, stern as a schoolmistress. My mother shrank in embarrassment, like a schoolchild caught cheating on a test. She had no choice but to open her shopping bag for Madame Marie's inspection. To my surprise, the inside was filled with crumpled newspaper. "Give it to me and stay here," said the tyrant. My mother surrendered her bag, which Madame Marie carried into the courtyard to the small shed that served as her kitchen. She soon returned. The bag was less bulky, but she seemed satisfied. My mother knew and I knew that she must have replaced the newspaper stuffing with real food. "Now you can go," she said more kindly. "But don't you ever, ever do that again!" And so it became clear that, no matter how limited my mother's means might be, her pride was not to get in the way: we were simply not permitted to go hungry.

FOUR

I WAKE UP late and lazy because it's Sunday.

There's a smell of bleached steam from the kitchen: my mother must be doing the weekly wash—now boiling the linen in a huge basin on the coal stove.

It feels good to lie in bed, to stare at the cracks in the ceiling. After a while, they become a meandering river with its many tributaries, like the ones on the map of France in my classroom.

When I've completed the rounds of my overhead landscape, I then take a tour of the walls. They're very interesting: every available space holds a painting. Above my pillow is a watercolor self-portrait of the painter, my father's best friend. He is handsome and wears a straw hat and a pleased smile. He looks toward the right, where he can see the tall mirror on the armoire, then, overlooking the long side of my parents' bed, a set of two small oil paintings he did when he was a teenager in Poland; both show a group of boys playing outdoors—one at winter games, one at summer games. Presiding over my parents' pillows is a small painting of me as a baby: stiffly bundled under the arms, rosy cheeks bulging, lips closed and satisfied as if I have just finished nursing, eyes calm. Then comes the window, with its

double set of curtains. Adjoining it, on the left wall: the door of
a cupboard; inside, its narrow shelves hold my parents' books,
photograph albums, postcard collection. The space between the
cupboard and the black pot-bellied stove has a large portrait of
my mother in a simple flowered dress of which only the top part
is visible, because it's really her face that's important; her face
looks strong and serious, as when she chooses food at a market.
You can tell she's the kind to invent the best-tasting dishes while
staring at a bargain price! And last of all, closest to me and the
painter's self-portrait, separated from us only by the space of a
door to the other room, is the largest and darkest oil painting:
it's of my father. All of him gets to be in the picture, seated on a
plain wooden chair behind a tall-legged plain wooden table. He
is very skinny; his pants are too short. He, too, looks serious, as
when he reads his newspaper, but here, exceptionally, he has no
newspaper; his hand is placed on a closed book, the only object on the table. Sometimes I think the book, not my father, is
the focus of this austere painting. I recognize the book: it's the
small *Illustrated Larousse French Dictionary*. My father would say that
someday he would know every word in that book. I never understood. They weren't stories; they were just words! But they made
him so happy, so proud to know them, that when he joined the
French Army, he took the book of French words with him.

MY FATHER! I saw him once after he left home. It was
a very hushed adventure. My mother had received a cryptic letter from him, telling her to bring a cake and cigars, and me —
by train to the city of Rennes in Brittany, where he was incarcerated as a prisoner of the Germans. Once there, she was to go

to a particular hotel and ask for the owner—at which point she would "begin to understand."

My first memory of that visit was the walk from the train station in Rennes. My mother had asked for directions from a woman who, it turned out, was returning from a shopping trip in Paris and was headed back home, just a few blocks from the station; she would show us the way.

She was carrying hat boxes and several other packages. Unlike my mother, my aunts, or Madame Marie, she was tall and slim and wore strong perfume and an elegant black coat with a white fur collar, high and broad in the shoulders, tapering down to her knees. I'm sure she had a hat to match, but I couldn't stop staring at her boots: high heels, black leather, lined with white fur folded neatly over the tops. Imagine walking in white fur at a brisk, confident step, excluding the springtime fragrance of lilies-of-the-valley in the middle of a cold winter! How extraordinarily kind of the lady to talk to us—let alone be our guide in a strange city! She kept talking to my mother, telling her how tiring shopping can be, and I hoped she wouldn't notice my old galoshes; if she did, she would surely be so horrified that she would immediately click her heels and leave us stranded. Madame Marie made pretty clothes for me, but she didn't make shoes. The fancy lady, however, paid no attention to me at all but only to the buildings ahead of us. She finally slowed down, then stopped in front of a very modest old hotel. My mother thanked her profusely, and we went in.

In a dimly lit apartment, all curtains drawn, we are sitting at a table covered with an ancient lace cloth. A jigsaw puzzle is placed in front of me, and I am admonished to put it together quietly. I stare at it: I've never before done such a complicated puzzle! My mind is still on fur-lined boots, but the puzzle picture is of a country house. The two women are talking softly, very seriously—something about camp regulations; something about an exception, and thank-you gifts of homemade cake and cigars, then about a Resistance network, and the owner of the café across the street. It's hard to follow. My mother keeps saying Thank you! Thank you! You're very kind! I understand! How good of you!

I'm collecting pieces for a window, but I find duplicates, as there are two windows; maybe I should work on the front door instead? The pieces are so small, though! It will take me forever. And what will happen then, when forever is reached and my puzzle is done? I'm too tired to figure it out. What I would like is for someone to give me a cup of hot cocoa, to tell me to take off my shoes and lie down for a nap on the sofa. Then, while I sleep, my galoshes will be replaced with lovely boots. Now the hotel keeper gets up; maybe she's going to the kitchen? No, she's going to the buffet. Maybe she'll get some pretty cups? No, she opens a drawer, searches, takes out a key and hands it to my mother, who picks up our suitcase and motions for me to follow.

WE ENTER a very narrow room with a narrow bed at one end, by the window, and a sink at the other. My mother checks that the curtains are fully drawn, puts the suitcase on the bed, opens it, and starts unpacking. I stand by the sink—a fine, white porcelain sink, so much prettier than our greystone one at home! My mother moves around silently, as usual, and I slip into a daydream, as usual: I have real boots lined with white fur turned neatly over the tops; my mother and I are living in the country house of the jigsaw puzzle, and it has a bright white porcelain sink.

I'm startled out of my reverie by a firm knock at the door. My mother rushes to the door, whispers something in Yiddish, is answered by a male voice in Yiddish, opens the door wide, and in comes a French soldier who quickly closes the door behind him and crushes my mother in his arms. I hold tight to the sink. What does this mean? Where does this leave me? Suddenly the soldier looks up, sees me, releases my mother, bends down, holds out his arms, calls my name. Now I can see! Under his cap: my father's face, my father's laughter! I run into his embrace. Snug in his arms, at last I remember; for the first time since we arrived, I remember why we made this trip. Now I don't care if I don't have boots or a porcelain sink; now I have my father and my mother and we'll be together again. We'll go back to Paris or even stay in this room, but we'll be a family again—forever. All is well.

My father stands and fills the darkened room like the sun of a new day. My mother and I are flowers blossoming in the light of his smile. He has gifts for us, he says, and out of his knapsack come several bars of pure castile soap from Marseilles, a rare wonder! We take turns smelling it in his hands; that fresh smell of soap; the hands we've missed!

A springtime of giggles, hugs, kisses, rounds of two-way, three-way embraces. The weather forecast: joy today, tomorrow, and forever after.

ONCE MORE: in the landlady's apartment, sitting at the same table with the faded lace cloth. This time there are just two

of us: the landlady and me. My parents have remained in the narrow room—to talk with each other, I am told. I should go on
with the puzzle, quietly. I'll try to finish the front door; perhaps
when I'm done, I'll be summoned to return to the parental room.

In the meantime, between spurts of collecting puzzle pieces
and trying to make them fit inside the door frame, I watch the
quiet woman busy herself; she stays in the room, dusting her furniture, shaking doilies. Aside from the wooden chairs at the table,
every piece of furniture is covered by some kind of textured
cloth: heavy spreads over the sofa, on the armchairs; doilies on
the buffet, on end tables; the lace cloth over the table; and on that
cloth, clusters of tiny, jagged puzzle pieces. Every now and then,
she goes to the window, puts her head to the brown curtain,
draws it ever so slightly, just enough to fit one eye, and quickly
lets it drop loose again. I wonder what she's seen—or not seen,
but I'm a well-brought-up French child so I don't ask. The large
room is so dense with furniture, objects, knickknacks, it makes
me sleepy; its textiled somberness exudes the scent of a warm
blanket you pull over your head to sleep in privacy. But I must
not fall asleep; I must stay awake to hear my name being called.

At last, I get bold and ask: "Madame, please, Madame, when
can I go back to my parents?" The landlady comes to the table,
across from me, lifts part of the lace cloth, opens a large drawer,
takes out all the silverware, dips a small rag in something I can't
see, then slowly, painstakingly, proceeds to polish every fork,
spoon, or knife that she holds up critically to her sight, one by
one, before returning it shining into the deep drawer. After a
while, she answers me: "You have to be patient. Your parents
surely have a lot to talk about; they haven't seen each other in a

long time, and God only knows when all this will be finished for good and all the soldiers will be back with their families, in their own homes!" I'm mesmerized by the silver's transformation, from dull to glossy, and I stare at each piece that rhythmically, monotonously gets lifted, polished, and put away. I must stay awake, so I start counting: one spoon, two spoons, three spoons . . . seven spoons, eight. . . .

My mother wakes me. I'm in the bed of the narrow room. I must have fallen asleep counting silver spoons! I see my mother already dressed, looking sullen. Where is my father? "Come, hurry up," she says. "We're going to the camp to see your father." Why did my father go back to camp? Did he go to get his things? But my mother doesn't answer; she just rushes me to wash and dress. I put on my galoshes, feeling like Cinderella after the ball. Cinderella was luckier, though: she had one glass slipper as a memento proving she had really been at the ball, had really danced with the prince. What do I have? I suddenly have a bright idea and insist on seeing the castile soaps from Marseilles that my father gave us. "They're in the suitcase," I'm told. "You'll see them later; we have no time now; we have to run or we'll miss your father before he goes away." And out we go, into the brutally cold early morning.

We stand with a crowd of townspeople by the gates of the prison camp. Long lines of soldiers are marching off, surrounded by German guards holding rifles and yelling "Schnell! Schnell!" In the grey stillness, the prisoners all look alike—all glum, all with knapsacks on their backs, caps on their heads, all looking straight ahead, dazed, marching, marching. "Why don't they look at us?" I ask. "Shh! It's not allowed," someone whispers. In a lower voice, I can't help myself but I must ask: "Where are they going?" A grown-up hand on my mouth: "Shh! To Germany." The lines go on endlessly, as if the prison had held every soldier wearing a French Army cap, every German guard holding a rifle. I stare, hypnotized, not knowing what I want most: to see my father or not to see him, checking every stranger's face that passes, holding on tight to my mother's hand. Suddenly, I feel her hand tense up, nearly crush mine: there, there is my father! I cry: "Papa! Papa!" He hesitates, stops for an instant, turns his head toward me—but quickly, the end of a rifle shoved in his back, he is forced to go on.

My mother and I are nearing the train station. She is holding the suitcase. I hope the castile soap is in it: I forgot to ask her; she forgot to show it to me. We pass a shoe store. In the window, several pairs of boots, including one pair small enough for me. I'm sure they would fit. I yank my mother: "Mama, Mama, those are the boots I want!" She yanks me back: "Don't be foolish; they're too expensive!"—"But Mama, they have fur. They're so warm; it's so cold now!"—"After the war, I promise, when your father comes back, we'll buy beautiful boots."—"When, Mama. When will that be?"—"When you're older."—"But I'm cold now. I want them now!"—"Walk faster or we'll miss the train."—"But they're little girls' boots; they're just right for me!"—"After the war, first Winter after the war! Walk faster, faster!"

MADAME MARIE is making a package in her tiny kitchen shed in the courtyard. She keeps rearranging cans of food until she is satisfied that she has fitted as many as can possibly fit in the cardboard box; then she carefully wraps it with parcel paper, seals it, ties it with strings paralleling the length, the width, asks me to hold my thumb tightly—keep pressing, don't move—so she can secure the strongest knot.

"Madame Marie, who is the package for?"

"For your father. I got them to register me as his godmother; that way, I have a right to send him packages, like your mother."

"Is Germany far?"

"Very far. But he can get letters and packages. You learn to write: you can write him letters. You learn to read: then no one has to read out loud the letters he writes you."

"Will he come back someday, Madame Marie?"

"But, of course!" she laughs. "I'll tell you a secret. When you were born, I made you the yellow blanket on your bed—for warmth and for good luck. When your father left for the army, I made him a blanket, too. I made it light enough so he could carry it in his knapsack, and I told him that whatever happens, he must hold on to it. If he does, he'll come back. He promised me that no one in the world could take that blanket from him; that he would bring it back home. So, don't worry. Your father will come back."

I look at my yellow blanket. I hold it close. It's Sunday, so Madame Marie may have gone to the public baths and then put on her prettiest dress to go out with Monsieur Henri to the Père Lachaise Cemetery that she loves so much because there are so many trees and cats, and so many beautiful statues on the graves of so many famous people. My mother is still fussing in the kitchen. Soon, since we're no longer allowed to go to the public baths, or any public place, she'll get me to wash my whole body at the greystone sink in the kitchen steaming from the bleached laundry. Then, she probably will write a letter to my father, and now that I can read and write she will ask me to add a few words. His few words to me are almost always the same: "My darling daughter, I look at your picture and wish I were with you and your mother. Be a good girl, and listen to your mother and Madame Marie."

But he doesn't tell me what he does, or what his German prison camp is like, and he doesn't send any photographs. (I would later come to know that the camp where my father spent four of his five-years' captivity was a hard-labor camp for Jewish prisoners of war.) He does, however, mention any package or letters he gets, and how happy they make him. I never know what to write. I always write the same things: that I'm well, that I like school, and that I hope he's well too, that I send him lots of kisses.

Now, I'd like to ask him if he still has his blanket, but I can't because Madame Marie said it's a secret. Secrets have magic; if you tell, the magic is gone. But I know and he knows. My father and I are protected by the same kind of gift: a blanket from our godmother. We'll keep the secret, always. He'll come back.

FIVE

1942: THE MONTH OF MAY started with traditional minibouquets of lilies-of-the-valley sold in the streets—white and green accents here and there, timid offerings of good luck for the few who could afford such luxuries. For the rest, they would have to subject themselves entirely to chance.

That month was barely done when June forced onto us Jews a stark symbol of reduced luck: a yellow star made of cotton, with the word Juif in its center. The star had to be purchased with clothing-ration tickets and displayed on all outer garments, over the chest, on the left, following precise instructions that it be tightly sewn, with not one loose stitch, and worn in public at all times.

All Jews over the age of six had to wear the yellow star. Since I was seven, both my mother and I had to wear it, except that on me, of course, it looked much larger.

THIS IS THE FIRST DAY I must wear the star to school. My mother has already gone to work. As I reach the bottom of the stairs, Madame Marie comes out of her loge to inspect me. Everything is right, every stitch in place. "Well, a solid gold star on a gold chain would look a lot better!" she sighs. "But in the meantime, be careful not to hide it: that's against the rule and could get you into deep trouble. And mind that you come right back home after school!"

As I go out the front door and turn left, I feel very strange, suddenly on display. I reason that if I stick close to the buildings, slanting my star toward them, maybe it won't be so noticeable. When I reach the little hardware store down my block, I stop to stare through the shop window at the familiar bright rolls of oilcloth by the door. But unlike other mornings, they don't invite me into the old daydream: my mother asking which one I would prefer as a replacement for our old one on the dining table; they seem indifferent, distant. I go on.

At the end of the block, I have to cross the street—or is it the sea, where every ship is visible? Somehow, I reach the other shore—which I quickly have to leave for another sea-crossing to yet another shore. Everyone must be looking at my yellow star, but I don't dare look up. The streets are peopled with faceless pedestrians all surely staring at me.

I've almost made it. I'm on the last leg of my voyage—the sidewalk leading to my school building, just a few transient hotels away. The only trouble is that now my star is exposed to full view of everyone on both sides of the street. Soon, though, I should be safely inside the entrance hall. If I just keep going, if I don't look at anything but the bottom of the walls on my right, soon I'll see the pink bricks of my school wall, then the few steps to the front door, then the linoleum of the lobby . . . but a burst of loud male laughter, loud German words, is making its way across the street, coming in my direction, getting louder, louder, closer and closer. I freeze in terror and this time I look up: four uniformed German soldiers are laughing coarsely, talking loudly, tittering. In fear, I lift my satchel and press it against my chest, tightly, with both hands; the star hides. If only they keep going on their sidewalk to the intersection behind me, by then I'll be by the school.

I start walking again, carefully, very quietly, hiding my star from German eyes, fixing my sight on my right: the pink brick wall should be coming up very soon. But as if suddenly their sidewalk had erupted, the soldiers rush onto the pavement in the middle of the block, like drunks ejected from a bar, unsteady, stumbling across the street in a full blast of human noise. And here they are, in front of me, blocking my way: huge, loud, drunk, swaggering. My satchel grows heavier, tighter against my chest. They are staring at it, saying harsh-sounding German words to each other, laughing. . . . Then with a rough, abrupt gesture, one of them grabs the satchel, throws it on the pavement, uncovers my star, yellow, naked, with all its stitches showing. That's the end of me. That's it. I did it: I broke the rule. They'll take me with them, very far away. I'll never see my mother again. Or Madame Marie. I hear crude, hard laughter; the soldiers grow immense; I shrink under the growing star. But suddenly they let me go — is it for something behind me? I hear a strange human cry and I look back only for a moment: an old woman is being dragged in the gutter by her long grey untied hair, her yellow star staring at the sky. I keep on walking faster toward my school, making a silent pledge: if this ever ends, if I get through it, I will someday come back to this very spot, wearing a solid gold star on a gold chain, the way Catholic girls wear their gold cross, letting it shine in full daylight.

I REMEMBER nothing from that point until recess.

We are then in the courtyard, free to run and play, a delicious time when we naturally regroup in familiar clans, and I'm about to join the girls I've known since those days we spent together in pre-school, on the other side of the wall. But something is wrong: they ominously gather into a growing group, facing me, the only one wearing the yellow star. In inarticulate fear, I back up till I hug the wall. Keeping their distance, they start to taunt me, yelling: "Go back to Palestine where you come from!" I don't understand: "But I don't come from Palestine! I'm French. I went to pre-school with you." That just makes them angrier. They scream, menacingly, coming closer, more and more of them: "You're a Jew! A Jew! Go back to Palestine! Back to Palestine!" I still don't understand: "But Palestine is where Jesus comes from, not Jews, not my family; they're from Poland!" That sends them into a fury. Everyone is saying something different, all at once, so I don't even know where to look: something to do with my using the name of Jesus, to which I have no right since I am a Jew, something about how France should rid itself of all Jews, and again: that they should all go back to being Palestinians. I try to imagine being a Palestinian, but the only thing that comes to my mind is our top-of-the-stove "Palestinian" cake-making pot. Before I can figure out how to use this in my defense, the mob is pushing me from the wall into the toilet shed, with its Turkish toilets, where one can squat over white porcelain-lined holes in the ground. Everything is happening fast: a mob of bodies is pushing me harder and harder till I'm thrown on the floor, face down against the toilet. I panic. Will I slip through the hole into the foul pit? But I'm choking and I can't think, shoved down till I can't breathe.

I WAKE UP in a bed, my mind a blank, my head heavy. Hovering above me, some women's faces in a hushed atmosphere of kind concern, relief. I begin to recognize them: the nurse, my teacher, the principal. Where can I be? I look around: it's the infirmary. The women whisper kind words: they're sorry about what has happened; they'll make sure it never happens again. But I don't know what has happened; I can't remember anything. I ask them why I'm in the infirmary. They look surprised, worried. Then the nurse says: "The child needs more time; let her rest." The others go away. If I don't move my head, if I just lie still, I can bathe in the kind quietness of the room and not think of anything, just enjoy the privilege of being fussed over by the soft-spoken nurse who brings me warm compresses and gentle words.

The nurse has now brought me to the lobby of the principal's office. I sit and wait for the principal's summons, still feeling funny in the head and the stomach, looking at the walls decorated with colorful pictures of girls dressed in French regional costumes. I'm worried: there are few reasons for a student to sit here. She could be on an errand for a teacher—a neutral act to be rewarded by a quick, formal thank-you. Or she could have distinguished herself by the enormity of her misbehavior, her

abysmal academic performance, or the excellence of her work—
all of which, with the appropriate choice of a frown or a smile,
would result in the same admonition for her to work harder and
behave like a well-brought-up French child. But none of these
situations applies to me at the moment, so why am I here?

The door opens and the principal invites me in, very
sweetly. I sit on the chair across from her. Her desk looks as
big as ever and, automatically, I lower my head, not knowing
what to expect. She starts speaking, kindly, sadly, but reassur-
ingly: "I'm very sorry about what happened. From now on, for
your own safety, you won't play with the other children during
recess. If you wish to go out in the courtyard, you'll stay close
to the recess supervisor at all times or, if you prefer, you may
spend your recess time in the lobby of my office."

I cannot bear the thought of not going outdoors during recess, but as soon as I am in the courtyard, I must stay close to
the recess supervisor—just stand by her, or follow her wherever
she goes to recite the rules of civilized behavior. There is nothing to do but look at the other girls chatting or playing without
me. I may only join them when the bell rings at the end of recess
and lines form to go back into the classrooms. In the brief commotion before absolute silence is restored, I am called names in
hissing whispers—teacher's pet! coward! Jew! I don't answer; I
am the first to assume silence. After a few days, I opt to spend
recess in the principal's lobby. I sit and stare at the pictures of the
girls in lovely costumes. My favorites are those of Alsace and Brittany, with their wonderful coifs. I daydream of living in those

regions, where girls wear colorful clothes instead of the dull uniform, the school smock I must wear as a Parisian schoolchild.

MY MOTHER is in the kitchen, washing dinner dishes; I am sitting at our dining table doing my homework. There is a knock at the door. As always, I let my mother answer it. She first says something peculiar; a man's voice replies with a nonsense word. I know what it means: a Resistance contact. My mother opens the door; the strange man comes in, is offered a chair by the table. He looks hesitantly at me, but my mother reassures him: "Don't worry about the child. She's used to keeping secrets." I feel very proud. Important. Grown-up. Indeed, I do know about secrets—good ones, bad ones, incomprehensible ones. A secret is what you never, never tell anyone, no matter what. My mother collects secrets, and so do I. My father's good-luck blanket; my troubles at school; our shortwave radio with its BBC station, taken out of its hiding place in the closet and returned to it at specific times; the passwords that open our door to strangers. No one could ever make me tell any of them.

SECRETS seemed to grow more numerous with time, but I remembered the Original Secret.

It was before we had been forbidden from being in any public place, when we could still relax in our favorite public place, the Park of the Buttes-Chaumont.

My mother sat on a bench, knitting as usual. I played nearby for a while, with the doll Madame Marie had given me for my birthday. Then, when I saw a girl I knew, I started to play ball with her, leaving my doll on the bench near the knitting bag.

We stayed within view of my mother, as was the rule. But after a while, my friend wanted to go off to the other side of the park, to watch the merry-go-round rides, and I went with her without asking my mother, for fear she would refuse. When my mother could no longer see me from the bench, she worried, interrupted her knitting, left it on the bench by the bag and the doll, and went to look for me.

She found me, scolded me all the way back to the bench. The knitting was still there, but the doll was missing. The scolding got louder: what had I done! The most beautiful doll I ever had, a very expensive one that had cost Madame Marie dearly! How could we face her? We had to find it; we wouldn't leave the park till we found it. Horrified at what I had done, I was determined to be the one who would spot it. We searched everywhere, and walked every main road, every meandering path of the park, looking at the kind of doll each girl was playing with — none of which was mine. I even looked in bushes, but eventually, we lost hope and walked home sadly, both of us feeling guilty, I for having made my mother leave the bench to look for me, and she for having left the precious doll unattended on the bench. As we neared home, she said: "We'll just go by Madame Marie quickly, so she won't notice anything. Don't ever tell her we lost the doll. It's a secret. I'll have to replace it, somehow, as soon as I can get the money together and find one just like her. Luckily, she was wearing a dress I knitted. I still have some of that wool left, so I'll make her a new one, and no one will be able to tell the difference."

While my mother was saving money from whatever further cuts she could make in our daily expenses, and whatever overtime she could get at the shop, I was scared, worried that Madame Marie would ask me why I didn't bring my doll to her apartment anymore. But luckily, she didn't ask. She was making so many garments and had scheduled so many fittings with customers in and out: there were deadlines, special occasions. I renewed efforts to make myself useful to her: to pick up pins with a magnet, setting them back carefully onto the cloth pincushion with just the heads showing; to gather remnants and bundle them by kinds; or to go on errands to get buttons. She was very busy; she didn't ask about the doll.

Then one day, my mother came home and told me to look in the knitting bag she carried. And there it was! A new doll, identical to my lost birthday doll, in the same starched white cotton dress hemmed with lace! "Don't say anything yet," she told me. She proceeded to spend long evenings knitting the identical dress my doll had last been seen wearing. Only then, pleased that order had been restored, did she allow me, and in fact urge me, to bring it to Madame Marie's loge. "As if nothing had happened," she warned. "Remember our secret."

It was a good secret. Madame Marie made the doll a new skirt and a new apron from my choice among many remnants. I was happy. I had learned that well-kept secrets could prevent disasters!

Since then, I had learned that there was one exception: a yellow star on outer garments could not be kept secret in public places. It was meant to identify a Jew as a moving target. Nothing could be done about it. It was outside the realm of secrets.

The square across the street from our Paris apartment

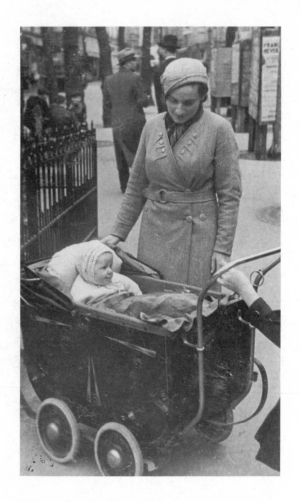

My mother and I. Paris. 1935

Doors to Madame Marie: the concierge's ground-floor apartment

The apartment at 90 rue Jean-Pierre Timbaud.
Our window is directly above the front door.

The bedroom door in our vacant apartment. Paris. 1985

Our Metro station, Couronnes, where Monsieur Henri
took me on the day of the round-up, July 16, 1942.

Henri Briard (Monsieur Henri). 1928

TIMBRE FISCAL 12 FRANCS
N° 396808 Serie B
CARTE D'IDENTITÉ

PRÉFECTURE DE POLICE Nom Mme Chotel

Prénoms Marie Gabrielle
Profession : Couturière
Né le 24 juillet 1883
à Saint-Brandrupt
département Vosges
Nationalité : Française
Domicile : à Paris
rue d'Angoulême

SIGNALEMENT

Taille 1m57
Cheveux ch[illegible]
Moustache
Yeux
Signes particuliers
Nez: Dos rect Base H
Dimension moy
Forme générale du visage ov
Teint mat

Empreinte digitale
Signature du titulaire : Chotel

PRÉFECTURE DE POLICE SERVICE de la CARTE D'IDENTITÉ Direction de l'Admon et de la Police générale

Paris, le 31 AOUT 1937
LE PRÉFET DE POLICE,

Imp. Chaix (B) — 1147-36 — (3-D)

Marie Chotel (Madame Marie). 1937

Painter Thomas Gleb. 1930s

My mother (left) with her best friend, Berthe Moulin, in the 1930s

My mother (far right) and father (third from right) with a group of
writer-and-artist friends, including painter Thomas Gleb (second from
right). My father wrote stories in Yiddish, and some were published
in magazines. They all enjoyed outings because everyone lived in
tiny apartments, so their only gathering places were cafés or parks.

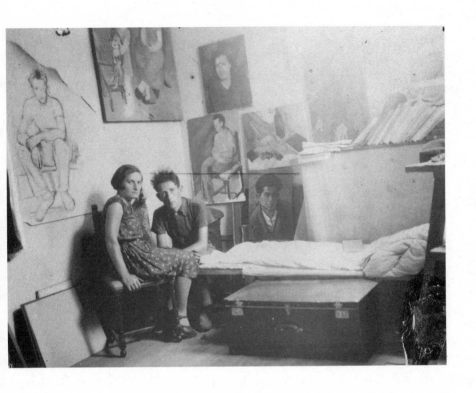

My mother and father at Thomas Gleb's atelier. Note the drawing
of my father and a painting of my mother. My parents' paintings
and family photo albums were saved during the war,
hidden in Madame Marie's basement.

As a toddler, at home on my Paris square

With my mother and father. 1935

Me, age four or five, with new shoes

In 1942, wearing a sweater knitted and embroidered by my mother.
My jumper was made by Madame Marie.

Monsieur Henri and Madame Marie

With my mother. 1942. The photographer, Maurice Daum,
was later deported with his family.

SIX

THERE *WAS NO* school on Thursdays. Officially, we were to stay home and do our homework. In working-class families like ours, though, this was the day parents expected their children to run errands. But in our yellow-star universe, my mother preferred that I spend my Thursdays with my cousins, at her sister Miriam's apartment. The Melczak family lived near the Père Lachaise Cemetery. Their crowded tenement faced a large courtyard off a small, dirty alley; the Passage des Amendiers.

It was a long walk. To get there, I took narrow side streets that made me feel smaller, less conspicuous. Eventually, though, I came into view of the wide boulevard I had avoided as long as possible. On the large island pavement between the sidewalks stood the Métro station of Père Lachaise with its ornamental wrought-iron art-nouveau entrance. The Living traveled in and out of the well-defined, large hole in the ground; the Dead stayed behind the serene stone walls of the majestic cemetery on the edge of the boulevard. German soldiers guarded everyone — dead or alive.

Before I crossed, I looked quickly to my left: a movie theater, now forbidden territory; I could imagine the womblike
hall, the rows of seats, the giant screen poised to hypnotize—
other children, not me, not my Jewish cousins—but I had to
move on; I had to leave the comfort of the narrow street. As I
prepared to do so, I could see how, into the wide mouth of the
large boulevard, streets on every side emptied their pedestrians,
their civilian bicyclists, into a flow of military motorcycles, cars,
trucks. It was dangerous to tarry; one mustn't tarry. I bravely left
the sidewalk, crossed the boulevard to the paved Métro island,
and from there, crossed the boulevard again till I had at last
safely reached the farthest sidewalk. On the corner to my right:
a popular shoe store with outside displays of bargain shoes. I
would have liked to linger, but one must not linger, nor walk
too fast, nor run. Like everyone, I walked on at an even pace, in
that neutral mode Parisians assumed when in sight of the occupants. A German soldier came out of a bakery, eating an éclair. I
made sure I did not quicken my step.

Past the bakery, the street narrowed till it was constricted
enough to enter the neighborhood slum, then it pushed me
into a dim alley that smelled of urine, onions, dirt, cooked cabbage. All at once, a medley of discordant sounds: babies screaming against a background of loud adult arguments, monotonous
hammering, popular love lyrics on a radio, someone running
down the stairs. I was almost there. A different fear tightened my
stomach; no longer the fear of German soldiers, who weren't
anywhere in sight anyway; just the familiar fear of poverty's
violence, of a sudden knife aimed at someone, of a child or a
woman being beaten, of the noise of pots being thrown down

flights of tenement stairs—the fear I always felt before I reached my aunt's door all alone. But that Thursday I was in luck: above the din I could hear my cousin's violin at the other end of the courtyard, serenading the sunlight in its outdoor prison cell.

A deep sorrow that has just been calmed, the music imposes a formal serenity, like the gardens of Versailles. I go toward it as to a fountain suddenly appearing on a square one suffocatingly hot afternoon. My cousin, like a fountain's statue, makes the music flow from his violin. The nervous disorder of tenement poverty fades out, is stilled for now. All I hear is classical music, in astonishing purity. My twelve-year-old Cousin Serge, short for his age, seems to caress his violin with his intense dark-brown eyes. When I am near him, everything else vanishes—all my fears, the German soldiers, even my longing for my father, for more of my mother. What remains is Music, divine, supreme. I come as a worshipper.

Serge has noticed me crossing the courtyard quietly, obviously wishing not to disturb him, not to stop the magic. He keeps on playing. Because he hasn't yet finished his piece. Because if he stops to greet me, he knows I will beg him to start again. I'm his best fan, his most ignorant admirer. I know nothing of music but this and what I hear in the streets. At home, the illegal radio is turned on only for BBC news. I have never gone to concerts, although my mother once took me to an opera. While she was ecstatic about it, I found it silly, terribly odd to hear overdressed people singing a conversation. But I am always thirsty for Serge's music; his violin bow draws a magic circle of daydream around us. I place myself into it, squatting at Serge's feet, looking up to listen to his face, his hands, the violin.

He smiles and plays. I daydream that we are both older; he on the stage, playing music; I in a front-row seat, listening. He has grown very tall and wears a black suit, a starched white shirt, a black tie, just like orchestra musicians in magazine photos; I wear a dressy maroon silk dress, my hair is up and my shoes are shiny black leather pumps. But nobody is really paying attention to anyone's clothes—so elegant. They're all in a trance, listening with open mouths, listening hard. I'm so proud that I whisper silently to myself: "This is my cousin, my own cousin, my first cousin, my best and dearest cousin, the one with the magical bow!"

To my great surprise, however, when the music finally stops, there is no applause. Coming out of a daze, I realize there is no one in the courtyard at the moment but two children: me, age seven, looking up at my twelve-year-old cousin, short for his age, dressed shabbily, who leans against the wall outside his apartment. As he removes his violin from his left shoulder, the hidden yellow star appears. Instinctively, I touch mine, to make sure it's still exactly where it belongs. Serge lovingly places his violin in the case. If only I dared, I would voice a protest: I don't want the violin to be hidden; I want it back resting on my cousin's shoulder. I don't want to move. I want to squat on this spot forever, in this squalid courtyard, waiting for the violin, listening to the violin, looking at the violinist, daydreaming of a marvelous future around a concert stage. But without the music, I am just an awkward frog in the presence of a secret prince.

LIKE A TRUE PRINCE, Serge knows how to enter a pauper's lodging as if it were a castle in which he feels totally at home. I follow him into my aunt's dark, cavernous, two-tiered apartment, where—miracle of miracles—the entire Melczak family lives, absolutely complete, no one missing. Two parents and five children. Aunt Miriam and Uncle Motl, their three sons: Maurice, 18, Charles, 16, Serge, 12; and two daughters: Sarah, 14, and little Henriette, not yet 3.

The apartment doubles as a shop where my uncle and his eldest son work all day on their knitting machines, the first objects you see on your left as you enter. Those large machines monopolize the narrow daylight coming through the only window in the whole apartment. Looking up across from them, you see a kind of loft that nightly accommodates a huddle of sleeping persons. To your right, the hearth of family life, where meals are made and served, guests are greeted, children admonished or praised, news circulated, and where you don't have to go far to fetch anything. Just ask; someone is likely to be near the object you want. It is so dark. At least one lamp must stay lit, even during the day, and you must watch your step, as the room is very cluttered with its central dining table surrounded by chairs and bordered by some single beds and a cooking area. Luckily, my Aunt Miriam always seems to be within range of a pot and ladle or a teakettle, making you feel cozy with an offer of tea or soup.

Aside from the pot and ladle on the stove, and the violin hanging in its case high on the wall, there is one other marvel in the room that attracts my attention every time I visit. It is a wonderful calendar. Every morning you tear off a square sheet with yesterday's joke to reveal today's date with today's joke! One of my older cousins always lifts me, reads the new joke out loud, and even lets me peek gently at tomorrow's joke. In my home we have just an ordinary calendar showing the current month's Christian holidays and saints' days. It isn't funny at all. Then too, in my home, there are only two people: a mother and a daughter; no father, no brothers, no sisters; it is lonely. I love to cozy up in my aunt's apartment, like a cat on a warm rug.

TODAY is different.

Serge and the other boys are gone (maybe to the public pool, where the brothers like to go) and my aunt has asked Sarah to take me and Henriette out for a few hours. That will leave just my aunt and uncle in the house. I wonder if they will get lonely. Sarah only asks at what time she should bring us back.

We cross the tenement courtyard—all its magic gone without Serge's violin—then walk through the small alley with its sharp stink till we reach the street with its more pleasant smell of fresh bread from the nearby bakery. At this point, we stop, not sure of where to go. In the "Old Days," we would have gone to the park above the Père Lachaise Cemetery, but now parks are forbidden public places.

Sarah cheerfully suggests that we walk on the wide boulevard, looking at shop windows on one side, then on the other. It doesn't sound as exciting as playing in a park or going to a movie, but we can't think of anything else.

We make a game of it. We imagine that we are under strict orders to choose one item from every shop window. A salesperson standing behind the display will surely overhear us saying: "I want this!" "That one!" She'll take note of our wishes and, since we can't enter the shop, will arrange for a delivery outside our front door later in the day.

My favorite store is particularly wonderful. It sells light fixtures, and its ceiling is covered with bronze chandeliers, ranging from the very ornate to the inordinately ornate. They make you think of movies with splendid châteaux, where kings, queens, and duchesses bow and curtsy to each other under gold chandeliers while the king's musicians play cheerful music. Henriette is so dazzled—forgetting the rules, holding up all her fingers, she cries: "I want ten! I want the biggest!" Sarah smiles and asks her: "And where will you put them?" "On the ceiling! On every bit of the ceiling!" Sensible Sarah is practical: "But there wouldn't be enough room for ten of them. Even if there were just two, the neighbors would get jealous and steal them the minute no one was at home." That convinces Henriette: if only she might have one, just one; Charles could nail it to the dining-room ceiling above the table, and it would be wonderful eating soup under it! We linger a long time at the chandelier store.

Walking slowly, we window-shop on both sides of the boulevard. After a while, though, Henriette begins to complain of being thirsty. We have little money, and anyway we can't go into a store (it is past the hour when Jews are allowed to shop), so we try to distract her: "Look, Henriette, a horse!" "A dog!" "Three birds on the bench!" She looks—one second per animal—then repeats her complaint: she is thirsty! thirsty! thirsty! In desperation, we pull her toward the shop window we have been saving for later, for when she has become unbearably tired or restless. It is a "doll clinic" where you can take your doll if her head comes off or her leg breaks.

There are all kinds of dolls. Some, from long ago, have light-blue eyes and blond hair, puckered lips, puffy pink cheeks, lacy hats tied with ribbons under the chin, and dainty long dresses. Having made their way back to health, they are waiting to be picked up. But there are also dolls' severed heads and headless bodies, totally unrelated, resting together. Henriette wants to know what would happen if you brought your doll to be fixed and were told to come and get her in a week—and then, suddenly, you had to leave town? Would the repairman keep your doll till you came back, or would he put it up for sale as a used doll, and another girl would end up with your doll? Sarah says that a man who runs a doll clinic knows how important it is to have your own doll, so he would surely wait a very long time for you to come back.

Henriette abruptly remembers that she is thirsty. We can't buy her any drink, we repeat; she will have to wait till we get back home. Well then, she wants to go home this very minute. "Not yet," says Sarah. "We still have two hours to go before the time Mommy told us to come back." Henriette is thirsty: that is that; and she is getting cranky about it. "Just get me some water!" she whimpers. "I want some water! I'm thirsty!" and she pulls at our hands as if they could pump water on the spot. Sarah is worried that her little sister will make a public scene—that we will be harassed as Jews. She starts negotiating: "Wait, stop crying. I'll do something. We'll get you some water in that bar across the street." She bends down, checks into the hem of her skirt, finds a little money. "Come now. We'll all go in together." So we go, Henriette, full of renewed energy, walking as fast as she can.

We enter the bar. At the counter: a couple of customers, drinking, chatting. They turn to look at us, stare at the yellow stars Sarah and I are wearing. Sarah asks the bartender if he would be kind enough to give the little girl a glass of water. But he has something else on his mind as he addresses Henriette, pointing to Sarah: "Is she a neighbor, or your babysitter?" Henriette is quick to correct him: "Oh no. She's my big sister, and this is my cousin!" "In that case," he points out, "shouldn't you also be wearing a yellow star?" Henriette patiently explains: "I'm not allowed; I'm too young. You have to be six. When I'm older, I'll wear the star." The barman turns to Sarah: "I'm sorry; I can't serve you." She puts all her money on the counter: "I can pay you. One glass of water, please." His voice has grown very cold: "I don't sell water. Please leave immediately." I start to protest: "It's not fair! It's not fair!" Sarah moves fast: pockets her money, grabs Henriette's hand and mine, and pulls us outside. Now she has two fussing children, Henriette repeating that she is thirsty, and I that it isn't fair.

Again, Sarah worries about attracting attention if we carry on in such an agitated manner. But when we ask to go home, Sarah says no, not yet. "Look, don't fret," she says. "We'll do something very nice, something special. You'll see. I'll think of something!" "But we're not allowed anywhere," I complain. Sarah suddenly seems very confident: "I have an idea," she says to me. "You and I are wearing the star, but Henriette isn't. If she were alone, they couldn't tell she's Jewish and they would let her in." "You're going to leave her alone?" I worry. Henriette has heard this: "Sarah, are you going to leave me alone?" Sarah calms us both: "No, of course not, but I have a plan. If you can only keep quiet, you'll see." She certainly seems to know where she is going, and she is going there quite fast; Henriette is almost running to keep up with us.

WE FOLLOWED Sarah's plan, and it worked! Lined up behind her against an old wall, we looked through the street-level windows of a small public library housed in the basement of the building. Sarah was pleased: "It's empty now except for the librarian. Henriette, you go down first, by yourself. The librarian will see you are alone and will worry about it and ask you questions. Don't answer right away; she'll try to make you feel good, show you some picture books before she asks you questions again. When she is very busy with you, Odette and I will go down." Henriette, glad to have such an important role, went down immediately. We stayed by the street entrance, waiting for the right moment. The afternoon was turning out to be very exciting after all: I was about to go into a library for the first time in my life!

A little while later, when the librarian looked up to see who else was coming down the library stairs, she immediately noticed our yellow stars. She quickly glanced around the room: no, there was no one but us and the little girl. She looked very kind but quite nervous. "Are you her mother?" she asked Sarah (who did look older than her age!). "No, but I'm her sister. I thought I'd lost her! Then as I passed by, I thought: she loves books so much, maybe she's in here! And she is!" On cue, Henriette begged: "Sarah, please, please read to me!" "Is that all right with you?" Sarah asked the librarian. "Oh, all right," said the librarian. "As long as you stay in the picture-book corner and mind the children. I'll go to my desk." Sarah was grateful: "You're very kind. We won't be any bother to you." Henriette and I said our most ardent thank-you's, then settled into our chairs, happy for the refuge, the quiet, the anticipation of a midday story-reading by our Sarah. In that younger children's corner, the chairs were little, but some of the books were quite large; open, they could cover our chests like shields. Behind that first layer of defense stood the bookcases, packed with books, and behind them, the old thick walls.

The fairy tale Sarah was reading us told of a girl all alone in a dark cave. She had taken refuge there from a giant, fond of eating small children, who was prowling the forest for his dinner fare. The little girl could hear his heavy footsteps above her, nearer and nearer to the cave. It was very scary! But then his footsteps went farther and farther away from the cave. The little girl was so scared she didn't dare move for a very long time, long after any footsteps could be heard. At last, though, she felt safe, but so tired that she promptly fell asleep, her head pillowed on a stone. I looked at Henriette — no, she wasn't falling asleep. She was wide awake, looking up at her sister in a trance. Sarah was reading from a large book; you couldn't see her star through it. You couldn't see mine, either, through the oversize book I held open on my lap. But I wasn't looking at it; I too was staring at Sarah serving us a feast of fairy tales, all so scary and wonderful, where good and beautiful children — or princesses—encountered terrible obstacles, horrifying dangers from evil-minded ugly creatures (or ugly inside, but disguised as beautiful and innocent to fool the truly good), but for our heroes, everything worked out in the end, usually with a joyful family reunion, a splendid wedding, or a coronation—or all three!—while the evil ones were severely punished.

Did we stay there forever? or just one hour? I can't remember. What I do remember is that I felt we had found refuge in a city cave, where we were guarded by large bookcases and a quiet librarian. Behind us stood the window and the door to the street, where danger lurked from booted giants and armies of hostile eyes. Here we were safe. My big Cousin Sarah was mesmerizing us with stories, my little Cousin Henriette had forgotten she was thirsty, and the woman librarian was pretending we were children like any others, that she hadn't seen our stars. She was at her post by her desk, and nobody dared come into our shelter. A little bit of Heaven, complete with gatekeeper!

BACK FROM SCHOOL the following afternoon, I checked as usual with my regular gatekeeper. Madame Marie looked up and saw me at her door, then burst into a smile that lingered long after she had returned her attention to the dress-in-progress at her sewing machine. That was a good sign. She probably had something special for me: a doll's dress she had just made, or some straight pins with colored heads, or else maybe she was going to send me on an errand to the buttonmaker. Protocol was strict: a well-brought-up French girl did not question grown-ups but patiently waited to be given instructions.

And so I sat on the tall stool and waited. Madame Marie fussed over a woman's dress she was close to finishing and she didn't chat. Silence with a stern look was always ominous, but silence with a lingering smile bode well. Whatever she might say would surely be worth the wait. And so I waited. And waited. She pinned the dress on the form—rather slowly, I thought. Then, she went to her dresser, came back poking hair pins into her braided bun—and finally, she spoke: "Let's go see what's in the warehouse today!"

Even though Madame Marie's hair was in impeccably good order, we didn't have far to go for our "outing": just some twenty feet across the courtyard, which, small as it was, had two distinct parts. The "residential" part faced the loge window: this was the shed that doubled as Madame Marie's kitchen. The space between that shed and the loge window was one of the three areas where I was allowed to play, the main criteria being that I remain within view of Madame Marie. The other two areas were the loge itself and the lobby. But I was forbidden to go by myself into the more "industrial" part of the courtyard, which had a couple of small warehouses under the guardianship of Madame Marie. So it was no small treat to be invited to accompany her to the warehouse!

It only happened twice a year, in summer and winter, when Madame Marie took me to see the fresh shipment of holiday decorations that would be stored there until all the orders had been filled. In winter, there were Easter baskets, toy rabbits, chicks of yellow puff; in summer, there were crèches and miniature snowy villages.

Madame Marie was very solemn, as on the rare occasions

when she went to church. In our very brief procession, I followed her from the mundane part of the courtyard into the domain of biannual mysteries.

She unlocked a door but did not turn on an electric light, as there was none. The large room had to make do with whatever daylight came from a narrow, elementary slit of a window that gave onto the courtyard. I thought it a proper setting for a lit candle, but quickly remembered that nothing of the sort was ever offered or even mentioned. Our eyes simply adjusted to the dimness, and soon we could distinguish everything well enough. Cartons were stacked along the walls, and the concrete floor resembled a newly planted field, with several rows of model snowy villages alternating with exemplary crèches, each arranged on a piece of painted cardboard. Madame Marie and I walked through the rows admiring the new crop of decorations. She had either obtained the right to give me one of the decorations or she would buy it herself at a bargain price; in either case, it was customary that I should not leave the shed empty-handed. It was even better than the shop-window game I had played with Sarah and Henriette: I could fantasize as to which item I wanted from the entire floor display, and I would indeed end up taking something home. It was wise then to examine every article in all its details. Madame Marie didn't rush me; she was also enjoying this ritual, urging me to take my time till I was absolutely sure which cardboard miniature I wanted.

What then was my wish: a village scene, or a crèche?
From where I stood, tall as Gargantua, I looked at one of

the village scenes. All the rooftops, all the trees glittered with snow; the houses clustered around the church as around a fire. That landscape radiated comfort and serenity. Such inner peace in those homes so tightly enclosed by slate roofs and wooden shutters! It must be nice to spend winter evenings safe inside, then in the morning to open wide the shutters and look out at the self-assured church pointing to the sky! Maybe I'd take one of those, the one with the most houses and the highest steeple. But no, that wouldn't be playing fair: I hadn't taken the crèches into consideration in making my choice, and they were so lovely! A few of them had just the suggestion of the roof and sketchy walls of a thatched barn, and you had to bend down or kneel to see what was inside, but most of them had no cover of any kind, the better for you to see the young Virgin Mary in her blue dress and with a golden halo, kneeling in adoration of her baby lying on a bed of straw. Kneeling on the other side of the baby was his father, Joseph, looking more like his grandfather. Behind the parents and their baby were a donkey and an ox. This was the basic set in every crèche, but sometimes there were also lambs and angels. It must be nice to have your mother on one side, your father on another, and friendly animals all in the same room! It would surely give me endless pleasure to stare at parents kneeling in adoration of their baby!

Just in time, just before I picked my crèche, I luckily remembered that the baby was a boy named Jesus, a Christian baby. It would upset my mother to have him and his parents in her apartment, so actually the only choice I had was of a snowy village miniature, the kind I saw on the occasional holiday greeting cards my parents would write or receive. But there were several different models; how should I make my choice? I first thought of leaving it to chance: closing my eyes, pointing my finger in one direction, opening my eyes again and seeing which village scene was closest to my pointed finger. But why should I leave it up to chance? It would be better, as always, to leave it up to Madame Marie. I knew she had come to Paris from someplace in the country, so I asked her which of the miniatures looked most like her native village. Without any hesitation, she walked over to the next row, picked out a set, and showed it to me dreamily: "You see this steeple? It's like the one on the church where I grew up." Well, that did it! I would have Madame Marie's church steeple in my own apartment. When I would tell my mother why the church was special, she would surely approve my choice, especially after reporting, for good measure, how I had resisted the temptation of choosing a crèche.

SEVEN

WHAT A STRANGE sight: Madame Marie herself in our bedroom, uncovering us from our deep sleep, throwing blankets off our beds!

The faint light of dawn awakens my first rational thought — today is Thursday, not the ordinary weekly day off from school, but *better* than that: actually the beginning of summer vacation, just two days after July 14th, Bastille Day. Madame Marie is very agitated. She whispers loudly: "Quick, put on a jacket, or anything! They're up the street . . . trucks filling with Jews. Come with me right away!" My mother starts to straighten her bed but Madame Marie has no patience: "No, Berthe, leave that. Leave everything! Come down with the child!" And so my mother grabs a couple of jackets — with yellow stars sewn onto them, and we go one quick flight down the spiral staircase. As soon as we enter her minuscule apartment, Madame Marie pushes us into the broom closet with orders to be perfectly still. It turns out to be just in the nick of time!

The front bell rings. We hear Madame Marie go to the lobby. She comes back, accompanied by several loud male voices. Now they explain themselves: they are conducting a surprise roundup of foreign immigrant Jews as part of a campaign "to rid France of Jewish vermin." (They have no German accent, so they must be French policemen!) Madame Marie loudly praises them: "It's about time! We've let those Jews take over our jobs, our houses, our money, everything! We've been pushed around too long!" They sound glad to be so warmly welcomed; this is not always the case, they say. "Some people, as French as you and me," one tells her, "resent the roundups, stick up for Jews and, who knows, might even hide them!" Madame Marie reassures them that she, too, can't understand how any Gentiles could possibly be taken in by these Christ-killers. She herself is from Alsace, and is therefore pleased to see—at last!—Germans and French working together to make France "Jew free." That's something worth toasting with a bottle of fine Alsatian wine—the very best!—one she has brought back herself from her own village. She is saving it for a special occasion, which this surely is! Won't they sit down for a minute, have a quick drink, a toast to their courage? "Just for a minute," they say.

In the small space where we stand, I can feel my mother's body tightening against mine. We hold our breath, sharpen our ears.

The sound of wine being poured, of glasses clinking in a toast, of Madame Marie pulling up chairs and stools around her small table; the sound of boastful talk, hearty laughter. Our bodies stiffen, our breath is muted; we become ears, nothing but ears.

Suddenly, a pointed question by one of the gendarmes bursts the bubbling chatter. "Where are your Jews?" he asks, and his companions fall silent. I think my heart has slipped into my stomach. Madame Marie answers in an oddly bitter tone: "You know how Jews are, always pretending to be poor, but the truth is they all have money; the husband is a prisoner of war, but his wife and child have gone off to their country house. Can I afford a country house or a long vacation? Anyway, I'm glad they're gone! Good riddance! I hope they don't come back. Let's have a drink to that, shouldn't we?" More pouring of wine, more easy-going chatter. Then an abrupt interruption—most surprising. A stern voice admonishes Madame Marie: "You know, Lady, what will happen if we find you've lied about your Jews? The same thing that will happen to them. We'll pack you into a truck full of Jews and you're off with them to the Vel d'Hiv. There you can wait with thousands of screaming Jews till the trains and the camps have room for you and for them."

In our closet shelter, my mother squeezes my hand too hard, but all I utter is a totally silent, ardent wish: "Madame Marie, don't let them take you away! Please, Madame Marie's God, please do something!" To my astonishment, I hear Madame Marie ask them: "Look at me! Do I look like an irresponsible, untrustworthy person? If my Jews were home, wouldn't I have brought them to you immediately?" The same male voice, still stern but not quite as confident: "Well, maybe you're right, but still, just to make sure you're telling the truth, we'll go up to their apartment. Please give us the key." Madame Marie sounds horrified. "Oh, dear," she says, speaking very fast. "You don't want to go near their apartment! You know how those foreign Jews are, especially Polish ones: rude, ill-mannered, keep a filthy house. Whenever I pass their apartment, the smell is so bad I have to hold my nose. If they open the door, I say whatever I have to say very quickly and get down the stairs as fast as my old legs will make it! I wouldn't want to have to go into their apartment! Those people have no sense of cleanliness, politeness, good manners! That's why it's hard for French—and Germans—to deal with them. Too bad you actually have to enter their apartments to get those Jews out. But I guess you can't count on all of them to turn themselves in quietly at the police headquarters! Anyway, here is another bottle, nearly empty; won't you help me finish it?" That said, she pours out a bit more wine—and a lot more words spouting praise, flattery, anti-Semitism.

Meanwhile, in the closet: our upright bodies stiff and still, our ears so sharp we could see with them; a slight pressure of the hand, a silent gesture takes the place of words. With quiet fingers, my mother has been trying to unstitch my star. Since we've had to follow the scene outside with exquisite attention, all accompanying thoughts, internal commentaries have come in short, compact heartbeats, such as one fleeting pang of dismay at Madame Marie's portrayal of Jews. ("How could she say such awful things about us? My mother keeps a clean apartment; we don't have a country house!") On the other hand, thoughts of another order—no, not thoughts, rather confessions of faith: Madame Marie is my godmother; she will save us. Whatever she is doing, whatever she says, however strange, it is surely to save us, and save us she will. True faith being absolute, my survival and that of my mother now guaranteed, I can turn my attention to the situation of my other two sets of relatives. With irrevocable certainty I know somehow that only one set will be spared while the other will be taken, will "disappear," never to be heard from again. When Fate announces itself, it does so with a solemn clarity that forbids any questioning of motives.

Which set of relatives will Fate take? The family of three on my father's side, or the family of seven on my mother's? The better-off small family with an only child, a girl three years older than I, or the much poorer much larger one, with a girl seven years older and another four years younger? "ONE will be taken." Which will it be? That question leaves Fate totally indifferent. In its silence, Fate leaves it up to me to answer. There is an inexorable deadline: I must make a quick decision. I figure that when people are taken away, disappear . . . so do their possessions. If my better-off cousin is taken, so will all the toys, all the dresses that are my birthright to inherit when she outgrows them. On the other hand, if Serge and his family are taken, there will also be nothing for me to inherit; nothing has been coming to me anyhow.

What a terrible choice, but it must be made, the way Sarah, Henriette and I had to pick one item out of every shop window we passed. Wanting all my cousins spared is like wanting all the items in the store while the quota was "ONE, only one," and now it is only one set of relatives, not more. And to make it worse, I must move fast, make my choice. . . .

Suddenly, outside the closet: sounds of policemen getting up, pushing chairs against the table, Madame Marie profusely grateful, thankful, full of good wishes, and so on. Soon it will all be over. I must hurry, pick the people to be spared: I opt for the family of my girl cousin who, as an only child, still wears and uses all my future hand-me-downs. It is an awesome moment: I have been reduced to a disembodied accomplice of Fate;

I have played my part; I can be dismissed. And now the search team is saying its good-bye and thank you. Soon after, Madame Marie opens the closet door and liberates us.

My mother bursts with expressions of gratitude and admiration which Madame Marie banishes as unwarranted; she has simply done the natural thing. But my mother does not let go; there is something that still puzzles her. "The Pope has not objected to the anti-Jewish laws, or to Vichy's anti-Semitic propaganda. It's like a mandate to Catholics not to intervene in whatever happens to Jews," she says. "How then do you reconcile what you did to save us with your own Catholic faith?" Madame Marie answers a little curtly, evidently eager to move on to other more urgent subjects: "Don't worry. Popes and governments come and go; only God is eternal. This is between me and God. If He thinks I've done wrong, He will let me know. Now: we must move quickly. The child has to be taken to the country [as was arranged in case of danger]; I'll fetch Henri from his night-shift job. He'll accompany her to the meeting place at the train station, where I hope they will find the other three girls. And you, what are your plans?" My mother answers that her concern is to go immediately (of course, wearing no star) to check on her sister, Miriam; beyond that, she will remain for now in Paris, with friends, and continue to work under cover in the Resistance. If Monsieur Henri will indeed take the child to the Gare du Nord, then she can have peace of mind.

My mother quickly left; Monsieur Henri of course soon materialized and firmly led me by the hand into the street. As we walked from the house, a couple of German soldiers stood watching truckloads of Jews pass by. In Monsieur Henri's huge hand, mine trembled with fear. His grasp tightened. A few steps later, when no one was nearby, he whispered: "Look at your feet and keep on walking. If anyone calls your name, don't answer, don't look up. Just keep on walking." I stared at my feet: with each step, they pushed the nearest bit of sidewalk just a bit, as if it were an aging, moving carpet that could no longer fly. And of course I did not look up. Nobody called, but even if someone had, I wouldn't, couldn't have answered. Still, I knew trucks were passing. Something heavy pressed the pavement, splattered invisible dark mud at my feet, made each step difficult to complete.

We went laboriously up our street for several blocks. At last we reached the wide boulevard with its two shores separated by its long island plaza where stood, beckoning like a lighthouse, the modest wrought-iron subway entrance of my neighborhood, guarding the open air-market stalls, still empty at that early hour. My feet were quick to respond: they wanted down, down. Going down the stairs into the underground corridors, I started to run but was immediately reined in by Monsieur Henri. I knew exactly what he meant: "Act natural!" Actually, I had always run down any flight of stairs, but ever since we wore the star, I had been well-trained to "look normal" in public, to "act natural" — that is, to have a measured, even walk, to look uninterested by anything I passed except storefronts or market stalls. So I quickly corrected my impulse, and one step at a time I descended the stairs, which one step at a time drew me nearer and nearer the underground corridor that would lead me to freedom. At last, my shoes hit the solid level floor of the corridor, and it was as if I had suddenly traded heavy galoshes for indoor felt slippers! All that was heavy and scary was up there, way above ground. Here I was on safe territory, underground like our cave during bomb alerts. In my "normal" universe, one always naturally descended into safety.

Yet another flight of stairs and we were on a subway platform. It was quiet; there were few people. I felt much lighter, glad to have Monsieur Henri to myself, a rare event. When the train came, it turned out to be one of those very luxurious Rothschild trains—always a special treat, surely a good omen. Automatically, I started to walk toward the last coach, reserved for Jews, but as Monsieur Henri pulled me to a more central coach, I remembered that I wasn't wearing a yellow star anymore. I could go anywhere, like anyone else—a most astonishing, wonderful feeling! If I had been alone, I would have gotten off at the next station just to try out yet another coach, and then repeat the ritual at each station. But of course, I couldn't do that, especially since a grey-haired lady wearing a black felt hat complimented Monsieur Henri on his quiet and well-brought-up "granddaughter." I hadn't thought of Monsieur Henri as a grandfather. My own grandfather had been expected to make his first visit from Warsaw to Paris that very summer to see his two daughters and their children. I had looked forward to seeing my only surviving grandparent, but I didn't think he would come now that the family was being scattered. Without the star, though, I suddenly acquired a French grandfather, big and strong as a mountain, and as unloquacious and undemonstrative as mountain folks. I was quiet and well-mannered in my happiness to have a family claim on Monsieur Henri, but our new relationship proved to be short-lived.

From the subway station we went up directly to the train station, then to the clock that had been designated as the meeting point for myself and three other Jewish girls. From there we would be escorted by a Gentile woman onto the train that would take us to our new home in the country. Amazingly, all four of us made it to the clock, and so did our Gentile escort. Monsieur Henri told me to be sure to listen to her. I should also, from the moment I met them, obey the grown-ups in my host family. After he wished me a brief good-bye and good luck, he was gone.

I took a window seat and looked out at the platform. People standing there were waving goodbye to someone they knew in the train, but no one was waving to me, nor to the other three girls.

When the locomotive at last set into motion, propelled by its triumphally mournful wail, the two-year-old Suzanne burst out crying. Her sister Paulette who was the eldest of us all by only a few months but was clearly the tallest, assumed the authority of a mother. Cecile and I, both seven, instantly took our place as the middle sisters. We had known one another all our lives. Our families were friends. Now that our mothers remained in Paris and our fathers were prisoners of war in Germany, we would stick together as a family of sorts. We had been rehearsed that if ever we left Paris in this manner, never under any circumstance were we to admit being Jewish. Our story was to be that our (Catholic) mothers were sending us to spend our summer vacation with relatives in the country, where the air was clear and the food was plentiful. It would be easy enough: none of us was wearing a star; our first names were French; we had no foreign accent and no outward sign of our Jewishness. We would stick together, whatever happened.

As we crossed the drab Paris suburbs, a polluted, fatal grey erased all traces of color. Behind me, fading into the distance, were clear memories of my mother, Madame Marie, Monsieur Henri, all my family, my parents' friends, the plaza with its statue, its drinking fountain, my school courtyard, the alley, the butcher shop. . . .

At every train stop, platforms repeated themselves, freighted with loneliness, all bearing strangers—children with suitcases, foreigners in soldiers' uniforms.

Patches of grassy green appeared, disappeared, reappeared: soft refrains of meadows—now and then a cow.

How long would all this go on? riding so far from home, into the indifferent world of others, the countryside of strangers? "One thousand years of the Third Reich," some voice somewhere in my head answered. What did one thousand years mean? How long was that? Some adult had tried to explain (my mother? Madame Marie?) that if somebody lived the longest possible life, one hundred years, and if, at the end of that time, a great-grandchild were born who would also live one hundred years, and if the same thing would happen to him, the whole thing ten times over, then we would reach one thousand years . . . and the Third Reich would be ended. I mulled this over, considered all my fingers, one by one. Ten times one grandparent followed by one great-grandchild. I didn't know how old my Warsaw grandfather was, but I didn't think it was one hundred, and I knew he had many grandchildren—some in Poland, some in Argentina, six in Paris—but to wait till he was one hundred? and had a new great-grandchild? The calculations were dizzying. My one point of reference didn't quite work, although it strengthened my sense of doom. I would never get to see the end of the Third Reich (or my mother again or my father or Madame Marie and Monsieur Henri or my aunts and uncles and all my cousins); I would just go on riding and riding, train after train, through a tunnel of greyness and darkness from which there would be no exit, ever. I was going away, leaving behind family, Madame Marie, friends, familiar streets. . . .

A great fatigue overpowered me.

WE ARE ENTERING a small townhouse, somewhere "in the country," looking for a "Madame Marie Raffin."

A strange woman ushers us in. She looks like a mother, limps, and uses a cane to keep her balance. She doesn't say anything but goes slowly enough, with us in tow, to let us stare a minute at a steaming pot of soup on the iron stove, a grandmother knitting nearby, then, still silently, leads us away from the kitchen into the backyard, all the way to the very back where, still silent, she lets us stare for a few minutes at the pigeons in the dovecote.

We are too shy to do anything but stare: steaming soup, knitting grandmother, cooing pigeons—life is good again! But here again we cannot linger; we are marched back into the house, across the kitchen up a staircase into a small room with a narrow window overlooking the street.

As soon as we are all in, the woman closes the door behind her, introduces herself as Madame Raffin, and says: "That pot of soup on the stove and the pigeons in the back of the yard will stay where they are. Listen carefully, do everything I tell you, and you will get to eat the soup and play with the pigeons. First: never, never say that you are Jewish, no matter what happens. From now on, you are Catholic girls. Second: I am going to teach you how to make the sign of the cross and to recite two prayers—the Lord's Prayer and the Hail Mary. When you have learned that and can also tell me your "story"—how your parents are Catholic; fathers, prisoners of war; mothers, working in Paris, sending you here to be in the country and get good food—then, and then only, will I open the door and let you go downstairs to eat and play. So, you'd better pay attention to me and repeat after me every word I say." And so we do.

We watch Madame Raffin make the sign of the cross, slowly, several times; then we imitate her and repeat after her: "In the name of the Father, and of the Son, and of the Holy Ghost. Amen." We remember our fathers, but none of them has a son, and what on earth is a holy ghost? What have we promised to do in their names?

Then Madame Raffin shows us how to kneel, and how to put our palms together with our fingertips pointing upwards in strange prayers. First the Lord's Prayer. The Lord, it turns out, is (again) a Father living in heaven, whose name is special. Then we tell Him to give us our daily bread and to forgive us; then something about temptation and evil. The only references that are clear to me are the idea of a distant and inaccessible father and the reminder for him to provide us with our daily bread (a fine idea!). We repeat that prayer many times, spurred by the desire to have it done with as soon as possible so we can go down to the kitchen and have soup.

When Madame Raffin is satisfied that we have learned the Lord's Prayer, she tells us to remember the soup and the pigeons and learn one more prayer as quickly as possible, pay attention, repeat word for word. We are more than willing. Behind us: the closed and shuttered window; in front of us: the closed door. The sign of the cross and the Lord's Prayer have not managed to open that door. Maybe the Hail Mary will!

The Hail Mary can be said only if you repeat the words without trying to understand them. Mary is "full of grace," the Lord is with her; she has a fruit named Jesus. She is the mother of God, which is a good thing to know. Also her French name is Marie, which is indeed a very good name. You can't tell from the prayer if she is near or far, and what we ask of her is not "daily bread" (that is for the father) but that she will pray for us now and "at the hour of our death." She is probably very nice and, wherever she is, she will kneel as we are doing, with joined hands pointing toward the Father in heaven and insist He provide us with our daily bread, preferably very fresh from the bakery, every day of our lives, although on this very day, even if there is no bread, we will make do with the soup which smells so strongly of cabbage, turnips, and onions. As to what she prays for "at the hour of our death," what can it be?

Madame Raffin makes us repeat everything we have learned: the Sign of the Cross, the Lord's Prayer, the Hail Mary. If any of us, especially the older three, makes a mistake or forgets a word, we must do the whole prayer again. By now, I begin to despair of ever seeing the door open, of ever getting out of this room, down the stairs, into the kitchen by the pot of soup. I am tired of kneeling, of repeating mostly incomprehensible incantations, and I am very hungry. We repeat and repeat every word Madame Raffin says. She goes through the prayers again, and yet again, and finally she tells us what she has in store for us: "When people ask you who you are and where you come from, remember to say that you are Catholics from Paris; your fathers are French soldiers taken prisoners and sent to Germany; your mothers have jobs in Paris and they sent you to my house as boarders because here the food is good and you can get the best Catholic education in France." Then she drills us, one by one, on the subject, till she is satisfied that we do not falter in reciting our origins. In spite of how quickly we learn, the door does not open. Perhaps it never really will, not until the end of the Third Reich; until then, we will stay on our knees, glued to the floor, without bread or soup, learning prayers for a thousand years . . .

Madame Raffin insists that this is the very last thing she will tell us before she opens the door and lets us go. It's about what will happen to us tomorrow. We need to pay close attention because she will say it once, and she won't ask us to repeat it, although it may be the most important thing for us to remember. We look at her and the door behind her and indeed pay very close attention to her words. She explains her plan of action: tomorrow, she will keep the little one at home to stay with her youngest boy. As for the three older girls, she will take us to the convent school. We are to follow her without talking. We will see the Mother Superior, who is also the school principal, and Madame Raffin will tell her that we are her Catholic boarders from Paris, but since we were caught in a bombardment and were just now separated from our mothers and are new to Vendée, she should tell the teacher nuns not to expect us to act normal for a good two weeks. As for us, during our first two weeks of school, we should refrain from asking any question on religion; we should just remember our basic prayers and the Sign of the Cross, look at the other girls and the nuns, and imitate them. Above all, we are not to ask questions of anyone but Madame Raffin, and only in the privacy of our home when we have come back from school. At the end of two weeks, though, she expects us to carry ourselves as any Catholic girls our age would do. "Do you have any questions?" she asks. We don't; we are numb; we just want to be released; we will do anything she asks. "Remember everything I have taught you here," she concludes. We promise.

Like a miracle, the door opens; we can still smell the soup.

EIGHT

OUR YIDDISH-SPEAKING mothers could not have invented a better refuge for us than the world of Chavagnes-en-Paillers! Everything about it was totally different from all we had ever known. Not only was it situated in deeply Catholic country, in the rural Vendée region just south of its pious neighbor Brittany, but its famous seminary and convent offered the ultimate in traditional Christian education to future priests and nuns. And here, the most revered animal was the pig, lovingly raised for slaughter.

We had imagined that living in the country meant living on a farm with cows, horses, and a barnyard, at some distance from the nearest neighbor. But that was not the case at all with our new home, which was like a townhouse shouldering its neighbors in a little procession of dwellings that stopped at the nearby church. Like a fallen halo, a small circle of townhouses surrounded the church, broken here and there by a narrow unpaved street which, like ours, led the faithful to the pews. Directly across from our house, stretching along the whole block, was the eerily quiet site of the seminary, surrounded by a tall stone wall, beyond which you could see the heads of bushes and the narrow windows shuttered at twilight. Still, the Holy Spirit did not hover in ethereal clouds; it dwelt in the solidity of time-honored traditions, processions, confessions, superstitions . . . and in the rough-hewn Calvary Crosses found at forks of the road. Here future priests and nuns and their guides to holiness found their way within strict stone enclosures and a rigid routine.

Like a mother hen, the church gathered the burg around her but managed to spread her protection a little farther into surrounding fields, woods, pastures, and here and there to a village or an isolated farm officially attached to Chavagnes-en-Paillers. The same pattern repeated itself in every one of the eight burgs in the District of St. Fulgent. At home, we soon learned that, of those eight, two were particularly relevant to us. The nearest was La Rabatelière, famous for its replica of an outdoor scene recreating the apparition of the Virgin Mary to three shepherd children at La Salette, and the farthest, eight kilometers away, was St. Fulgent. Madame Raffin would speak of it as "the country I come from," which made it sound much farther, like Italy or Spain. Before getting married to a wheelwright from Chavagnes, she had worked at the train station of the town of St. Fulgent, where her high school education had landed her a clean office job rather than farm work at her village of La Basse Clavelière, two kilometers from St. Fulgent, or as a domestic at some local chateau, as her birth mother had been. But in the language of rural France, le pays (the country) was that geographical unit of only several kilometers where your childhood, like that of your ancestors, had taken place. So Madame Raffin was right: she had married a "foreigner" from Chavagnes-en-Paillers and was now living in exile from her own *pays*, which she seldom visited.

For our part, we at once took Chavagnes-en-Paillers as our own *pays*. Not only did the *pays* we quickly adopted have an elite status, but so did our host family. Few of the local children, unless they chose a religious vocation, even graduated from parochial elementary school. Our foster mother was an exception: she had attended a public high school in the city and was therefore respected as a "cultured lady." And indeed, she valued education and good handwriting and watched over our progress at school.

WE FITTED COZILY into the hub of the town. To go to the girls' school, though, we had to walk some distance through open countryside before we reached the convent. On the way, we might come across some farmers walking an ox or a cow or riding in a wooden wagon drawn by oxen.

Within weeks of our arrival here, "Paris" had become just a short word, as light as a single goose feather, thought of but seldom pronounced. But how we relished every occasion to repeat that many-syllable word, a whole marching band of pride: "Chavagnes-en-Paillers." We live in Chavagnes-en-Paillers! Our school is in Chavagnes-en-Paillers! This is the church of Chavagnes-en-Paillers. At the head of the regional procession, the priest and the altar boys of Chavagnes-en-Paillers. . . . Aside from Marie, Jesus, Joseph, this was the word we most often repeated. It clearly stated: "I am here. In this world. Here I am. See: In Chavagnes-en-Paillers. Chavagnes-en-Paillers."

IN THIS EARTHLY paradise, our daily life centered around three enclosures: the home, the convent school, and the church—and the outdoor areas adjoining each of these buildings: the backyard of our home, the school courtyard, and the pavement in front of the church.

Our house faced the seminary. The window pane in the upper part of its plain front door was covered by a lace curtain. The red-tiled greyish-white stucco house seemed to limp. On the second floor, narrow windows with wooden shutters were not quite equidistant from each other, making the row of neighboring houses look crosseyed. But entering the Raffin home: it would take you only a few seconds to cross the two ground-level rooms and find yourself opening the door to the back yard. Fully enclosed by a stone wall, it felt invitingly private. First came the well, then beyond it a center path divided the compact flower and vegetable garden which scrolled to the pigeon house in the back. At that point, turning and looking back at the house: it bore no resemblance to the front. Every detail looked carefully done, the decoration lovingly individualized. Against chalky grey walls, windows and door were framed in a finely balanced design of small pink bricks, matched by the salmon-pink rafters of the sharply pointed, red tile roof. In this *pays*, gardens were natural outdoor chapels, little islands of private beauty, of peacefulness; the street would not betray their presence to a stranger passing by.

It was wonderful to propel yourself onto the wooden swing hanging from the big tree by the shed, to start swinging hypnotically, like a pendulum, surveying your territory: the well with its pulley; the garden with string beans and tomatoes; the pigeon house full of cooing pigeons; and through the little window of the shed you passed as you swung near its top, a loft full of apples drying, grain for the pigeons, miscellaneous stored objects. Such a sense of well-being!

The most beautiful of all buildings, though, was not our house viewed from the back yard, nor even the church from any angle, but our convent school, especially its grandly serene façade. We would arrive there early in the morning, in bunches of girls collected along the road. A stone wall partially hid the convent school from view. On either side of the wrought-iron gate, a pillar of layered brick and stone held up a symbol of the Church of Christ: the half globe topped by a Greek cross of four equal arms. Beyond a large courtyard, a one-storey ground-level white stucco building was neatly divided by four doors and four windows; each of them with a white cross built into the frames of the glass panes.

But first, as we entered into the courtyard, we turned right, to a statue of the Virgin, to whom we prayed to start the school day. Behind her was the open hangar we used for lunch and recess. There we could eat, talk, and take shelter from the rain. It was there that we had what limited freedom we could expect (though the nuns supervised from a certain distance, trusting their interpretation of loud noises or body language to tighten supervision and discipline).

OUR TEACHERS belonged to the Order of Ursulines, which specialized in the education of girls. Their habits were austere. Covering their heads: very simple black kerchiefs over stiffly starched white cowls tied under the chin. All that showed of their bodies were their faces and their hands—but oh, how we watched those! We had learned to read our daily fate in them: a smile, a scowl, a slap. Every nun was different. One was sweet and meek like the Little St. Theresa; another was hard as the nail in the feet of Jesus on the cross; yet another was the down-to-earth "practical" nun, who did all the shopping and took care of the vegetable garden. She was like Lazarus's sister Martha, who quietly worked hard to prepare a good meal for the visiting Jesus while their dreamy sister Mary sat at his feet and listened to him. Each nun, according to her background and her personality, was assigned a particular role. Each filled a specific niche in that strange household of the convent house, but most of the nuns served on the staff of the attached school. It was a quaint family of many sisters and one Mother Superior, all of whom were the spouses of the dead Jesus, whose wedding ring they wore. They called us "My child," "My children," which made sense if you remembered that we were the children of God, whom they had married in the person of Christ.

On the surface, everything was orderly, soothing, slow. But there were haunting mysteries, both in the way of life of the nuns and in their teachings.

In the classroom, the only sound was the voice of the teacher introducing or repeating a set of rules—of religion, behavior, basic arithmetic, or simple natural sciences—or that of a student repeating a lesson learned by rote. But as soon as we were released into recess or lunchtime, we burst into conversations, giggles, shouts, laughter, whispers and every kind of noise known to the human voice. As for us recent refugees from Paris, we were careful to follow Madame Raffin's advice. We listened hard and spoke little. We hoped to learn how the classroom teachings applied "in real life," since often the talk at recess actually related to the lesson preceding it, which inevitably thereby lost its simplicity.

One rainy day, the religion lesson had concluded that it was a virtue to disdain money and earthly possessions. In the hangar, an animated discussion followed. A peasant living alone in near poverty was rumored to have buried a treasure of gold coins and jewelry, and one girl swore she caught him once digging in his orchard, about to add to his treasure, but she had made a pledge that she would never reveal the spot to anyone, so she couldn't tell us.

Many questions came up. Since he lived the life of a poor peasant and kept his treasures buried in the ground (and therefore useless to anyone), was he being virtuous? If he died without telling anybody where his treasure was, and no one got to make use of it, then had he lived a good life by thus removing a temptation from others? The general feeling was that, on balance, the peasant definitely weighed more heavily on the scale of evil, which would make him drop down into Hell. The question was: did he draw others down with him? If so, how? One girl reasoned that if the very rumor itself became a source of gossip or envy, then it created a pool of sins in others. And, of course, even if he counted only one sin in all that, the peasant was bound by religious duty to report it to his confessor. If he did report it, wouldn't the priest advise him to give his treasure to the church, the convent, or charity? If so, and if his treasure still remained buried, was he then committing a sin of disobedience? And then again, how did he accumulate his treasure? Did he steal it (a sin)? Did he overcharge for his goods or underpay his workers (sins)? If, however, he simply denied himself all pleasures, was that denial a sin or a virtue? (Since not to want, not to indulge in earthly goods was supposed to get you a lot of good points!) Such a complicated accounting and weighing of sins and virtues was bewildering and endlessly fascinating!

You had to watch your step every minute of the day. Not only did you have to recognize one sin from another (there were different kinds: some mortal! some not so bad), but then you also had to get God back on your side by saying the appropriate prayers. And how many to say at one time? How often? Like Parisian prescription drugs to cure you of an illness? Sometimes you prayed straight to God, but at other times it was wiser to ask for the intercession of saints (the famous ones, or your patron saint). The Virgin Mary was a good choice: Mother of God the Son, but not the wife of God the Father, she seemed nevertheless to exert great influence on Him. There was something else that would help matters: you could do good deeds. You had to figure out how you could do something good for somebody, but this didn't always work. Sometimes you'd see an old lady carrying a heavy load. That would be a good target. You'd catch up with her on the road and ask: "Can I help you? Can I carry one of your baskets?" But most of the time, the old lady would be tersely cranky: "Why

do you want to help me? Do you see me dropping my load?"
or "Run off, you nasty child, trying to make a spectacle of me!"
The only ones who were dependably responsive to our efforts
to perform good deeds were the nuns themselves. They always
said yes to whatever we wanted to do for them. Lucky for us!

EVERY NEW DAY brought new wonders: more Bible
stories from the Old and the New Testaments and exemplary
lives from the Book of Saints; gossip about neighbors or the
local count's family; church rituals, with a priest who dressed in
splendid robes of varying colors; the grandfather of our house,
who carved reeds into whistles, acorns into playhouse pots and
pans; the grandmother, who mended our clothes and bed linens,
or the times when all of us children were sent formally into the
garden, probably to provide privacy for grown-ups. There, we
would gather around the well and scare each other describing
the ghost who inhabited the bottom of the well. Someday, when
he felt like it, he might get into the bucket we were drawing. It
would be so heavy that we'd have to ask someone to help us with
the pulley. Then as the bucket would finally surface, the ugly
ghost would leap at us, throw us on the ground, and strangle us.
You were never sure what a new day would bring!

I was happy: I belonged to a large family, with a father and
mother, a grandfather and a grandmother, two brothers, three
sisters. I was a child among children, praised or reprimanded like
the others. And I was also the child of the Virgin Mary, Mother of
God, without, strangely, becoming the sister of her child Jesus
(nobody was, not even the Ursuline Sisters, who were sisters

only to each other—or acted as if they were!). And, like every-one in the whole world, I was a child of God the Father (not of the God Jesus-son-of-Mary, whose father was variously Joseph, God the Father, or a bird called the Holy Ghost). I lived with my family on rue du Calvaire, named after the Calvary Cross to our left at the fork of the road. I loved the grey stones of the semi-nary, the convent, the church, and our Calvary; they made me feel like a native of Chavagnes-en-Paillers. They were mine and I was theirs, and it would always be that way.

Still, days of innocence are always counted, even in a Ven-déen Garden of Eden! Suddenly, a snake spurts out a poison that confuses the mind, troubles the soul, crucifies the heart . . . and causes a pain that cries out that nothing will ever be the same. The snake had lain in wait for me for a long time, without my noticing its presence.

WE FULFILLED Madame Raffin's expectation that, after a very short time, all four of us girls should easily pass as born-Catholics. The little one stayed home with Madame Raffin and her little boy and did whatever two-year-old children do (some-thing that, at seven and eight, we had long forgotten). The rest of us—the three eldest—were full of zeal, always eager to please our teachers, Madame Raffin, the priests, the saints, the Virgin Mary. With a respect slightly tinged with terror, we even remem-bered that most awesome of the religious mysteries: the Holy Trinity, the three persons of God in One. We had noticed that whatever was really important to remember came in numbers. We could recite many lists: the twelve apostles, the fourteen Sta-tions of the Cross, the seven mortal sins opposed to the seven principal virtues, the seven sacraments. Then came the sequence of three sets of Mysteries of the Rosary: five Joyful, five Sorrowful, and five Glorious—and of course, the ten commandments. As for the prosaic aspects of daily life, we didn't cause anyone any particular trouble. We listened to the grown-ups and tried to make ourselves helpful. Everyone seemed quite pleased with us.

I became obsessed with keeping a detailed accounting of my sins, which I tried to balance with good deeds. It kept me very busy: sometimes it was difficult to know exactly which sin (or how many at once) I had committed, or if what I thought was a good deed really was one. But it was vital to keep track of it all so you could report it properly in the confessional booth. You could atone for your sins immediately afterwards by saying the prescribed number and kinds of prayers. But even so, when you died, when all but saints died, there would still remain so many sins to atone for that, unless you were obviously evil and therefore thrown headlong into Hell, you had to put in time in Purgatory. There, little by little, as you prayed and atoned for your sins, you would gradually, step by step, go up a ladder of purification that led to Heaven. It could take many years till you left Purgatory for ultimate union with God, whose Paradise offered Eternal Joy. We were urged to be compassionate and to offer prayers for the souls in Purgatory, to help shorten their sentence. Still, it seemed like a good idea to come to Purgatory with as light a load of sins as possible!

One day, on the way home from school, I was giggling along with the other girls, passing tidbits of gossip like pieces of candy, when a village girl told us that her mother's new baby had just been born dead and everyone was upset because he hadn't been baptized in time and so would end up in Limbo. I didn't dare ask what "Limbo" was, so I kept quiet. Someone else said: "It's not his fault, though, so God won't let him suffer." That was of small comfort to his sister: "Yes, but don't you think it's awful to be in Limbo forever and ever, with no chance ever to get into Heaven, let alone Purgatory?" Another effort at consolation: "But the baby is too little to know anything about that. And Limbo anyway is a place where you don't feel anything: it's neither cold nor hot, dark nor light, and no one feels either hunger or thirst." "Does that mean the babies don't cry?" "Well, maybe they still do. Even if they're not hungry or thirsty, they may want somebody to hold them." "But who would there be to hold them? Are there any grown-ups there?" "Yes," said an older girl. "All the good savages and pagans who never got to know about Jesus but lived good lives before the missionaries converted them, in China and other countries, they end up there, too. So they could hold the babies." And that's when the Snake bit me. It was so sudden and sharp a pain that I lagged behind the others and as silently as possible left the main road for the first bushy path into the thick woods. When I was at last alone, I sobbed uncontrollably.

My world was shattered. There was no point in balancing venial sins with good deeds, no point in minding the arduous practice of virtue. I wouldn't even get into Purgatory. I was doomed to end up in Limbo, with crying babies and good savages who didn't speak French. Forever and ever for all eternity! It wasn't fair! And all because I wasn't baptized. If you weren't baptized, not only would you end up in Limbo after you died, but while you were alive, anything you did as a Catholic, like taking Communion at the Sunday Mass, or going to confession to get a penance for your sins—none of that was valid. Even if you did it with all your heart, no matter how much you believed, it was as if you had done nothing Christian at all; it didn't count. How terrible! How I envied the baptized girls; how I'd make a trade and take on all the sins of my classmates if only I could be counted as baptized just for wanting it so much! But envy was a sin, and taking on other people's sins was probably a form of arrogance for which the priest would scold me at confession. Oh, but anyway it didn't matter, since I wasn't baptized! I couldn't be cleansed of my sins by confession, or have my soul purified by taking Communion. Surely this must be Limbo on earth! How awful! At least stillborn babies didn't know enough to fear Hell and long for Heaven, and neither did the Chinese pagans before missionaries came to save their souls. But I was old enough and I knew enough to feel wretched about all this. I would do anything to be at least let into Purgatory, even if I had to stay there five hundred years! I was ready to make any kind of bargain with anyone of sufficient influence with God to intercede in my favor and let everything be as if I had, in truth, been baptized at birth, as everyone here took for granted. To whom should I turn? I needed to get to the church as soon as possible. There, in the Divine Presence, the answer would make itself known to me; surely if I prayed with all my heart, God would send me a sign.

I ran to the church, rushed up the steps through the tall open doors, turned to my left, dipped my fingers into the font of Holy Water, made the sign of the cross, dashed farther to the left, past the beautiful stone baptismal font to the wall full of religious paintings. I thought it would be good to position myself in front of Stations of the Cross, so I could be humbled by the sufferings of Christ. But I had trouble: Christ, after all, knew His suffering was temporary, while for all eternity He would sit on a throne to the right of God Himself, accepting adoring praise from all His loyal subjects. And I, meanwhile, would be in a never-ending Limbo, where it is neither dark nor light, cold nor hot, midway to everywhere and nowhere, a place of neither joy nor sorrow, with crying dead babies and foreign savages. I would never get to see the Throne of God, with Jesus on his right, and the Virgin Mary as Queen of Angels, and all the angels and archangels in their finest robes and prettiest wings! Again I was overwhelmed with grief: there was no point in anything. Ah but wait! Despair, loss of faith is the worst sin against religion! I mustn't let myself yield to it. I'm in enough trouble. I must pray harder, harder!

I tried, but I soon got distracted from my prayers. Kneeling just a few steps from me, at the altar of the Virgin Mary, an agitated peasant woman, dressed in the long black clothes of mourning, was praying out loud: "Madame Marie, please intercede for my husband! He is not all that bad. He was just drunk. In his right mind, he wouldn't hurt a fly . . ." Ah! . . . The clouds had suddenly parted and light poured into my soul! Yes, of course (I had forgotten), the peasants call her "Madame Marie," out of affectionate respect. That was it! I was saved! The Virgin Mary had the same name as my own godmother. I wasn't baptized, but I did have a godmother whose job it was to offer me protection and guidance. It didn't matter that our relationship had not been formalized; she had already acted on it and saved me from the police roundup. It didn't matter that she never spoke to me of religion. I knew she was a Catholic, and now I even knew what that meant. I was learning to be a good Catholic like my own Madame Marie. She was clever; she would find a way to save me from Limbo; she would talk to the other Madame Marie, the Mother of God, who would speak to Him and intercede for me. Now that my Madame Marie was in on it, it would work. I was sure of it. I was so happy, so grateful, that I knelt next to the peasant woman and ardently prayed to the statue of Madame Marie, two persons in one, just as the Holy Trinity was three persons in one. This way, whenever I would pray to the Virgin Mary, my own Madame Marie would slip into the statue, and both in one would help me. With that double protection, I felt the omission of formal baptism with the subsequent doom of Limbo forever removed from my future.

After many prayers of thanks and solemn promises of special devotion to the Virgin Mary, I felt free to resume my normal activities: identifying and counting up all my sins, even those of thought or omission, and trying to estimate the value of each intended good deed.

I ran down the steps of my good church, then I skipped joyfully home—my home, my Calvary Street, my seminary across the street, my family, my burg of Chavagnes-en-Paillers. Madame Marie was with me. She was in the church. She was in every statue, every picture of the Virgin Mary. She would take care of me. I would go into the garden and whisper the news to the ghost in our well. He would never dare to cause me any harm.

EVERY BEDTIME, my roommate and I had a special ritual of our own. Actually it was Cécile, with whom I shared the small room and the bed, who had initiated it and who daily performed its opening act. At first I was frightened, but I quickly got used to it. As soon as the door closed behind us, Cécile was twitching on the floor, deep into agonized convulsions, terrifying to witness. Just as suddenly as it had begun, it was all over and she stood up calmly. The first time it happened, I was on the verge of calling for help, but she explained that again she had committed the horrible sin of gluttony (a mortal sin at that!) and was mad at herself for yielding to temptation; she wanted God to know she felt terrible.

After the ritual convulsions, we prepared ourselves for bed. Then came the solemn act of the evening, directed by Cécile but performed by both of us.

We took our posts facing the open window, she on the left and I on the right. The children's sleeping hour came about around twilight, that exquisite moment of the day. "Look," Cécile would say, pointing outside the window. "We're alive; everything is beautiful. Let's thank God." We prayed a thank you. "Tonight," she would add, "a bomb could fall and we could die, so we have to make sure everything is in good order. Odette, can you picture your mother's face?" It would take me a few seconds till my mother's face was comfortably hovering just outside the window. I would then nod yes. "Tell her all the sins you committed today. Ask her to forgive you, and say good-bye." I would. Then was the turn of my father's face. This came even faster, as it was the photo of him in his soldier's winter cap and coat which Madame Raffin had placed on the mantelpiece. I repeated everything I told my mother, only faster, because he never smiled and I knew he was growing terribly distant. Then it was Cécile's turn to say good-bye to her parents; she didn't need directions, so I kept perfectly still until she was done. It was indeed so beautiful outside. The wall of the seminary seemed to guard something safe, soft, inviting! When both of us were done, the apparition of our parents, who one by one had listened to us, forgiven us, and bid us good-bye, dissolved—our mothers went back to occupied Paris, our fathers to German prison camps. Cécile closed the wooden shutters, and night entered our room. We embraced in a strong, comforting hug as we recited together the ritual goodnight Cécile had worded: "If we die tonight, may we meet in Paradise tomorrow." Then we climbed into bed, Cécile first, against the wall. We promptly fell asleep.

I was on my back, staring at something blank straight ahead of me. The first in a rapid succession of thoughts was that we had died and were already in Paradise. I wasn't terribly happy about it, although I was grateful it was neither Limbo nor Purgatory. I thought my arrival premature and would have preferred to make my grand entrance as an old grandmother, after a splendid funeral attended by masses of relatives and friends. My second thought, however, was that the blank space didn't reflect the glory of Paradise. At that point I would quickly remember a trick to ascertain whether I had really died and landed in Paradise. I would turn my head to the right, where I knew that in our earthly bedroom there was a small chest of drawers; no one—at school, at church, or elsewhere—had ever mentioned that there were chests of drawers in Paradise. As soon as I caught sight of our chest of drawers, I was filled with happiness. It was a new day and we were alive in Chavagnes-en-Paillers!

MADAME RAFFIN would occasionally make us write letters to our mothers. We reluctantly wrote brief notes that we copied from each other: "I am in good health; hope you are too; everyone here is very nice; I do my homework; I love the pigeons; if you come to visit, please bring my doll. Love, your daughter."

One day, Madame Raffin told me that my mother would visit us at Christmas time. I had mixed feelings. I longed to see her. She would kiss and hug me, then would open her suitcase and take out my doll. But I also feared she would want to take me back to Paris.

The weather turned cold, the roads slippery, and we entered the Christmas season in its full beauty. At school and at church, we helped the nuns set up the wonderful Nativity scenes, with real hay for baby Jesus to sleep on, and Mary and Joseph kneeling in adoration of their child. The music teacher chose the girls with the best voices, who then got excused from regular classes to practice harmonizing Christmas carols. The rest of us were urged to concentrate on our lesson, but we could hear the singing in the hall and it cheered us up.

I spent a lot of time either inside the church admiring the crèche, or just outside, window-shopping at the bakery or the variety store.

The bakery showed its double allegiance: the traditional French *Buche de Noël*, a chocolate-frosted cake shaped like a Yule log, as well as the traditional regional Holiday bread, a giant *brioche*. Filling in the spaces all around the cake and the bread were small, colorful tins of sugar-coated candies, and little cardboard boxes prettily decorated with peaceful winter scenes, packed with sugar cookies. Now if I were forced to choose just one thing, what would it be? The cake would be delicious, but once eaten, nothing would remain, while if I picked a tin of candies or box of cookies, after eating its contents, I could keep the container. What should it be: candies or cookies? I knew a baptism was coming up soon. All the children would then get a chance at picking up candies thrown outside the church after the ceremony, so there was no point in choosing candies. That left the cookies. Which box should it be? There were three different pictures. I decided to choose the one showing a snowy village with a church very much like ours. Suddenly I remembered Madame Marie's giving me a choice of Christmas scenes: a snowy village or a crèche. This year, I didn't have to decide which one to take home. I could leisurely look at both: a picture of a snowy village very much like my own Chavagnes-en-Paillers, and a real crèche in my own church.

The day finally came when my mother entered the front room where I stood in the corner, waiting. As she opened her arms to me, the room, the house, the burg shrank. I charged into her embrace: my mother, my mother's coat, my mother's cologne, my mother's small suitcase (that maybe held my doll!). I was eager to show her everything immediately, but she said no, first she had to meet the Raffin family, as she had never met them, and they were so good to me and the other girls. I should go outside and play. We were always sent outside when grownups wanted private time! "But Mama, Mama, did you bring my doll?" She had, and she gave it to me. I was beside myself with joy: my own doll, the one Madame Marie had given me, the one that got lost in the Park of the Buttes-Chaumont and then was replaced by my mother without Madame Marie ever noticing, so it really was the same doll all along. How I had missed that doll! I ran outside to show her everything.

I sat my doll beside me on the swing and held her tight while I propelled us high off the tall branch. Now she could look up to the loft and down into the pigeon house below. After a while of swinging and looking up and down, we saw my mother come out of the house. She was smiling, her gaze lingering over the garden. Then she spotted me on the swing. That's right, that's what my mother looked like when she was happy, her smile as warmly inviting as her embrace! I smiled back, and there were just the two of us in the garden. And my doll. I was flying high into the tree, then down closer to the garden path, with my doll next to me and my mother coming closer: pure happiness!

"Well, my little girl," she said. "Madame Raffin and I have had a good talk. I told her how much I miss you, and how I'd like to find a way so we can live together here in Vendée. She said she understands and she will look for a place for us, and as soon as she finds one she will let me know." "In the burg of Chavagnes-en-Paillers? Or one of its villages? We'd be together and I could still go to the same school?" "No. That wouldn't work out. It's better to go where nobody knows us. We'll have to make absolutely sure that they can never, never guess we are Jewish, and to do that, we'll need a new last name. Which name would you prefer: Petit or Grand?" It sounded exciting, like playing house or Joan of Arc: "Petit!" I answered. "And what will my first name be?" "You don't need to change it; it's very French, but I'll change mine to Marie." "Like Madame Marie! and Marie Raffin!" "Yes," she sighed. "It's the name of those two good women, but it's also the French way of saying Miriam—your Aunt Miriam, my sister who was taken away." I was on the verge of asking what had happened to my aunt, my uncle, and my cousins on that terrible day in July, but my mother's expression said no, don't ask. So I didn't. Still I was glad she had chosen Marie as her new first name. Now that name had become more powerful than ever: two good Catholic women named Marie, my Jewish mother (alias Berthe and Bronsha), and my Jewish Aunt Miriam, all with the same French name as the Mother of God, the Queen of Angels. How it simplified everything! From now on, when I prayed to the Virgin Mary, all the other "Maries" would line up exactly behind her and all slip into one picture, one statue of the Blessed Virgin, whom I would beseech to give me and my loved ones the most vigilant and all-encompassing protection.

MY MOTHER says yes, she does want to see the bakery, the church, the Calvary Cross, the convent school. We bundle up, with her fussing over my knee-length winter socks that don't stay up because of worn-out elastics.

First I show her the Calvary Cross. She wants to know what it is for. "If you're on the road and you need to pray, you can do it here," I tell her. She doesn't see the point: "But you're just a block away from the church!" I had never thought of that. Maybe it's because of the seminary? Or to give its name to our street? I'll have to ask.

We go to the church. No one is inside so it gives me a chance to give my mother a full guided tour. Here is the font of

Holy Water: you dip your fingers in it and make the sign of the cross. I show her how. She tries to repeat after me, but she does it all wrong. So we move on. Here is the baptismal font, where a baptism is to take place later in the day; we might catch it on the way back from the convent school. On this side is the second half of the fourteen Stations of the Cross, showing Jesus carrying his cross, falling, being disrobed, being nailed on the cross, dying, being taken off the cross and placed in the tomb. The first seven Stations are on the other side. Here is the confessional booth: You kneel behind the heavy curtains and tell the priest your sins.

My mother looks worried. "And what if you don't tell everything?" she asks. "Then," I answer, "you carry more sins into Purgatory, where you have to stay a lot longer before you get to Heaven." "What does Purgatory look like?" she asks. "It's a spiral staircase. As you pray and repent, you get to go up a step at a time. Look, Mother, after the priest forgives you, you kneel here, at the small altar to the Virgin Mary, and say your prayers so you spend less time in Purgatory." As we pass by the main altar of the sanctuary, she says she knows it's for the Mass, doesn't ask any questions, and moves on quickly. Which is just as well, since we finally get to what I wanted most to show off to my mother: "Look, look! The crèche with the infant Jesus, and his mother and father kneeling in adoration, and the ox and the donkey blowing on the baby to keep him warm!" But to my chagrin, she seems ill at ease. We move on. "This is the altar of St. Joseph, Mary's husband," I announce. She is perplexed. "It's good for a mother to have a husband, but why do they have separate altars? It's like separate beds. Is the whole family together only at Christmas?" "No, also at other times, when Jesus is a bigger boy; then it's called The Holy Family. But Mary and Joseph always have separate altars, one on each side of the Main Altar. You can go to them any time, by yourself, without a priest. For the Main Altar, you need a priest." I made her look up at the pulpit, with its spiral staircase, and she wanted to know if Purgatory had the same staircase. I didn't think so, but by then I sensed that my mother had exhausted her curiosity and her tolerance, so I rushed her through the first half of the Stations of the Cross, at which she barely glanced, and soon we were going down the steps of the church and out.

Now that we had left sacred territory, she let out a sigh of relief and a heartfelt comment: "It's so dark and musty! All those paintings, statues, objects! So much gold and silver! It reminds me of an old lady's room, where you can hardly move around because it's so crowded with knickknacks, photographs, souvenirs, all from long ago. Like the old lady herself, who hasn't gone outside for years!" I looked back at the church and suddenly it seemed oddly shaped, as if it squatted.

I HAD GREATER success with the bakery. My mother marveled at the giant brioche; she said white bread was hard to get in Paris.

I then led her to the variety-store window display. She was amazed at the large sizes of pots and pans and silverware, but what held her attention the longest was a display of charcoal-grey wool. I recognized that look: it was as if she were seeing through the wool to a finished sweater, a dress, a hat and scarf. If I had but one choice, would I pick the wool as a present for my mother, or would I treat myself to that beautiful rosary—

the one with mother-of-pearl beads and an ornate silver cross that I had been coveting for some time? Again I looked at the religious objects grouped on the right. Among the devotional pictures, missals, first Communion candles, Christmas greeting cards, cozy crèches, and snowy church steeples with sparkles, were several rosaries. One was very plain—wooden beads on a thin cord, with a simple wooden cross (probably for nuns or monks); one was elegant, with alabaster beads; another, with glass beads, was a popular kind at school. But yes, my own favorite still was the silver chain with mother-of-pearl beads.

Suddenly I feel someone staring at me. It's my mother, now suggesting: "Let's move on and go see your school."

On the way there, Maman is enchanted with the beauty of the countryside: wintering meadows alternating with small woods crisscrossed by creeks, and here and there, a large farm with smoke coming out of the chimney, or a little village with its small houses all huddled together in the cold. I am very proud of everything she admires and I tell her how beautiful it is when it is not winter. "Every day you pass by here?" she exclaims. "It's so much better than Paris!" She is very pleased, as if this aspect of my moving to Vendée has never entered her mind until this very moment.

When we arrive at the school, she refuses to go past the enclosure. She explains that she is not ready to be introduced to the nuns as my Catholic mother from Paris. She might not yet be that convincing. It's different with the Raffin family or their neighbors. With them, it's easy to get by with small talk, but teacher-nuns must know very little outside religion, so that's probably all they talk about.

Under the circumstances, my brief "tour-guide" speech is delivered outside the entrance gate. I point to the top of the half-globe on each pillar holding the gate: "Here is a cross, not the Crucifixion cross but the Greek cross; the globe and the cross together represents the Universal Church. "The what?" she asks, "Is that the same as the Catholic Church?" "Yes," I reassure her. "It means the Catholic Church is everywhere in the world." She looks far from being reassured. I show her the pretty statue of the Virgin Mary, to whom we pray before we start school. Then I point out how cleverly the cross has been designed into every door and every window of the convent school. She tells me it's hard for her to understand all this fussing over crosses and statues; she finds it all very complicated, but when we'll be together, I'll have to teach her so that no one will guess she is not Catholic. I promise.

On our way back, I tell her the names of trees we pass, names of fish that can be caught, names of flowers, names of mushrooms and how to know the poisonous ones (Usually they're much more beautiful!). She is very pleased that I've learned such practical things. Encouraged by her approval, I report on other nonreligious matters. I notice that she is very curious and interested. I'm glad to answer her questions.

"What do you drink at dinner?" "The children drink apple cider and the grown-ups drink wine from our wine barrels in the cellar of the garden shed." "Where do you get the water for cooking and washing?" "From our garden well." "What do you do for heat?" "Well, there is the fireplace in the kitchen. The coal stove is also in the kitchen. Grandmother Raffin sits by the stove when it's on. She opens the oven door and puts her feet up on it when she's cold. Then, in your bed at night, you can keep your feet warm on a brick or an iron that's been heated and wrapped up in towels. It's important to keep your feet warm."

At home, we just had a pot-bellied stove in the bedroom and a regular coal stove in the kitchen that was used only in the winter, so my mother is fascinated. She considers the peasants very resourceful. "Oh yes, they are very clever. For instance, at a fancy meal where there's going to be a dessert, you clean your plate with a piece of bread. You turn the plate upside down, and there you are. The bottom is a clean dessert plate!" Mother is very impressed; she's eager to get a plate and try it herself. "And you know what else they do that's very clever? If you have a loose tooth, they don't take you to the dentist. Madame Raffin ties a long string to your tooth. Then she ties the other end to the handle of the back door. She slams the door shut, you scream, and there is your tooth. Out!" I can't tell what my mother thinks of that one!

To save myself and make sure she is still interested in what I am telling her, I decide to get back to the subject of food, which always seems to keep her attention. "Mama, you'll still be here after Christmas Day. On that day, the pigs get slaughtered and the women come together to make blood sausages, headcheese, patés, and to cure the ham so it can get smoked by the fireplace! But best of all, they take the fresh blood, simmer it, stir it, throw in all the leftovers from the other charcuterie, stir it some more, and cook it some more. And it gets eaten at the end of the day, and it's delicious!" My secular mother, whose parents were strict Orthodox Jews can't contain her astonishment: "That I would surely like to see. Maybe Madame Raffin will invite me?" I think she will. People like it when you are interested in their way of doing things!

Getting close to home again, we pass the church. It looks very festive as the baptismal party comes down the steps, all bundled—parents, godfather, aunts, uncles, cousins, neighbors —and the baby, dressed in a long white lace robe and a lace bonnet, crying in his godmother's arms. I'm thrilled: I didn't miss it! A swarm of candies flies from the open church portals and lands randomly on the pavement. The children, positioned at the foot of the stairs, make a run for the candies; so do I. Triumphantly, I show my mother my pickings: pale blue sugar-coated almond candies; "See, it means it's a boy!" She is horrified, confiscates them, and draws me away. "It's not sanitary! You'll catch an illness." "No I won't. Look, everybody else is doing it." "They're used to it. The peasants spit on the ground and animals leave their droppings on the road. If a candy falls into the spit or the dropping, and then you put it in your mouth, you could catch their illness. People with TB spit a lot." I am in tears: "But that's not fair! It's my candy." My mother softens: "Where is the nearest water?" "Well, it's either the Holy Water in the church or the water from our well." "Let's go inside the church; everybody is outside now." So we enter. My mother dips her fingers in the Holy Water, sprinkles it on the candies, then wipes them off on her sleeve. She has baptised my candies and given them back to me, purified, so I can eat them.

CHRISTMAS MORNING, after the beautiful Mass, we had a crowd of Raffin relatives in the kitchen. Madame Raffin used her cane for a variety of purposes other than to steady her limping walk. Now, she used it to orchestrate the delivery of the traditional *crêpes* meal, pointing here, chasing a cat there, knocking on a door to call someone, banging on the floor to show her dissatisfaction with young helpers. The coarse rye-flour *crêpes* were eaten in prescribed sequence. First, powdered with sugar, then spread with jam and finally with honey. Everyone was very jolly—eating, chatting, gossiping. Afterwards, when we had a chance to be alone, I asked my mother: "Wasn't that wonderful?" To my surprise, she admitted disappointment. She thought a country Christmas meal would be a feast with roast meat and marvelous mushroom dishes. She was really obsessed with food, so I reminded her that Madame Raffin had invited her to go with her the next day to the neighbors for a whole day of cooking up every inch of a just slaughtered pig. She perked up.

My mother has now gone back to Paris and the natural order of my life has returned. In my regained Paradise, I join all the children of the Raffin household, all six of us—two native boys and four transplanted Parisian girls—for the local New Year custom. Children go from house to house, reciting the traditional phrase of blessing: "Happy new year, good health, and Paradise at the end of your days!" In return for being blessed, the house-holders give the children treats of candy or small change.

It's a beautiful cold morning. My foster brothers and sisters and I are dressed warmly. We cheerfully recite the blessing in chorus, faster and faster at each new home. We fill our pockets with candy and coins. We are always eagerly and well received, as it is a bad omen if your house is overlooked by the children. We are important! I am happy!

NINE

I WAS FETCHED to join my mother in the small village of
La Basse Clavelière near St. Fulgent. I must have said good-bye to
Chavagnes-en-Paillers, but I have no memory of doing so. What
I do remember, though, was that I took into my new home the
photograph of my father in uniform, my rosary, the few holy
pictures I had begun to collect—all of which I brought with me,
together with my selection of favorite saints and martyrs and, of
course, my guardian angel. His presence was of great comfort,
now that I knew he was under obligation not to abandon me.

This hadn't always been the case. There was that terrible
time in Chavagnes-en-Paillers when I learned that a guardian
angel was assigned to every Christian in the course of the baptism ceremony, and at the very same moment I recalled again
that, contrary to what I pretended, I had not been baptized.
Again, this dreadful secret obstacle to being a Christian like any
other! It was so unbearable I had to find a way around it. The
surest way was to pray to the statue of the Holy Virgin—standing for herself as well as for all my other Maries, including my

Aunt Miriam and my mother, Bronsha. I prayed hard and long, reciting two rosaries, and calmly waited for a sign, an answer. Of course, it came—in the form of a very simple reasoning I had overlooked. Madame Marie had declared herself my godmother; therefore, ceremony or not, it was as if I had gone through the sacrament of baptism and received all the privileges that came with it, including the right to Communion and to Purgatory. Since my godmother was responsible for my soul before God, she must also have been given the right to choose a guardian angel for me and to stay in constant and direct communication with him. And so it became clear: that if my guardian angel accompanied me everywhere, and if everywhere I went, I encountered the Virgin Mary in statues, pictures, stories, prayers, litanies, rosaries, then Madame Marie would also be with me at all times, wherever I might be. And she would naturally protect me.

My mother and I moved into the little stone house she had rented. So did my whole invisible retinue: Madame Marie as the mentor of my guardian angel hovering above my right shoulder; the Holy Virgin, wearing her blue dress, accompanied by that gentlest of saints, her husband, St. Joseph, holding carpentry tools; St. Francis of Assisi, speaking to birds; and St. Thérèse de Lisieux, covering with roses the miniature body of Christ resting on the crucifix in her arms. My father in his winter army coat and cap tried to join us, but my mother confiscated his photograph and hid it. "Don't talk about him," she warned me. "Here we are known as Marie and Odette Petit. But he is still a Melszpajz, and that's the name I have to use on his mail to Germany. It's too foreign a name; the peasants would give us trouble. If they ask, we'll tell them that George Melszpajz is a family friend of Alsatian ancestry. But it's best to avoid talking about him, or even about Paris for that matter; they don't like Paris here. And it's not a good idea to talk about Chavagnes-en-Paillers, either. It will be hard enough being strangers in a village, so we'll try our best to make them forget. We'll talk about them and whatever is very important to them, always respectfully, politely. We'll participate in all the village events. We want them to accept us."

So my father had to hide in the linen chest.

Our little cottage was actually larger than our Paris apartment. It had the traditional main room with its fireplace, a wooden table and benches, two single iron cots, and two cupboards, one for dishes and food and one for linen and clothes. The tiny adjoining room had a ladder leading to the attic. It also had a brick cooler for storing perishables, and an area my mother had set up for washing ourselves, our clothes, and our dishes—next to a strange-looking stove she had concocted from a discarded pail and pipes. As for the attic, it was used by an old spinning wheel to scare me with visions of ghost spinners, by my mother to dry apples and onions and winter clothes, and by mice to dance through the night.

It was winter when I arrived. I had worn out my Parisian galoshes, so my mother took me to the town of St. Fulgent and bought me two pairs of wooden sabots—one plain pair for everyday and one black-lacquered pair for church—with one pair of felt slippers to go into either one of them. I was delighted. The toe of each sabot pointed up like a prow of a ship; you could go through muddy paths while your feet stayed dry. Then when you reached your home, you'd slip out of the sabots, leave them at the doorstep, and enter the house in your felt slippers. Before I was allowed to enter my house, though, I had to wash and dry my hands and face, using the pail of water and the towel my mother had set up outside on an old crate. She was strict about keeping as much dirt and mud as possible out of the interior of the house. And that applied to mice, too, who were not allowed to remain long in our straw mattresses, which we would often take outside to unstitch one side and empty out the straw. All the mice would scamper. Then we would stuff in fresh new straw, sew up the open seam, and for a while our nights were blessedly quiet.

WINTER EVENINGS were lovely in our cottage. At the fireplace, I stirred the embers to uncover yet another roasted chestnut. The black iron caldron hanging in the middle steamed with the comforting smell of cabbage and onion soup. My mother would place two potatoes under the embers, where they would bake overnight so we could eat them the next day. Our self-satisfied, self-absorbed cat "Bijou" purred incessantly, steadily, loudly, as if she were a toy whose wind-up mechanism could go on for hours. Then, as the embers got dimmer, Mother lit our petroleum lamp, which I much preferred to our Parisian electric light. She would let me adjust the flame, but she didn't like me to carry the lamp because I had once dropped it and stepped barefoot on the broken glass during a night she could not forget. It had seemed that my foot would never stop bleeding. To her horror, my mother realized there was no one we could wake in the middle of the night for help, no doctor, no clinic, and that she had nothing resembling a first-aid kit. No matter how hard she pressed towels against my foot, they reddened with blood. But the whole episode did not lessen either my love of running around barefoot except under the harshest winter conditions, or my fondness for the petroleum lamp. Nothing was cozier than the lamp on the wooden table in front of a slowly dying fire monitored by a satisfied cat. When the flame was just right and the last chestnut was eaten, my mother would sit and read a while before she went to sleep. I relished such opulent well-being.

Winter passed and we spent more time outdoors. Sabots were put away and slippers were lined up inside rather than outside the cottage. I was urged to wash myself more thoroughly and more frequently before entering. On very hot days, a potato sack hung over the opened door to keep the heat out, and inside, hanging from the ceiling over the table, an unrolled strip of yellow flypaper gradually blackened with dead flies.

The back of our house faced the village center. Although of ambiguous shape, neither quite a square nor a circle, that small area was clearly recognizable as the gathering place for the villagers, the way that the Church Plaza was the town's outdoor assembly spot. Stone houses clustered around our village center, some facing it; some, like ours, turning their back to it. Those houses that couldn't fit into the odd space just straggled along on its periphery. All the villagers were close to that center so that, if anything happened, anyone in the village at the time could be present within minutes. The well and the winepress—communal property of the village—were located in this central area. It was here, too, that the villagers gathered for one of their liveliest forms of entertainment: the forced mating of cows by the breeding bull—accompanied by loud daunts, appeals, jeers, laughter, cheers, vulgar comments, with the spectators' excitement rising to a pitch in perfect accord with eventual bovine progress.

Like other village children, I went to school only sporadically, more often in winter than the other seasons, as it was considered wise to keep children indoors then, preferably far from home. We went together, the handful of us still in grammar school, a two-kilometers' walk to the church of St. Fulgent, at which point we separated: the boys had reached their parochial school and the girls had another two blocks to go. If an oxcart drove by on the road to St. Fulgent, the boldest among us would sneak a ride by crouching on the back of the cart; the rest would go on, trudging along, singing folk songs.

As in Chavagnes-en-Paillers, the convent house was separated from the school building, but there was nothing grand or harmonious about the St. Fulgent parochial complex—or for that matter about any of the town's architecture. Harmony, symmetry, architectural beauty were the exclusive rights of the local château and its aristocratic family. And yet the small town of St. Fulgent had the important status of being the county seat. The main road that cut through St. Fulgent led north to Nantes and south to La Rochelle. Religious processions took place there, collecting worshippers from other nearby burgs and villages along the way. The train station, where Madame Raffin had worked as a young woman, and the buses that came twice a week brought mail, packages, passengers. So perhaps St. Fulgent did not have to make a point of pleasing the eye: naturally, and for solid reasons, it attracted peasants from all over the area. Its plain-looking parochial schools served schoolchildren from a number of surrounding villages as well as the sons and daughters of the town's craftsmen and merchants.

Winter was the best school season. We were divided into two classrooms: one for the little ones, the other for the older girls. At prescribed times within each classroom, the older children helped the younger ones. At other times, students were either silently listening to the teacher or repeating in chorus what she had just said. The regular routine in clement weather had us kneeling in prayer every hour or so, but in winter we were each provided with a footwarmer to keep us warm at our desks. A stack of embers layered the bottom of a small iron crate, and an iron grill cover let out the steady heat. You placed your slippered feet on it and drifted into mellow daydreams of instant hibernation. So as not to be separated from your comforting footwarmer, you were not required to move from your desk as often as in the good season. Gone were the days when you had to get up frequently not only to kneel in prayer, but also to stand in front of the class reciting a fable by La Fontaine, or to go outside to play in the yard. The footwarmer even elicited some kind attention from our usually callous teacher. Like the other nuns, she was dressed in the same long, black habit regardless of the season, but in winter she also wore a heavy knitted black shawl. Sensitive to cold, she was always sneezing and blowing her nose and coughing, but what we hoped for never happened: she never got laryngitis and lost her voice. So, whether it was for our sake or out of self-protection, Sister Augusta would often interrupt the class to make the rounds of the footwarmers, stirring the embers in each to encourage or revive them. We felt wonderfully pampered.

Good weather, however, always changed our teacher's mood. Reenergized, she reverted to her bamboo rods as disciplinary tools. At the slightest infraction of any rule, the slightest sign of inattention, she armed herself with a rod. The designated culprit whose name was called had immediately to hold open her hands, palms up together, to be lashed with the rod till the nun's wrist hurt her too much to continue. After the rod was put away, the punished student was allowed to place her hands on the desk or on her lap—and to spend the remainder of the day distracted by the pain.

At rest, the bamboo whips stood behind the teacher's desk by the blackboard. We hated them. Some mornings there were fewer of them, or even none. The teacher would contemplate her loss, giving us each in turn a long, accusatory look. By the following day, the supply of bamboo sticks would be fully replenished.

One day, just as the bamboo rod was about to hit her uplifted palms, a girl quickly withdrew her hands; the rod hit the desk. The nun angrily ordered her to resume the sacrificial pose. The girl did so, but again, at the last second, eluded the punishing stick. After several such failed attempts, the furious nun, increasingly frustrated, got up from her desk, bamboo whip in hand, and directed herself to the desk of the girl. She was waiting there, looking repentant, but as the nun drew near, the girl quickly got up and started running around the room. The nun, encumbered by her long, black habit and the bamboo cane, ran after her. All of us delighted in the undignified spectacle of middle-aged Sister Augusta chasing around the room after a ten-year-old girl. Suddenly, everything happened at once: the bamboo cane hit an open window; glass broke; the classroom door opened; the Mother Superior unexpectedly came in; Sister Augusta stopped in her tracks and looked sheepish. Class was dismissed early. The incident was never openly mentioned again.

IN GOOD WEATHER, we village children were the privileged ones. We were needed in any number of farming activities and so were excused from school. The town children, whose parents for the most part were artisans and merchants and lived in St. Fulgent itself, had no such official alibi. They still had to make their way to school every morning.

In the villages, the children were expected to do certain tasks: girls were to watch the cows, or help the women in the vegetable gardens and the kitchen, or carry baskets of food to the men in the fields. Boys were to help the men with sowing and plowing, curing tobacco leaves, repairing wine barrels, and fixing tools. Children of either sex could bring the animals back into the barnyard at the end of the day or could run errands and transmit news and messages from one village to another. It was not essential that the child belong to the family needing the work done; any child at hand would do. Children seemed to be part of a collective free-labor pool. We got paid with a food treat—and an excuse from school.

When not working, we played. Our playtime took a variety

of forms. For our freest play, we would race to the adjoining forest. But we also had more formal games that we played in the village itself. One such game, popular with girls, was hopscotch, where the goal was of course Paradise, that eternal attraction. Another girls' game was similar to pick-up-sticks. With chalk smuggled from school, we drew a circle on a spot of hard ground. Into the circle we threw bundles of sewing pins with different colored heads which we had managed to obtain from our mothers. We then bounced a ball to dislodge as many pins as possible. You had to keep count of your gains and losses until the last count, when the circle was empty of pins and the winner declared. Another game was played by both boys and girls. Where the earth was malleable, we dug two rows of small holes facing each other. Each player had a pile of small stones; the player whose turn it was would distribute his or her stones, one to a hole, in sequence. If one of your stones filled a hole, you collected all the stones in that hole. When all the holes were empty, the child with the most stones was the winner.

To all such formal games, I much preferred going to the forest, running with the other children to that magical place reputed to be the setting for Rabelais's *Gargantua*. We had games of make-believe. The favorite was to pretend that we were Chouans, the royalist Vendéen insurgents in the French Revolution, fighting the Republicans with pitchforks made of cut branches. We always won for God and King and made Vendée proud.

Or we challenged one another to climb to the highest branches of trees to raid birds' nests, to pierce the eggs with a nail and eat them raw while sitting on a branch. On the ground around the tree trunks, we could collect mushrooms, the older children teaching the younger children which mushrooms were safe to eat, which ones were poisonous. Other such lessons included distinguishing between benign and dangerous snakes; or the different kinds of wild greens, those that could be used in salads and those that should not even be tasted, those to approach cautiously to see if they were thorny or prickly; and what kinds of spider webs not to break, for fear of arousing bad luck. This last bit of knowledge was particularly important: walking on a road, you could suddenly be stopped in your tracks by an invisible power. Behind you, a friend would say: "What's the matter? Keep going." "I can't," you'd protest. "It's a Thread of Mary." This was a peculiar kind of spider fabrication: a straight line going from bush to bush across the road, hardly visible, thin, but strong as a thick rope. Since its name was associated with the Virgin Mary, back luck would follow if you broke the spider thread, accidentally or not.

We grouped ourselves according to age, so we were roughly divided into two groups: under age seven, and between 7 and 12. After age twelve, girls joined their mothers in very long days of repetitive work in the barnyard, the garden, and the home. Boys joined their fathers in occasional work that demanded muscle and strength, and in spending the rest of their time drinking and playing cards, or hunting and fishing.

Grown-ups were not, as in Paris, solicitous of children; they did not constantly inquire if we were in need of food, drink, rest, company, or entertainment.

Through the children's grapevine, I soon learned how to satisfy hunger and a sweet tooth. If there were a good smell of food, you could first try coming to the door with the child of the house and saying: "We're hungry," in the unlikely chance that you might be given something to eat. But you were most likely to be treated with the Vendéen folk saying: *Mange un poing et garde l'autre pour demain.* (Eat one fist and keep the other for tomorrow.) Which still left you a few options. You could get into an orchard if the fruit was ripening and simply pick some, whether or not it was totally ripe, and hope you didn't get caught. Or you could go into a house temporarily empty of adults, look in the food cupboard and see what you could find of jam, lumps of sugar, or honey. In one such much-pirated home, when we opened the cupboard door one day, we leapt away in terror. Glued to the inside of the door was a picture of an immense eye staring at us: the eye of God. We quickly closed that door and tried our last-resort approach. We went to the home of the kindest woman, the mother of a friend who worked as a waitress in the café at the St. Fulgent hotel, and who was therefore more citified. We claimed terrible toothaches. She gave us a look of doubt but still went to fetch the local cure for toothaches: for each of us, a lump of sugar dipped in brandy.

My friends and I would play hide and seek, pick berries, tease each other, sing folk songs, and generally do whatever children do wherever and whenever they have the chance, except that we had more time and more freedom than I could ever have imagined!

There was always something interesting to watch: a farmer at his plow or sowing seeds in his field; the farmer's wife milking cows; older men repairing tools, or fishing by a stream, or curing tobacco leaves; two young goats playfully banging heads; chicken's necks being severed from their bodies with one blow of an ax; or freshly killed rabbits being skinned on a barn doorpost.

But to me, the most wonderful sight was that of a man using a scythe at haymaking time, the man's entire body following the movements of the scythe, slowly, surely, with a hypnotic, rhythmical swish, swish, swish. He was at one with his tool, with the stalks of wheat, with the earth, alone unto himself, complete. Just watching a man and his scythe at work together was as awesome as watching the priest at the altar performing the mystery of the Mass. I couldn't imagine anything I wanted more than to hold a scythe. But that was strictly forbidden to women and children. The division of tools was very clear: scythes were for men, sickles were for women and children. So, as second best, I longed for a sickle.

Sickles were used to cut grass or do the harvest in out-of-the-way small plots of land, odd fragments of inherited property divided and again divided down the generations of peasants. These fields were too small to warrant using harvesting machines, or a team of workers, or even a single man with a scythe. Still, it would be foolish to let them remain untilled, unproductive; so they were the ideal places to send children to work with sickles.

One day a farmer asked me if I would go work a very small plot up in the hills. Would I ever! I must have radiated zeal. So he gave me a sickle, told me what to do and where, and off I went.

I was ecstatic. I had been entrusted with a sickle and with a job to execute and complete on my own! This was different from other children's tasks I had been given until then: running errands, peeling potatoes, shelling peas, sweeping, minding the fire, going to the well for a pail of water, even watching cows in the pasture. Here I was, eagerly going up a hill with a sickle in one hand and, on my shoulder, a hunter's satchel which my mother had filled with food and a bottle of cider. It was a beautiful day; the landscape was friendly. My grip tightened on the sickle's wooden handle. I was ready, like a medieval knight, to face any encounter, overcome any obstacle, and come back triumphant, having fully accomplished the task assigned by my lord.

I reach the top of a hill and locate the small field. All around the field—so many trees, such peacefulness! Down below—the Vendéen patchwork landscape, fields of all dimensions bearing different crops and belonging to heirs of the handful of intermarried peasant families. Such a cheerful-looking quilt! The sky, like a good farmer, seems very close to the earth. I am alone with benevolent Nature. "Here I am!" I shout as I brandish my sickle at the field. Then the grass and I enter into a dance of mutual politeness. I bend down to a spot of grass; it yields and lays down its blades. I move on to the next spot of grass. We repeat the same steps in exactly the same way, keeping the same beat. I am in a trance and keep going: another spot covered, and another, and another. Can I do yet another? Maybe I should stand up, straighten my back, stretch? No. Not now, not until I cover more of the field. And I go on, and on, until I fear the sickle is bewitched and will not let me stop. I call on the saints to deliver me from that irresistible magic of work, not dull homework or errands but real work in a real field with a real farm tool. They come to my help, and I stand up to contemplate the full measure of my accomplishment. Nearly half done! Now I can take a break, eat, drink, maybe sing a song.

I hear a churchbell ring the noon hour, and I kneel to say the Angelus. "Pray for us, oh Holy Mother of God. . . . Hail Mary, full of grace . . ." I have a strong sense of Her responsive and kind presence covering the hill with protective grace. Marie is with me. She will make me strong.

I resume my work, sometimes singing a song, sometimes reciting the litany of my good luck. I live with my mother; I have a cat; I speak patois like everyone; our village has won the Month of Mary shrine contest; Simone is my best friend, she lives two houses away; I'm eight, old enough to be entrusted with a sickle, with a real job; when I grow up, I'll use a scythe when no man is looking.

Mid-afternoon: my part is over. A grown-up will later come to collect the fresh fodder. My right hand is sore from holding on so tightly to the handle of the sickle, but I don't care. I feel victorious. I was entrusted with a sickle; I used it well. I promised to do a job; I did it well. I look all around me: I see the day ripening, the sky rising, the sunlight softening. On the verge of fatigue, a burst of energy mixed with tremendous pride: I did it, I did it. I'm alive, strong, capable, trustworthy. I'm a village child! This is very important. I must tell someone—someone

very important. Right now, before the sky changes, before twilight comes. Suddenly, I know who that person is: it is me, years
from now—a grown-up weighed down with grown-up worries
and a heavy spirit. I summon my future self. She comes and I
solemnly address her: "Remember this day, this moment. Never
forget. Look at me, standing by my work, sickle in hand, satchel
on my shoulder. I finished my day's work. I was trusted. I am a
village child like the others. I am one with this field, this sky, this
sun and, below, with my village, my town, my church. Look.
I'm alive! Look at me. I'm happy! Don't forget this moment, ever.
Remember this day. I am you when you were eight and very
happy. Don't forget!" My future self promises not to forget.

I HAD PASSED my initiation and had proven myself a
good and very willing worker. I was now a full-fledged village
child. My mother had also done well. She was quick to learn
how to grow vegetables in our garden, how to make patés, headcheese, soap, vinegar, a makeshift wood stove. She was admired
for her ability to unravel any piece of knitted clothing and use
the wool again to knit a full layette for a new baby. All this
ingenuity came naturally enough for her—poor working-class
women and peasant women learn equally quickly to make the
best of whatever is at hand.

But not everything came naturally for her. Nothing in her
Jewish Orthodox childhood or in her adult years as an atheist
had prepared her for our present Catholic life. At church, she
watched me closely to know when to kneel, sit, stand, and cross
herself. Her gestures were not smooth. There was always a sec-

ond's hesitation, an expression of muted bewilderment. Back home after church, we would hold a ritual session of evaluation: what had she done wrong? What had she not understood? And I would explain over and over again what I knew, what I had been taught was the proper way. She would ask why this? and why that? Sometimes there was a catechism answer. When there wasn't, I would repeat what I myself had been told by the nuns and priest: some things will not be known to us until we are dead—a thought that brought her no comfort whatever. We had a tacit understanding: she didn't argue against my Catholic beliefs; I didn't fuss over her pagan lack of faith. But we both accepted that I would teach my mother the basic principles of Catholic beliefs and all the related prayers, gestures, rituals, popular devotions, and superstitions. It amazed me that she, who was so astonishingly quick to learn anything practical, was so slow to turn into a credible Catholic!

Another aspect of our village life which turned out to be difficult for both of us, though surely more for my mother than for me, was the villagers' attitude toward the occupying German soldiers. My first memory of their arrival was akin to that of the unexpected coming of a circus troupe.

My friend Simone and I were playing by the entrance of the village when barking dogs signaled that something strange was going on in a very large field across the road. We went to see. As soon as we arrived, we were transfixed by a sight so futuristic that we at first thought it an apparition. Closed and silent, huge silver-colored trailers faced each other in two even rows. Suddenly they ejected doors, stairs, porches, tables, soldiers. A camp fell into place very quickly, everything carried out with the greatest efficiency.

German soldiers had French money, so they immediately bought fresh food from the peasants. Some of the officers also bought the right to sleep on a comfortable feather-bed mattress inside a farmhouse or village cottage, its owners moving in with a relative or making do in a hayloft for the duration.

The soldiers were jovial, loud, self-assured. They were eager to befriend us children and offered sweets that we had been warned not to eat for fear they might be poisoned. We did accept the chocolates and candies but, instead of turning them over to our parents, we hid them. You never knew about grown-ups. They could change their minds tomorrow, decide the sweets were not poisoned after all, and still not give them to us—in which case it made more sense for us to keep them secretly, safely from our parents.

FEAR OF POISON, of curses, maledictions, illness, and death kept villagers in a constant state of anxiety. They defended themselves as best they could.

Against illness, the local healer would bring his own choice of herbal medicines and a wooden box containing leeches. Infusions would be long and complicated to prepare, with a very strong smell. They were administered at regular intervals, which had to be odd-numbered, usually five or seven times a day. The leeches fascinated me. Carefully choosing a handful of slimy creatures from the mass of blood-sucking worms mulling around in the box, the healer would arrange them strategically along the veins of the patient's naked arms. The leeches attached themselves eagerly to the skin, nursing on blood at its pores. It was strange to see an older peasant woman's naked arms! I had never seen married peasant women's naked arms; women that age wore long sleeves and black cotton stockings under long black dresses.

Most of the cures focused on blood. Leeches were used to draw out the bad blood that was believed to carry the illness. In cases of weakness or anemia, a drink of blood from a freshly slaughtered animal was highly recommended. The blood, of course, would make you strong. To obtain that remedy, you could go to an old widow who lived just two houses from the slaughterhouse in St. Fulgent, and who therefore could guarantee the blood's freshness. The old lady was also known for the high quality of her canned preserves. My mother would chat with her a good long time in the hopes of catching a recipe or two for those preserves she would buy. Later, at home, she would analyze their contents and not be at peace until she had created a credible facsimile.

What my mother of course would not do in case of illness was what all local peasant women did. Whether or not they had called for a healer, they lit a votive candle at a church altar to their most trusted saint with an ardent petition to cure their loved one.

A case of poison, a run of bad luck, infertility, or an unexplained death, all were attributed to the forces of Satan and his cohorts, experts in disguise, craftiness, and witchcraft. In those cases, it was not sufficient to light candles; it was also necessary to ferret out Satan's accomplices.

To my astonishment, I learned that the most dangerous, because the most elusive, of Satan's emissaries was the Jew. He could look deceptively like anyone else and could pass as a Christian. As such, he was in the position of satisfying his traditional hatred of Christians by causing them to die, or at the very least by interfering with their reproduction, their health, and their prosperity. Poisons and curses were common weapons in his arsenal.

In this regard, our local priest made himself useful to his parishioners. From his Sunday pulpit, he explained that the Jew, acting on behalf of Satan, used various means to distract the Christian from his true moral path. For instance, everyone knew Jews were the major makers of movies, which featured adultery and other forms of human depravity. Paris was infatuated with those movies. It was therefore imperative never to go to Paris and especially never to let our young go there. Another field dominated by Jews was the garment industry. The skin-tight and revealing knitted bathing suit was a devilish invention of the Jews. There were even Vendéens vacationing on the beaches of La Rochelle wearing those obscene bathing suits. And so La Rochelle was to be avoided at all cost by all pious Fulgentians.

It was strange hearing all this! Because of Jews, the people of the villages and the burgs must not go to Paris; they must not go to La Rochelle; they must not see movies; they must not put on a bathing suit. How they must hate Jews for preventing their traveling and enjoying themselves! My mother was in the machine knitting trade—which made sweaters and bathing suits—as were my uncle and my older cousins. Aside from my father, everyone else we knew worked in a garment shop or at home, mostly on coats and suits. Did we really sabotage Christians' chances at ending up in Paradise? Ah, but wait. Madame Marie, my very Christian godmother, was a seamstress. Was that the same as or different from the garment trade? She made clothes for everyone, Christian or Jew. And she wasn't the kind to harm anyone. But neither was my mother. It was so confusing!

To further complicate matters for me, it turned out that placing temptations on the Christian path to moral purity, as bad as it was, was a relatively mild accomplishment of Jews compared with their ultimate goal of bringing death to Christians, apparently an old habit dating back to the Crucifixion. Jews were not only the instruments of Satan; they also were the Angels of Death. They poisoned wells, put curses on innocent people, and caused epidemics and fatal illnesses. It was therefore wise not only to take precautions but to keep a safe distance from them. The problem was: since Jews could pass as ordinary people, how then could you recognize them? Everyone knew that because of the war and German efforts to eradicate all foreign Jews from French soil, some Jews were living in the country, passing as Catholics. How could you accurately identify your enemy in order to defend yourself and your family? The priest advocated a very simple test: if a Jew, even one mistaken for a Christian, so much as crossed the threshold of your house, someone in your family would soon die. Then you would know for sure that you had been dealing with a Jew.

I walked away from church that day, a heavy tombstone in the middle of my soul taking up too much space, too much air, too much light.

I tried not to think of Jews, but there was no way to bring the matter to rest. Gradually, I found myself seeking out chores and errands so I would be too busy to play with the other children. What if they discovered my mother and I were Jewish? What would they do to us? And was it true that, as Jews, we were in league with Satan and that he was using us to hurt true Christians? And if it were true, then what was the Christian thing to do about it?

In my predicament, I increased the number of prayers, of good deeds as negotiating points, of visits to church, of all efforts at getting the saints on my side so they would send me signs that everything would be all right.

Then the Marchands' cat gave birth to five black-and-white kittens. As soon as word got around, all the village schoolchildren went to fetch the newborns. Following an old local custom, they brought the five unwanted animals to the oldest villager, the widower Père René.

Soon, the whole procession—the dozen children, the old man, and the five, blind newborn kittens, ended up across the way from my house. I came out to watch. They settled on the edge of the small black pond to my right. It was black because of cows' and horses' urine streaming into it from the Charpentiers' stable and barn. Adjoining it, directly across from our front door, was a large vacant lot filled with cabbagelike weeds which was used as a public outhouse. Mint grew on its walls. On our left, next to our small vegetable garden, was a stone structure that housed the brick oven. If it weren't for this smell of freshly baked bread, you might not be able to withstand all the other smells, but as it was, with the proximity of human sweat assailing you, you abandoned yourself to the intense sensuality of that August moment. The water was very still: the frogs and toads that croaked nightly were hiding somewhere. Perhaps they too were overwhelmed by the torpid air.

The long-awaited event began. Père René threw the kittens one by one from the warmth of his body into the coldness of the pond. Satisfied with his performance, he carefully followed their progress. His smugness was that of a privately well-informed horse-race addict. "Just look at them! Not even a day old, and blind at that, thinking they can swim their way to safety. They're sure dumb!" The children laughed. Père René went on recording his observations: "There goes one! Mark my word, that one by the reeds will follow. What did I tell you? That spunky little one is still going; it would have made a nice cat. Throw him a stone, Jean. We'll see what he'll say to that! Ah, so you're scared, my little one, eh? Won't be long now. Serves your mother right for whoring with the first-come tomcat!" Finally, Père René announced: "Well, children, now it's all over. I have to take a nap." And with that, he left. The children ran away in a flock to play on the cobbled road. I went back in my house and hugged my cat so tightly that she struggled out of my arms, scratching indiscriminately.

The drowning of the kittens did not strike me as a good portent. I was still looking for a sign, for a good omen that we would not be discovered as Jews, that we would be all right.

My mother had to mail a package of food to Madame Marie —something she did regularly in exchange for my godmother's managing to collect my mother's food rations and sending us some money in trade for them. The post office was in St. Fulgent, so that morning, my mother and I walked to the town together. Once there, I would go to school while she spent her time in town, doing various errands. In the afternoon, we would come back to the village together.

The sky is full of clouds, so there aren't many children in school today. The teacher in the little ones' class, who never misses a chance to take her girls out in a field to look at the clouds, comes into our classroom and talks to our teacher. Then we all go out to the field. When we reach the field, we know exactly what is going to happen. When the nuns clap their hands, we look up at the clouds. "What do you see?" the nuns ask. The littlest girls cry out: "Oh, that's a bear!" "No, it's not! It's a very furry dog!"

"Now, now," says their teacher. "Look again, very, very carefully." Playfully, the clouds have changed shapes. "It's a woman in a long dress and long hair!" "Good, you're getting warm!" says the teacher. "Look again. Is she wearing a crown?" Of course she is. We can all see that very clearly. "Now look, look very quickly; she might go away. Is she holding a flag with a cross?" "Oh yes, yes, there it is!" "Come now, girls, what saint is this?" Everyone yells at once: "St. Ursula!" It never fails. It always turns out to be St. Ursula, the patron saint of teachers of young girls, like our nuns of the Order of Ursulines.

It is frustrating, ending up seeing exactly what our teachers want us to see, as if God Himself is communicating to them through the clouds. After the nun's victory, and a prayer to St.

Ursula, we start to return to the convent. I linger, mulling unhappily over the fact that, once again, St. Ursula has triumphed over bears, dogs, and miscellaneous earthly apparitions. Just to make sure she is still there, I turn my head, looking to the clouds, and I see a mosaic of round shapes. As the clouds keep moving, so do the rounded masses, some of which become more oval. A picture is slowly forming, beckoning me to watch its creation. It begins to look like a peasant grandmother, face down, with her hair in a bun. Whatever is she looking at by her left hand, while her right hand is somewhat raised, apparently moving something? Oh! It is, it is! It really is! It's Madame Marie at her sewing machine!!

The apparition is shortlived but it fills me with happiness. Surely this is the sign I've been waiting for: Madame Marie in the sky, busy at her sewing machine. She is at her post. She will protect my mother and me.

Later, when the bell rings the end of the schoolday and I go outside, my mother is waiting for me with two straw baskets. I look through them. There is a variety of foodstuff, a loaf of bread sticking out, a set of knitting needles, a bottle of lamp oil, a roll of flypaper. It feels like Christmas! We walk through a few blocks of St. Fulgent, pass the church, the café, the slaughterhouse. We exit the town and, immediately past the cemetery, we take the long dirt road that leads us back to our village. My mother hands me a basket to carry. It's light; it's almost empty. She spreads some cabbage leaves. We walk for a while. As usual since we live here, she doesn't talk much. I make up for it and chatter incessantly. An oxcart passes us by. When it is nearly out of sight, my mother looks around. There is absolutely no one on the road or in the nearby fields. She motions to me to follow her quietly. I do so. We find ourselves in a field full of rutabagas. My mother shows me how to pull them out of the ground in a seemingly random fashion, one here, another a few feet away. I am to place them in my basket under the cabbage leaves. My mother shoves hers under her store purchases. It occurs to me that we are stealing, committing a sin worth confessing, though if pressed, I would surely not admit to doing it at my mother's bidding!

We're back on the road and all is well. Madame Marie will get a package of good country food—lots of meat, sausages, lard, patés. We'll have a supply of rutabaga, a loaf of fresh bread, enough oil for our light, and a new roll of flypaper to replace the old one so overcrowded with dead flies. My mother will have the new set of knitting needles she kept saying she needed. And best of all, I will take back to the village a wonderful secret, the most potent of all possible good omens—an apparition of Madame Marie at her sewing machine in the burg's clouds. We are safe.

With my foster family in Chavagnes-en-Paillers.
Clockwise, from top: Cécile Popowicz, Jacques Raffin, Paulette Klaper,
Suzanne Klaper, Jean Raffin, and me. 1942

In La Basse-Clavelière, 1943, on my way to school from the village

A street in La Basse-Clavelière showing a typical old-style Vendéen house

The convent school in Chavagnes-en-Paillers

The Catholic Church in St. Fulgent

My mother's visit to Chavagnes-en-Paillers. Winter 1942

La Basse-Clavelière. 1943

My school photograph. 1943

Berthe Moulin, at far left, visited us in La Basse-Claveliere in 1943.
The peasant woman and man on either side of me were Madame Raffin's
adoptive parents. They also knew and kept the secret of our Jewishness.

My father as a volunteer in the French Army.

He is smoking his pipe, third from right, center row.

My father's photograph, which I had throughout the war.
He later told me he had lost his French Army cap
and had replaced it with a Russian soldier's cap.

TEN

1944: *WE HAD* completed our second year in La Basse
Clavelière. It was May again, that month set aside from all others
as the Month of Mary, who reigned over it in all her glory. For
that entire month, the Holy Virgin was not confined to her altar
in the town's church; she appeared in every village, where she
held open house every day. Her home in La Basse Clavelière was
Père René's barn, partitioned for the occasion: cows crowded
on one side, the Virgin's altar on the other. On top of the many-
tiered shrine was a small statue of the Blessed Virgin in her light-
blue robe and her golden crown. All month long, the villagers
kept bringing her offerings of flowers and prayers. At the end of
May, she would officially be declared "Queen of Heaven."

I was walking to school with the dozen other village children, on the long road to St. Fulgent, when we saw a meadow
brushed in silver glitter. We had heard that sometimes night-
flying planes would drop a bright layer of thin strips of silver
tinsel over meadows. There were rumors the strips were explo-

sive, so cautious people did not touch them. But we could not resist, as it reminded us so much of the silver foil wrapping of chocolate bars. We figured school could wait another day and ran wildly to harvest the light surface crop of metallic strips that lay like thin yogis on beds of pointed blades. The sun smiled at them. Soon, a myriad of silver giggles rose and fell and were picked up and tossed in the air again. A quiet boy sat by a tree, counting and re-counting his treasure while the rest of us, unable to hold on to our fragile loads without much crushing and wrinkling, sowed new trails of silver behind us. Eventually, the futility of overloading ourselves forced us to stop. One by one, we left the grass and went to the side path.

One little girl, with a torso as shapeless and bloated as a frog's, and legs and arms as thin, covered her dress and hair with silver, then stretched out her neck and squeaked: "I'm a queen, a queen! No, I'm an empress!" A small group sitting around a mole hole was arguing about the length of the strips. An older child, one of the altar boys, stated with conviction: "It was from a German plane." But he was immediately challenged by a younger boy. "You can never tell," he said. "It could be from an English plane. My uncle said the English always hated the French; they invaded us and burned Joan of Arc. He said our worst enemies are always our neighbors, and France has the Germans on one side and the English on the other. So it could be either. You can't tell for sure." "Well, German or English, what difference does it make?" asked the altar boy, quickly adding: "In any case, the Holy Virgin will protect us from all our enemies. Let's go back to the village and decorate her shrine so it shines like the church. She'll like that!"

Patient as ever, the Virgin Mary let us toss silver strips onto all the tiers of her shrine. Most of them fell on the lower tiers, brightening the white cloth or accenting the flowers in vases. The cows were out for the day, but their warm smell lingered over the roses. A sheep dog came in to see what was happening. Someone whispered the alarm: "Old Père René's dog! Let's go!" But before anyone could leave, a dry old man was blocking the barn door, pointing at us with his six-fingered hand. In a voice stern as Judgment Day, he scolded: "Not in school? Not in the fields? The day's still young and there's plenty of work to do, but are you helping your parents? No, you're here disturbing the Virgin, making a mess of her shrine!"

"Oh no, we're not!" said the oldest girl. "We're making it pretty for her. Look at the silver: we picked it up in the field to decorate her shrine. It will be the prettiest shrine in any village!"

Old Père René softened. He left the barn, grumbling: "All right, all right! Anything to get out of the good, hard, healthy work that God's planned for us ever since Adam left the Garden of Eden!"

On the village square, I saw my friend Simone; she was about to skip into the number six of the hopscotch when she saw me coming. She stopped playing and quickly walked away. I caught up with her, and the two of us walked silently for a while. Then Simone explained: "I can't play with you anymore. People say you and your mother are Jewish and you came from Paris to hide from the Germans, who are helping us make France Jew-free once and for all." She sounded as if she had been personally betrayed. But then, softly, she asked: "Are you really Jewish?"

"Jewish? How could I be Jewish? People gossip about any-one who's not from the village! Lots of Catholics like us have left Paris since the occupation. My mother's shop closed; she couldn't find work. Food is rationed. There are curfews and sirens and you have to rush into bomb shelters. It's just awful! And be-sides, Germans are Protestants. We wanted to be where it's quiet and peaceful, with lots of good food, and where everybody is Catholic. So we came here."

"I knew they were lying! You're too nice to be Jewish. Then we can still be friends. You know what? I forgot to tell you I have a brand-new baby brother, and that silly, mean black horse of Grandpa's finally croaked. He's so sad, Grandpa is. He's going out of his mind. Says it was a real Christian horse and should be buried in the cemetery, in the family plot. He's really crazy, my Grandpa, and he hates kids, too. He says women and kids are what kills a man. You should see this new baby! I think he's the ugliest yet. They're all like that at the beginning, before they get to be really cute! Did you ever have a brother or a sister?"

"No, my father died in the war."

"And you didn't have any other fathers?"

"Yes, the first one, but we don't know anything about him."

"Your mother really didn't have any other babies, not even one that died?"

"No."

"Then maybe she can't have any more. That happens, you know."

"Can I see your new brother?"

"Sure. Mom's so nice now. She thinks her new baby's just beautiful and she says she was blessed with fine children. But in a month, she'll say she's cursed with us and doesn't know what sins she's committed to be punished this way. She doesn't say that when Dad's around, though, because he just says, quietlike, that he knows. But come quick: the house smells good; everybody's brought cheese and sausages!"

We raced each other to the plain greystone house squatting in the sun. When he saw us, the grandfather removed himself and his pipe from the doorstep where he had been sitting. He stood up, coughed, spat, and farted almost at the same time and mumbled loudly between his toothless gums: "Kids! And they're still making them! In the Garden of Eden, they didn't have any kids and it was the only time man was happy. And if it hadn't been for a stupid, nosy woman, he'd still be happy!"

Simone stuck her tongue out at him and sneered: "Your horse's dead and no one's going to give you another, ever!" From inside the house, a woman's voice called out: "Simone, come here! You be nice to your Grandpa. He's old and this here is his farm. When he dies it will be ours, so you stop bothering him and come and make me a cup of tea."

Like all the houses in the village, this one had two rooms. The main one, the largest, had as its focus a huge fireplace with a hanging cauldron and a long wooden table with benches. Against the walls were many straw-mattress beds, a few cupboards and, towering over everything, a tall, carved four-poster with three down mattresses and innumerable pillows covered with embroidered cloth. The bed, a family heirloom, was the pride of the house. A thin woman was resting there with her sleeping baby.

"You see, Odette, how I've been blessed with fine children!

And Simone there, what a good little woman she is. She can keep house, watch over the little ones, garden, and milk cows just as well as I can. Another few years and she'll make the best farmwife in the whole county. But then, I don't know how I'll manage without her! Listen, dearie, be good and do me a favor. Take Simone's place in the pasture this afternoon, so she can stay here to do the chores around the farm and help me prepare supper. I'm still too weak for all that! Will you go?"

"Of course. I'd be glad to."

"Simone," said her mother. "Look by the fireplace and take the best blood sausage, a good slice of ham, and a piece of rye bread. Then fetch a bottle of cider from the cooler. Remember to replace the bricks against the hole as tightly as you can, or all the food will be as warm as the barn!"

Simone did all she was asked and put the food and drink into a linen satchel she handed me. Her mother had a last bit of advice: "Now, Odette, as soon as you get there, you find yourself a pile of rocks in the stream and make sure it's deep enough to hold a bottle in place. And then you put your cider in there and it will keep cool all afternoon. You know where the cows are right now: in the field in the back of the house. Take them to the stream, and thanks a lot!"

When I reached the stream, I first settled my four cows and closed the gate behind them. Then I attended to the cooling of my cider. In the stream, mirages of frogs appeared and disappeared on stands of water lilies. Tiny birds paused on the most delicate branches of trees hovering over the soft-spoken, lightly breathing body of water. I threw off my Parisian rubber sandals and ran knee-deep into the stream, trying my most quiet, catlike best to catch a frog. But either my fingers were not long enough or the frog could hear me sigh from suspense because as soon as I thought my hand had reached its goal, it only touched vacant air or the leaves of a water lily. But for all that, it was a really fine day and there were other things to do besides playing with such silly creatures. So I got out of the stream and dried my feet by running in the meadow, stopping now and then to gather wild-flowers. After a while I had a large enough bouquet to bring back to the Month of Mary altar. I was very pleased with it and confident it would be well received.

I became thirsty and went back to the spot where I had left my cider bottle. A quick look around: the gate was closed and all was well with the cows—with so much water, grass, sun, and shade, there shouldn't be any trouble. They took very good, leisurely care of themselves.

The bottle of cider was in place and marvelously cool. Not far off was a frog—was it worth trying? I crouched precariously and pretended with all my might that my hand was invisible. Maybe that would help. But suddenly the sound of footsteps coming behind me made me jump and almost lose my balance: the cows!

No, it was not the cows. The children of the village were walking towards me at a grim, deliberate pace. Simone was among them. They looked ready to chop down a sturdy tree, in the quiet way of farmers about to do what they must do. The children and the sun appeared so final and immovable, it immo-bilized me. I just stood still and waited. For a second, I was distracted and called out: "Simone . . . the gate . . . quickly! Toinette will run out!" My friend broke away from the group, kicked the cow back into the meadow, and closed the gate. No one else had changed position, so Simone ran back to her place, just slightly behind the others.

When they had come within six feet of the stream, they formed a silent half-circle around me, blocking me where I stood, the stream behind me, and at my feet a bouquet of wild-flowers, a satchel, a bottle of cool cider, and a pair of rubber sandals.

Shattering the silence, the oldest boy shouted in a deep, threatening voice: "You thought you could fool us! We're not dumb. We don't let Jews slip away. We know how to recognize a Jew. If a Jew enters your house, someone in your family will die."

"And that's what's just happened!" screamed a younger boy. "You damn Jew! As soon as your mother rented that house from my parents, my brother Maurice got sicker from T.B. And now he's died! He's died! It wasn't enough that you crucified Jesus!"

I felt as if I had been whipped and it hurt terribly. I shouted: "I? I didn't kill Jesus! I'm only nine and I'm not Jewish! I'm a Christian! A Christian!"

The oldest boy screamed: "Let's throw her in the water! Let's shove her pagan face into the water till she drowns!" They all rushed towards me: "In the water! In the water! Throw her in the water!"

I knew in my guts they meant every word they said. I must run away from the stream, run like a flash, run anywhere even if they caught me. In a flurry of self-defense, I threw everything around me at my foes: food, cider, rocks, flowers. Then, holding my sandals in angry fists, I beat a path, pushing the younger children aside, and I ran, ran with all the strength of terror and anger. They were running after me. I ran faster, away from the stream, anywhere away from the stream. Still, they caught up with me at the hedge of a pasture, breaking loose into an orgy of beating, scratching, spitting, screaming: "You killed Maurice!" "Don't you dare call yourself a Christian!" "You killed Jesus! If you could, you'd kill us all!" "We'll tell the Germans. The Gestapo will get you!" "Let's throw her in the thorn bush!" Better than the water, I thought. Anything is better than drowning. But it stung terribly as the bigger boys rolled me into the bush and then, finally satisfied, just left me there.

Like hunters done with their prey, they recovered the calmness of the idle day. Silently, they separated, and one by one disappeared in the vastness of their world. Only Simone lingered a while, and then went back to the stream meadow to gather the cows and reclaim the satchel.

WHEN I THOUGHT they had all gone, I pulled myself out of the thorns, bruised and sore all over. By the bush was a clearing of thick grass and sunshine. I just lay there on my stomach, still as the earth. After I regained enough courage to lift my eyes, I saw a small daisy within hand's reach. Or was it really that near? Would I make a noise that might bring them back?

I stretched out a hand and reached the daisy. Pulling out the petals, one by one, I recited silently: "They're gone, they're not gone, they're gone. . . ." And when the last petal indicated that they were indeed gone, I knew the danger had passed. I got up, straightening my blue cotton dress. It was torn in various places.

What would my mother say? She'd be angry with me. Luckily, I still had my sandals from Paris. Mother would have been furious had I lost them.

I needed a lot of protection, so I knelt down, made the sign of the cross, and prayed: "Thank you, God, for saving me. Please also watch over my mother. And Blessed Virgin, Holy Mother of God, Queen of Heaven, dear Madame Marie, I thank you, too. I'm going straight to you in the barn with my bouquet of daisies and cornflowers!"

As I walked back to the village toward the sunset, I lingered at each field I passed—those beautiful fields that changed color and smell every day and month of the year! At one point, noticing an old woman gathering twigs to make a broom, I was on the verge of offering my help (and counting it as my day's good deed) when I remembered what a sight I must be—hair tangled, dress torn, sores all over. I figured I would really scare the old lady; how could I explain my sorry state? I made myself very still and slipped behind a tree till the old woman had long passed.

What really hurt the most was that all the children had been against me, even my best friend Simone. They blamed me for Maurice's death. But he was going to die anyway; Mother kept saying that. You couldn't live with T.B. forever, and he had been bedridden since even before we came to the village. How could they accuse me? It wasn't fair. I really was a true believer. I said all my prayers, attended Mass and confessed my sins regularly, took Communion, did very well at catechism. So what was wrong? I automatically placed my hand on the left side of my chest, but no, the yellow star hadn't been there since I left Paris.

Maybe, though, it was God's punishment because I told a lie, many lies all to the same end: that I was not Jewish but Catholic from Paris. God punishes all liars. But what else could I do? My mother had been so emphatic: "You must never never tell anyone our real name or that we are Jewish and that your father my husband is alive in Germany in a Jewish prisoner-of-war camp. This is a matter of life and death. But I trust you. I know you can keep secrets." The priest said we must obey our parents. So what could I do? I could not confess to the priest! My mother had trusted me with a grown-up secret. Of course I would never tell, no matter what, even if I had been thrown into the stream and pushed down till I drowned. The problem now was how it would be between me and the village children. Would they ever play with me again? Would I have to walk to school alone? Or worse, if they didn't believe me, if they still suspected us of being Jewish, would they really denounce us to the Gestapo? If so, we'd end up first on a truck, then on a cattle train, going somewhere far away where no one ever hears from you again— like my Aunt Miriam and Uncle Motl and my cousins in Paris.

NOW IT WAS DUSK and the air had cooled. My cotton dress felt thinner and more torn. The village was going through its end-of-the-day ritual in which, as usual, I had no part at all—no farm chores to attend to, no baby brother to rock to sleep. Just my sad mother, spending her evenings quietly reading or knitting, looking lonely or worried. I wasn't that eager to get home, especially today when she would panic over the way I looked, so I walked slowly back to the village, careful to avoid anyone along the way.

Thank God! Here was the door to Père René's partitioned barn! I came in from the cold twilight and threw myself on my knees by the altar of the Virgin Mary.

There she stood in solitary serenity, wearing her blue robe and her golden crown, on top of the shrine shaped like a multi-layered wedding cake. Every tier, covered with white embroidered cloth bordered by lace, was filled with flowers in vases, pots, old milking cans, small barrels. Our Lady's calm presence, the flowers, the mooing of the cows on the other side of the temporary wooden partition, all began to soothe me. After a while, I remembered the fading flowers I had long been holding and placed them in one of the red clay pots farmers used for liverwurst or head cheese, beside an unwieldy bunch of yellow roses. Something cold and silvery slid down my hand. I jumped up and looked all around. Streaks of silver pierced the semidarkness as if the moon herself had come in to worship and had broken into a thousand tears.

I was overcome by the moon's sadness, by the beauty of those silver strips we had had such a good time gathering only that morning, and I began a long, breathless half-coherent prayer: "Our Lady of Mercy, have pity on me. I didn't kill your Son. I couldn't have. It happened long ago, and I'm too little. You know all that. You know I love Him as I love God and more than I love you, as it says I should. Holy Mother of Christ, why did Simone join in on the beating? She's my friend! Friends don't beat up on you; friends are on your side no matter what. Holy Mary, please pray for me and my mother. Please protect us. Forgive me for lying. I couldn't help it. My mother made me promise to keep our secret. But the truth is, I am indeed a Christian.

And the proof is that God just saved me, as He did before, when Madame Marie wanted me saved. But now I'm scared. I don't know what they'll do to us. Please watch over us, intervene for us, pray for us, have mercy on us, protect us. If God is mad at me for lying, please explain everything to Him, ask Him to forgive me. And then, from Heaven, please send me a sign that I've been forgiven for lying, that you will protect me and my mother from the villagers' harm. Please, please send me a sign!"

Words had exhausted me. I stopped praying but kept sobbing. It wore me out. I would soon suffocate or faint. The barn was very stuffy and languorous, filled with the stifling fragrance of the bouquets and the warm, penetrating smell of cows. My whole being was slipping into the oneness of the smell, the rich, potent smell. I thought I'd faint when suddenly I was startled by a sound. I jumped up, turned around. Someone stood in the darkened barn. I was afraid it was the oldest boy, the leader of the group, but I could make out the hunched figure of a bony man leaning on a carved stick clutched in his left hand. He held a lit candle in his right hand, which had one too many fingers. I realized it was Père René and I worried terribly. "Oh dear," I thought. "How long has he been here? Could he have heard me? What was I saying? Did I give away our secret? Will he tell the others? Will he go to the Gestapo?" I stared at him but his face admitted nothing.

He took his time looking me over, then he spoke: "You are a sight! Oh, those kids! Always getting into fights over nothing! Come now, child. Make yourself useful. Help me light the candles for Our Lady. Then, you'd better get yourself home! Your mother's been looking for you everywhere. She's upset. You'd better have a good excuse. Come on. If you hurry, I'll give you a tumbler of warm milk fresh from the cows to get you on your way!"

WHEN I GOT HOME, my mother was sitting on a suitcase outside our house, looking forlorn. She was horrified to see me so bruised, and I wondered what she was doing outside. We traded stories. She spoke first, very fast, in a low voice: "A terrible thing happened while you were gone. I was accused of being a Jew because our landlord's son died! They evicted us. But worse, I'm worried that they may have denounced us to the Gestapo. I was waiting for you. I was so worried, but I didn't want you to find the house empty when you came back. Now I have to rush to St. Fulgent and speak to the Comte; as the mayor, he's the only one who can save us."

And save us he did. The Comte de Grandcourt covered up our just-revealed secret Jewish identity, and we of course said nothing of learning that he was active in the Resistance. He publicly denied we were Jewish, claiming he knew through personal contacts that we were good Catholics from Paris and that he even had the papers to prove it. The peasants pretended it was true. My mother acted as though the villagers had never even wished us ill. I gave it a try also, but in my case it didn't work right away.

I began to avoid the other children. On the days I did go to school, I left a little earlier or a little later than the others so I could walk by myself. But once at school, I was ill at ease. Though no one ever made reference to the day of my close call with drowning, eviction, and deportation, I felt my classmates were cool and distant, and I was uncomfortable. Something had snapped between us. They had ejected the stranger from their midst, and I had lost my trust. Soon, to my mother's dismay, I would also lose my voice. At which point I stopped going to school altogether. Instead, I went to the forest.

TO HER GREAT surprise and immense delight, my mother had recently stumbled on a private library of French literature at the house of an old lady who lived behind the wine-press. It had been stored there by her grandson, who had been studying in the city but was now away in the army. She let my mother borrow any book she wanted, claiming she herself had no patience for literature of invention. For her, the Word of God was enough; all the reading material she needed was her cherished prayer book—a family legacy.

Until I lost my voice, I had considered those books to be merely my mother's distractions, but now I too began to read in earnest. Unlike her, though, I didn't read at home.

In the morning, I would stuff a book, a piece of bread, and some apples in my canvas shoulder bag, go spend the day by myself in the forest, and come back to the house at dusk.

We lived in the *bocage*, the wooded part of Vendée. It was a privileged setting for reading French literature, especially *Gargantua*, which Rabelais had written long ago when he lived around here, long before Bas-Poitou was called Vendée. Rabelais's forest was populated by giants with huge appetites. They must have eaten a lot, but there still was much left to see in a forest dense with great numbers of varied trees, with sudden clearings, many waterways, abundant animal life, vegetation of all sorts—mushrooms, berries, thistles, wildflowers—and, flying through it all, owls, bats, birds. And haunting its shadows were generations of elves, giants, ghosts, apparitions of the Virgin.

Our forest also had human noises. I learned to identify them. After gunshots, a man's victorious cry: surely a hunter had caught a hare or a bird. A shout of triumph by a stream: a fisherman's hook had caught a fish. The sound of giggles and struggle in the rustling grass: a young couple had caught each other.

School taught us that military history had always favored our forest. During the "Wars of Vendée," local royalists had valiantly fought—and lost—fierce forest battles to stop the Revolution. Now, German soldiers on their way to the nearest village noisily drove through the woods, their horse-drawn carts covered with camouflage canvas. Or, on foot, an occasional band of cautious young partisans bathed in the river.

Aside from Rabelais, I read whatever my mother had just read—Montaigne, Molière, Rousseau, Pascal, Racine, Corneille.

Reading gave such deep pleasure, particularly relished in full solitude after an exhausting tree-climb—to settle at last on a branch, clearly far away, above it all. Imagine it! No one to bother you, to ask questions, to make demands, to criticize, to expect something. Forest, book, solitude, satchel of food and drink: nothing more was needed—except more and more books to satisfy a ravenous, Gargantuan appetite for reading!

Only one regret: I felt sorry for my mother. She was so upset that I had become mute. There were times when I truly wanted to say something of comfort to her, but nothing would come out. She tried, talked, asked questions. At times I thought

I had answered her, but she would bemoan loudly the fact that I kept silent.

Although I couldn't say a word, I didn't mind listening to others, especially to my mother. It was soothing to hear her voice.

But one day my mother confided in me. Flattered, I listened in silence as she described her problem. It was about a letter she had just received from my father. She had written him that she was reading a book of poetry, the first one she had come across since she lived in Vendée. This odd book, *Jocelyn,* was unlike anything she had ever read. It was actually a novel in verse, by the French Romantic poet Lamartine. It was about a young seminarian and the teenage girl, disguised as a boy, whom he rescues and shelters in the Alpine forest where he lives in a grotto—a strange subject, but somehow my mother liked reading it.

She then read me passages from my father's letter. He made a passionate case for Poetry: how poems speak to the heart and soul, fortifying one in times of adversity; how poems can be learned and recited silently to oneself during long hours of hard labor; how their hidden meaning can also be understood and shared by your comrades. And finally, he told her that Lamartine was one of the great French poets, that he had never read *Jocelyn,* but if she could manage to buy a copy and send it to him, it would give him double pleasure—reading French Poetry and reading the very book she herself had read. Poetry was a bridge that would bring them closer.

I was listening, very interested. For once, the words didn't add up to a reproach, a loaded question, or a list of chores for me to do. These were my father's words about Poetry, my mother's words about a book, a book whose subject immediately fascinated me. But what could she want from me? Where was the problem? She finally worded it. When she read Yiddish Poetry, it would sing to her. With this nineteenth-century French Poetry, though, she wasn't sure she was "singing along" to the same music Lamartine had written. Maybe it was her accent, or the fact that she was simply not born in this country. The problem, then, was that she couldn't figure out if Jocelyn was good enough to send to my father. She needed someone to read a passage from it aloud. The last thing she should do was to bring suspicion on herself by asking a neighbor or the priest to do her this favor. She didn't want to call attention to being a stranger, and she certainly couldn't tell anyone about her husband in a German P.O.W. camp. It was a nice day, so she thought that if we just sat together on the doorstep, I could read aloud from the book for a while. That would help her decide if this were the kind of musical Poetry she and my father loved. I shouldn't worry. I didn't have to talk. All she needed was to hear the sound of Lamartine's words. That's all. Even just five minutes would be fine, after which she'd excuse me from the rest of my chores for the day.

My mother took the book and went to sit on the doorstep. I sat next to her. She handed me Jocelyn, which I opened at random. I read silently to myself. It turned out to be a journal description of Jocelyn's idyllic day with young Laurence. They had joyfully rolled down hills together, played hide and seek, and then had run until they found themselves, exhausted, lying side by side, daydreaming quietly near a lake in a valley.

Did he ever discover she was a secret girl? If so, then what did he do? If he became a priest, he couldn't marry her! And if he didn't marry her, what would happen to her? Orphan girls with no guardians were sent to convents. Maybe after a while, she would run away from the orphanage and come back to her beautiful forest—to live there by herself? She could play and run by herself, close to Nature and God, then lie down exhausted, filled with sweetness and love for everyone and everything.

I felt myself overcome with an exalted happiness tinged with soft sadness. From some distant space on the step next to me, a soft voice said: "Read me this page." I started to read silently: "And life, pounding our breasts like a drum, / threatened to gush and overflow our souls. . . ." Then a muscle made itself sharply felt, tightened in my throat, something was wanting to gush and overflow, a strong drum was beating in my chest . . . and suddenly I heard a voice read aloud: "And life, pounding our breasts like a drum, / threatened to gush and overflow our souls. . . ." And the voice continued, line by line for pages and pages, sometimes hitting the right-hand margin like a wave, sometimes ascending grand mountain tops or slowly rolling down into pastoral valleys. The music, stronger than the words, propelled me into a hypnotic trance. Finally, overtaken by an immense, exhausted calm, I closed the book. I felt as if I had gone through a mute and invisible, seemingly interminable fit of uncontrollable sobbing, followed by the usual but always unexpected soothing sweetness of all-encompassing tranquillity. Only then did I realize that the voice I had heard reading Lamartine was my own.

"It's beautiful!" I said. "Daddy will love it."

My mother's face was radiant. In my mind, I could also see my father's face, under his army winter cap, just like the photograph, except that he was smiling at us. Still under the spell of Lamartine's romanticism, I felt that all distances, all boundaries had dissolved. My mother, my father, and I were together again as a family: we were one, united by Poetry. We would rejoice in the very same words, the very same music. Poetry was stronger than the Germans, stronger than the war. It was so strong, it gave me back my voice.

I now found it pleasant to spend my days reading at home. After a while, my mother talked me into going back to school. I returned to the nuns' classroom with some degree of excited anticipation. Now that I had discovered Poetry, I had invisible wings. I could fly anywhere. The reciting of litanies came close to the reading aloud of Poetry, but it had nothing to do with Nature or freedom. A litany was a kind of extra-polite request for protection, a supplication to the Virgin, a major saint, or the heart of Jesus. It made me feel good, at one with the other girls as we chanted together. But it had nothing to do with my own Jewish mother, my faraway Jewish soldier-father; it didn't sing of the trees and clearings of my forest, nor of the exhilarating freedom that came from running whenever, wherever, I wanted to run. I much preferred Poetry!

IT WAS A VERY hot day and I wanted something light and easy to wear. The only summer dress I could still get into was one that had been too long on me when I left Paris. It was a simple, sleeveless cotton dress with a flowery print which

Madame Marie had made for me. I went to school in a cheerful mood, dressed in something of Madame Marie—something real, tangible, that harmonized with my favorite memory of her: sitting at her sewing machine like an advertisement for stability, usefulness, serenity.

The way to school was pleasant. I was running late and so I was alone, but no matter. The countryside between La Basse Clavelière and St. Fulgent was even more exquisite than this time last year. In the fields bordering the road I found blue wildflowers as dainty as those printed on my dress.

As I neared the convent gate, I could hear a chorus of prayers. I entered the courtyard very quietly and tried to find a discreet place in the crowd. Furtive glances of shocked astonishment from my classmates, both of my village and elsewhere, immediately made me uncomfortable. What had I done wrong? Was my dress torn? dirty? Hadn't I combed my hair? Did I suddenly look Jewish? As we lined up, two by two, to go into the classroom, I hoped someone would tell me. Instead Sister Augusta yanked me by my ear out of the line and forced me to sit on a bench facing the wall, with my back to the class. When she rang a bell and all chatter ceased, she made a public example of me. It turned out that I had no respect for the Church, God, or my fellow human beings. I wore a more than frivolous dress, surely from Paris, that Capital of Sin. My arms were totally naked. How did I dare come to school in such immodest clothing? When I tried to defend myself by saying that was really my only cool summer dress, I was soundly accused of insolence and was sentenced to remain in the same spot without moving for the rest of the day. I could hear giggles behind my back.

I sat unhappily. Hours of dull class time passed. I was not released at morning recess nor at lunch, when Sister Augusta stayed in the classroom to monitor me. When we were alone, I complained of hunger. She didn't respond. Then I asked to go to the latrine. She didn't respond. I began to beg "Please! Please!" She didn't respond. Then suddenly, I stood up and tried to make a run for the door. She got there before me and blocked my way. She pulled me, crying and screaming, into a dark closet, where I remained till school was over.

The very next day, my mother, so angry she hadn't spoken a word on the way to St. Fulgent, burst into the Convent House, where she made a scene confronting the Mother Superior. Pointing to me as a major piece of evidence, she accused the nuns of extreme cruelty and told them she had no choice but to take me immediately out of their school and transfer me to the public school. We left the convent in a huff, before the nuns recovered from my mother's verbal assault. I felt avenged.

FROM ONE DAY to the next, I went from Purgatory to Paradise. My new school was small, secular, and devoted to the ultimate reign of reason and the pleasures of literature. In the one classroom were thirteen pupils of both sexes and of all elementary school levels. Except for me, they were children of civil servants or aristocrats. Our teacher was a warm and indulgent woman whose apparent main goal in life was to encourage and nurture our curiosity and imagination. In the nuns' school, our rewards for obedience and conformity were gold paper stars which, when accumulated, could be redeemed for religious pictures; in this public school, our individual progress was monitored all week. On the last day, we were ranked according to our degree of individual effort and the progress we had made that week. Thus ranked, we lined up to choose a book from our teacher's private glass-door bookcase library. Naturally, everyone's current favorite was the book our teacher had read from that very week, but it would be taken by the child who was ranked first. Miraculously, each week another one of us ended up first, so at some time or other, we all got a chance to borrow the week's "best seller." Our teacher lived in the other part of the house, where she invited us in winter to gather around her potbellied stove to warm ourselves and our lunches.

We adored her. Unless you were dreadfully ill, you didn't want to miss a day of school. She made every one of us feel intelligent, capable, and cooperative, even the handicapped boy whose limbs went into every direction if he tried to get up from the wheelchair his mother brought him in every morning. The teacher would publicly admire his zany sense of humor and we all looked up to him. She didn't claim a monopoly on questions, unlike the nuns. On the contrary, she was always eliciting our own sets of questions. And she discouraged us from repeating after her or reciting pat answers: "You're not parrots! Parrots don't know what they're saying, and we don't know what they think." She would remind us: "You're boys and girls! You have minds of your own and words to go with them." Still, for all that emphasis on originality and spontaneity, she drilled us till, like parrots, we could sing every word of every stanza of the

"Marseillaise." We imitated her fierce patriotic fervor, and like her, we beat our fists on our desks to punctuate the rhythm of the French anthem.

One day, we could hear German soldiers coming up the road singing a rowdy German marching song. Though it was daytime, our teacher closed the shutters, then the windows. But the soldiers were loud, and we could still hear them as they passed by. In our indoor silence, we looked at her. She was looking at us sadly. Then, she sighed and began to beat her fists on her desk. We listened carefully—and understood. We too began to beat our fists on our desks, in unison with her, at first softly, and then louder and louder, marking the rhythm of the "Marseillaise." Fully protected by our devoted teacher and the closed windows with shutters, we felt like heroes on a battlefield ready to slaughter our enemies, to spill our blood into overflowing rivers of French blood that would irrigate French crops for the abundant harvest of Peace that would come to all survivors of the holy carnage.

I was nine and a half, fluent in both French and patois, equally at home with secular French literature and the *Lives of the Saints*, by my mother's side in our cottage, or alone in the forest or the Church. My relations with the other village children had resumed, but strain remained on both sides, especially after I had transferred to the public school where I was the only student from the village. Still, life was marvelous, especially at grape or wheat harvest time. I was overjoyed to be part of a team—men, women, children—picking grapes, throwing them into straw baskets, then throwing those baskets into buckets filling up with grapes. Or to follow the harvesting machine driven by the men and, together with the women and other girls, bend down to glean the stalks of wheat left behind in the fields.

THE WEEK'S LESSON was on the five senses. We made noises; brought objects with interesting shapes, smells, textures, tastes; had guessing games: "My object is round, sometimes white, sometimes yellow; it has many layers; it tastes very strong when it's raw, but it makes for a delicious soup when it's cooked with other things. What is it?"

Our classroom filled with a motley of objects, plants, even insects and worms in boxes. Nothing of that kind had ever happened in the nuns' school!

All week long, the teacher read from an anthology of French Poetry. I coveted that book and determined to work at my fullest capacity every minute of the week to earn first place in line at the glass-door bookcase on Saturday morning.

As a special assignment, to culminate that week's work, we were to show how proud we were of being Fulgentians. We would do so by praising our "pays," and our praise song would be oral, in five parts, one for each of the five senses. We would name all the sounds we liked, and describe what smelled good to us, tasted good, looked good or felt good to touch.

I thought about our assignment all the way back to the village, looking at everything I passed on the road. Once in the village, I made the rounds of all ten houses and their attached barns, barnyards, vegetable gardens, orchards. I stood by the winepress, then by the well, even by the black pond across our house. I took a walk to the forest, then through the forest up to my favorite reading tree. I stared, I listened, I touched, I smelled, I tasted. It was wonderful. I felt I was claiming my territory, enumerating all my possessions. And then I began:

I love my *pays*. I love all the sounds of the barnyard; the ox-carts; the grandfather clock; the church bells ringing of Mass, Vespers, weddings and funerals; the chanting of Sunday Mass; singing at harvest time; men's drinking songs; impertinent courting songs; and, for lively dancing, all the homemade instruments (made from reeds or other plants), the violin, and the accordion.

I love my *pays*. All the smells of the barn; of the village oven; of the weekly stew cooking in the cauldron; of the grapes being pressed for wine in the winepress; of the flowers at the Virgin's altar during the month of Mary; of the cow dung to collect on the road and bring to the manure heaps; the smell of spitting tobacco; of church incense; of freshly cut grass; of bales of hay.

I love my *pays*. And the taste of the cow's milk still warm from her udder; of the licorice plant picked on the way to school; of cool cider; of the holiday brioche; of mushrooms in the woods after a rain; of blackberries, gooseberries, currants before and after they are turned into jam; of fluffy egg-white "snowballs" floating in a sea of rum; the taste of fireplace-roasted chestnuts, roasted pine nuts, baked apples, baked potatoes.

I love my *pays*. And the look of homemade butter or homemade cookies with their homemade decorations traced by a spoon or a fork; the look of lightning tearing up the sky; of the oxen's wooden harness; of handmade patriotic rosettes, circles within circles of blue, white, and red ribbons worn for the procession of the Virgin of Peace, so pretty, a small statue set on a bed of flower petals and carried from village to village in petition for Peace; and the picture of St. Denis the Martyr, holding in his hand his severed head, complete with bishop's hat; and, over our supper plates, the golden flypaper blackened with dead flies.

I love my *pays*. The feel of a full pail of water, drawn from the well, being carried to the house; of a cow's warm breath; of nettles accidentally encountered; of a young brook's fresh water in cupped hands; of a frog caught by the leg; of a ladybug on the back of your hand; of lice caught and crushed; of the beads of the rosary, held and pushed away, one by one; of hopping in a potato-sack race at the fair.

I was out of ideas and hoped I would remember at least something for each category. It was dusk, time to go home. On my way there, I kept counting on my fingers, making sure I had taken every sense into account, a whole handful of senses. Then I remembered hearing something about a "sixth sense"; it was something mysterious.

That night, I asked my mother. She said the sixth sense must be fear. When I got to bed, I passed in review a list of my fears:

The fear of sneezing seven times in a row, at which point the devil gets my soul; of seeing a corpse rise out of his coffin at a funeral; of putting out my hand in the traditional gesture of reconciliation, and of having the friend I longed for spit in my hand, in the traditional gesture of nonreconciliation; of the cows in my charge being bewitched into madness by a trick of sorcery; of being denounced to the Gestapo and, chased out of the village, of walking with my mother to the train station on a long one-way journey East; of being beaten unconscious, then drowned in a river or a well; of the nightly ghost-spinner in my attic; of someone drowning my cat, or stealing my black-lacquered Sunday sabots; of the priest guessing I am not really baptized and refusing to give me Communion or absolution.

That Saturday morning I was first in line at the bookcase and took the anthology of French Poetry home for a week. Lamartine had only a few pages; there were so many other poets!

READING REMAINED my favorite activity. I delighted in all manner of printed matter, from the down-to-earth *Farmers' Almanac*, with its phases of the moon, propitious planting times, proverbs, jokes, herbal remedies for everything from nausea to melancholy, to the wondrous *Lives of the Saints*, celebrating the bizarre fate of early church martyrs and medieval saints—young virgins with their breasts cut off; men beheaded, or roasted, or beaten with clubs, or slain by swords, or killed with knives, or thrown to the lions, or dragged with their hair tied to a racing chariot; all of which proved their faith in God and their devotion to the Catholic Church. Those were exemplary Christian lives—as was the life of Christ. One was to live in imitation of those lives. I wasn't sure, though, that it wasn't just a manner of speaking, as no one in my village, or the neighborhood, or the town, lived that way.

Then there was French literature in all its glory: Rabelais's imaginative world of excesses; Montaigne's Epicurean tolerance; the troubles of kings and queens and ancient heroes in the plays of Corneille and Racine; the tales of Flaubert and de Maupassant describing poor people and peasants; and most of all, best of all, Poetry. I never had enough of it. It wasn't necessary to understand every word; you could listen to its melody, its rhythm. You could read it silently to yourself or aloud to a cat or a cow if no one was around. You could make grand gestures if that was called for.

I even discovered something between prose and poetry: a book by the "other" St. Theresa; not the little one of Lisieux with her roses, but the big one, the "Great St. Theresa," the Spanish Theresa of Avila. Her book was The Interior Castle. I looked at the first pages and the epilogue. Everything in between seemed too difficult, but on the very first page was my salvation, the metaphor on which St. Theresa built her philosophy of a proper Christian life: "We consider our soul to be like a castle made entirely out of diamond or of very clear crystal, in which there are many rooms, just as in heaven there are many dwelling places." And in the epilogue, she says: "Once you get used to enjoying this castle, you will find rest in all things, even those involving much labor, for you will have the hope of returning to the castle, which no one can take from you."

This was grander of course than: "The heart is like an apartment." Madame Marie was a concierge who lived in a tiny apartment on the ground floor. St. Theresa of Avila was a great lady, a prioress, who lived in a very large convent. So to her, the soul was like a castle. Was the soul more lofty than the heart? Should I put the apartment inside the soul, or beside it? Maybe inside would be safer.

RUMORS OF JUBILATION in the streets of St. Fulgent. My mother drags me there; she doesn't want to miss it. People are screaming that we have won, that Paris has been liberated. My mother is terribly excited; I'm not. On the way home, walking the familiar road from the cemetery to the village, she chatters incessantly. And once back home, she begins a litany of what is soon going to come to an end for us: the oil lamp, straw mattresses, cooking in a cauldron, staying warm by a fireplace, using chamber pots, kneeling in church, making the sign of the cross, wearing sabots, trying to understand patois, drawing water from the well, pretending her husband is not her husband or my father. Everything will change when we get back to Paris, the City of Lights, with its ornate street lamps and indoor electric lights; when we get back into our apartment with its sink and running cold water, its toilet room, its two-burner hot plate for summer and its coal stove for winter. My father, my aunts and uncles, all my cousins, our neighbors, our friends, all will come back. There will be many parties where everyone will speak Yiddish again. The bedside table will fill up with Yiddish newspapers and books. As for me, my mother reassures me that I will have a normal life again. I will wear galoshes in winter and sandals in summer. I will go back to my elementary school, where the only language spoken is French. I will go to Jewish summer camps and, on the weekends, to Jewish clubs. On Sundays, instead of church, we'll go to the neighborhood bathhouse, take a weekly shower, even an occasional bath. In the afternoons, we'll go to the movies. In the stores of liberated Paris, we'll buy French-milled soap, vinegar, wine, butter, sausages, ham, bread, aprons, skeins of wool, and at the streetstands we'll buy freshly roasted chestnuts, hot crêpes fried just for us, or lovely ice-cream cones, depending on the season. We'll go to museums, concerts, plays, lectures, spend the day in a park. Paris has everything. La Basse Clavelière has been a desert to endure.

I WAS CRUSHED. I didn't want to go to the City of Lights, my mother's utopia. How could I leave my village, the road to St. Fulgent, the detour to the cemetery, the slaughterhouse next to the café, then around the corner, my beloved church? How could I leave my church? and all my saints? How could I leave all the farm animals, especially the cows and my own cat? How could I leave my vast forests; my immense collection of fields and pastures; all my wildflowers, mushrooms, birds, fishes; all the trees I climbed and those I hadn't yet climbed? How could I leave when I would soon be ten, nearing the age of the great event of menstruation when all the already initiated girls sat in a circle by the village well and, upon your presenting evidence of menstrual blood, introduced you to the new order of things you were to face, namely how to avoid being raped? How could I leave before my confirmation, all dressed in white like a bride? And supposing I found out I really had a call for the religious vocation, how could I miss entering the Order of the Ursulines in Chavagnes-en-Paillers? How could I not speak patois anymore? not hear it either? How could I live without a fireplace, or a chamber pot, or a basin and pitcher for washing up? How could I be cooped up in an apartment building? lose all my freedom? live where I don't belong?

I did not want to leave. I prayed a great deal to all my saints. I recited many rosaries. I spent much time going up the highest hills with a book of Romantic Poetry, looking at the patchwork of my *pays*, begging God for a miracle that would spare me from a return to Paris, that would let me stay in La Basse Clavelière till I entered the convent in Chavagnes-en-Paillers.

This time, however, my request was not granted. In my despair, I remembered St. Theresa of Avila. My soul was a castle with many rooms. It was fully portable and conveniently invisible; therefore the highest degree of privacy was guaranteed. I would hide all my treasures in those rooms. One room would hold my St. Fulgent church; one room, our cottage, complete with fireplace, oil lamp, and attic; another would hold my public school teacher's classroom with its glass-case library. There would be courtyards, too. Some would be filled with farm animals; others would hold aviaries; some would have ponds full of fish and frogs; yet others would have vegetable gardens and orchards. The main problem was the forest. I didn't think it would fit, even in such generous proportions as St. Theresa granted the Interior Castle. The best I could do was to fill one of the courtyards with a few forest trees—birds' nests on their branches and mushrooms at their feet.

Though I would let priests, nuns, and saints hide in the church of my Interior Castle, there was one saint I knew I could openly take with me: St. Joan of Arc. There had been no trouble in transferring her from the nuns' school to the public school, where she was portrayed differently but was equally important. The nuns had stressed her devotion to God and church. In the secular school, she had an earthy character: she was a strong, intelligent, spirited young peasant, driven by her desire to free France of its British occupants. She was a true partisan, full of patriotic fervor, great courage. No wonder. Like Madame Marie, Joan came from Lorraine!

ELEVEN

WITH A HEAVY STEP, I followed my mother up the stairs of the Métro station. Eluding me was that miracle I had prayed for that would whisk us back to La Basse Clavelière. I didn't want to look up at the exit; I didn't want to exit. I wanted us to go into reverse: through the concrete tubes of the subway into a series of trains, then into a bus that would let us off once more on the church plaza of St. Fulgent. From there, we'd make our way back to the village. But no, it wasn't likely to happen. Here we were, about to surface on an asphalt sidewalk of my old neighborhood!

We had traveled a long time, for days, loaded with food-stuffs from the country. We had packed everything into old carton suitcases tied with rope or into sheet bundles. I was carrying one of those bundled sheets with knotted ends that I kept pulling forward over my right shoulder. In my left hand, a large canvas bag; hanging from my left shoulder, my beloved satchel. My mother was so loaded down I couldn't get close to her, but I followed all those bulges at her back and sides. They held something of St. Fulgent and my village.

In spite of her load, my mother quickened her step as we went up. Suddenly I heard her shout: "Odette, Odette! Look, look who's here!" I looked up. One face came into focus. Everything around it instantly blurred, making way for the large, rough kindly features of Monsieur Henri. I couldn't believe our good luck! He had no way of knowing on which train we would return within a range of two to three days' journey. But there he was, our own Monsieur Henri, standing tall at the exit! At my mother's cry, he ran down, briefly greeting us on the stairs, exclaiming: "My, how Odette has grown! She is such a big girl now!" Then he immediately transferred the bulk of our bundles to his own hands and shoulders. I started following him like a chick her mother hen.

A MEMORY: when I was very little and got burned with scalding water, Monsieur Henri carried me in his big arms to the pharmacist down the block. Now he is carrying my village on his back, on his sides. Two and a half years ago—half my remembered life—he had been the one who walked me down the subway, rode with me to the train station, and said good-bye before I boarded the train that carried me and three other Jewish girls into the relative safety of Catholic Vendée. Now that the war is nearly over and Paris has been liberated for two months, Monsieur Henri is carrying sausages, patés, hams, preserves, and other delicacies from my village back into our apartment.

Santa Claus of foodstuffs, St. Joseph the husband of Mary, Monsieur Henri my protector, you lead me back into my old world just as you led me away from it. You lay out the sidewalk in front of my shoes; you open streets I had forgotten; you line up the stores on my block: the pastry shop at the corner, then the tripe shop, then the hardware store with its rolls of oilcloth, its pots and pans, its display of magazines.

Looking to the left, I see our town square with its water fountain, its pissoir, its statue, trees, benches, a couple of old people, a mother pushing a baby carriage. It seems so unnatural. Until this very minute it was all gone. But someone has put it back just where it was, in front of the chain manufacturer and the convent school—like a stage set kept in storage for the duration of the theater's closure.

Now we reach the wooden front door of our building. In its upper part, there's still the historic bullet hole from a long-ago insurrection, but it is not as high as before. In fact, as I enter the lobby, everything seems a bit smaller than I remember. Holding my breath as when unwrapping a birthday gift, I dare to look at the loge: Madame Marie is still at her sewing machine! Maybe she never moved from there all the time we were gone. Maybe that's why we survived; from that very spot, she managed to hold the Vendéen ground under our feet and an invisible tent over our heads. Her machine, her table, her loge are smaller than ever, especially since there is a new piece of furniture: a huge peasant bed that somehow has made its way into the tiny apartment to claim nearly half the space. In the other half, there is still space for much hugging and rejoicing, and even for a measured backing away from me the better to point out how tall I've grown, what a "big girl" I am. I'm not sure I like all these comments on my size. I fear it implies a potential loss of important privileges, but how I love hearing the voices of Madame Marie and Monsieur Henri!

Now I can't figure out how I made them fit inside the statues of the Virgin Mary and St. Joseph so they could protect me. Madame Marie is really very round and wears a sizable apron to protect her roundness from dust and spots; she's not at all like the slim Virgin in her Sunday church best, that impeccable blue dress! And taciturn Monsieur Henri exudes a gruff kindness, not the effacing serenity of St. Joseph! How real they are, how marvelous it is to share the same small space, breathe the same air! These are their arms, their legs; with these moving body parts, within my very sight, I can see them walk, pick up objects, close a door, rewind the wall clock; in their own voices they say words I don't expect, not the words I had to lend them when they lived inside statues. They are at last liberated from the statues, and I am liberated from holding them there safely and secretly. I no longer have to keep them alive in my mind as I did during our years of exile from each other. I'm so relieved I feel as if a volcanic lava of underground tears has suddenly dried up and a sweetly delicious lassitude has followed.

With Monsieur Henri and Madame Marie, I am Odette Melszpajz again. A native of Paris, a child of my neighborhood. I speak French, not Vendéen patois. My "village square" is across the street; it has a Wasserman fountain, a pissoir, a statue of "The Thinker," some benches and trees. My "forest" is a long walk to the Park of the Buttes-Chaumont, my local cemetery is the Cemetery of Père Lachaise. I am home, and that is that.

OUR NEXT-DOOR apartment remains silent; no one seems to be home. My mother asks Madame Marie what has happened to our neighbor, the young woman whose wartime lover was a German officer. Did the French arrest her, shave her head, and force her to walk her shame in the streets? Madame Marie is totally reassuring: "Don't worry," she says. "They didn't have a chance; I took care of that. She's safe, out in the country till the situation calms down. It's not fair: those who did the most harm will surely get away, especially if they have money on their side. It's the little people they'll pick on, as usual. Your neighbor didn't denounce you—or me. She was just young and poor, dazzled by a bit of luxury. She just enjoyed going to the opera in a fancy dress, escorted by a soldier in uniform. Not many young Frenchmen around anyway during the war."

I GET REGISTERED in my neighborhood school. Since the academic year starts in October, I've hardly missed any time. My mother explains to the principal that my education was severely disrupted when we lived in Vendée. The nuns' school offered very little outside of a religious education, while the progressive public school concentrated on lively and informal discussions of French literature and social studies. What got left out of my education were all the other standard subjects: arithmetic, physical sciences, geography, and history. Do I at least know my multiplication tables that are printed on the inside cover of every student's notebook? My mother is unsure. Heads turn toward me: I keep an embarrassed silence. The principal asks a few other odd questions: What is a delta? Where are the French coal mines located? I have no idea. However, when she asks about Molière or Corneille, I can answer at length. This is obviously confusing to her and she isn't sure in which grade to place me. Finally, with all kinds of warnings to the teacher about my "case," she sends me to the grade appropriate to my age.

I know I can't ask my mother about it, so I will go find out for myself. I cross the wide boulevard: there, at the corner, is André's shoe store. On its outdoor stalls: rubber rain boots, felt house slippers. Rue des Amendiers. I pass the pastry shop. Not much in the window. Corn bread. Not as good as rye peasant bread, but I don't mind it, though everyone seems to long for that expensive white bread—"real" French bread you see in the bakeries of fancy neighborhoods.

I keep going on that familiar street till it's interrupted by the narrow cul-de-sac, Passage des Amendiers. As before the war, the alley feels dark, ominous, and smells strongly of bleach, onions, cabbage, and urine. All the windows follow me, staring at my back till I'm about to turn into the dreary courtyard where, I've been told, my aunt Miriam, my uncle Motl and my cousins Sarah, Serge, and little Henriette were rounded up on that "Black Thursday" of July 16th, 1942, to be put into a truck; from there to the Vel d'Hiv, then to Pithiviers and Drancy, and eventually to Auschwitz. And they've not come back. I have to see for myself. Maybe my mother's telling me a story. Maybe she doesn't want me to know that only one or two of them have come back—but they are blind, crippled, or mad. She wants to spare me.

I go into the courtyard. First I pass the loge of the concierge, staring from behind her lace curtains. I go toward my aunt's apartment in the far left corner of the courtyard. Something seems wrong. A big Frenchman comes out, stares at me. I ask about the Melczak family, with five children. He knows nothing about them; he's been living here with his family for over two years. "Did any Melczak ever come back?" I ask him. "No, never!" he assures me, then goes back into my aunt's apartment.

I stand outside the door, waiting for something else to happen, waiting to hear long-ago familiar sounds: my uncle's knitting machine, Henriette's giggles, Serge's violin. But the door remains mute. Maybe my mother is right after all.

Still, I can't understand. I know that the oldest son, Charles, tried to hide but was caught also. Have they all died in concentration camps? Or are they late in returning, like many people, like my father maybe if he is still alive? What about Maurice, who joined the Resistance fighters? Will he show up again when the war is over everywhere, not just in Paris? If not in his home, now occupied by strangers, at least in ours?

IT WAS STRANGE, not knowing whether people had died. In Vendée, all the dead lay neatly dressed in wooden coffins. They let their relatives carry them on their shoulders, inside the coffins, first to the church and later to the cemetery, where the coffins would be lowered into the ground. Then everybody would say prayers over them and go home. Thereafter, any time they wanted to, the mourners knew just where to find their dead. They could even bring them flowers.

My cousins' family was gone. Not alive like my mother and me. Not dead like the dead who have coffins and graves. Just gone without a trace. I went home disheartened.

But I came back, many times. I didn't mean to, but somehow I would find myself near the Passage des Amendiers and would be drawn automatically to turn right into that dark alley. Then I would just stand still, on the edge of the courtyard, staring into space, waiting for something to happen, some sign of my family's return. Eventually the concierge's rustling lace curtains would startle me out of my reverie—and I would go home.

And again I would be back. Finally the concierge took the initiative. She opened her door and, from her doorway, asked me what I wanted. "My cousin's violin," I answered. She simply shut the door. But this was not to be our last confrontation. I came again and again. Each time, she seemed more irritated, more eager to get rid of me. "What do you want this time?" she'd ask. "Serge Melczak's violin." "Why would I know where it is?" "You're the concierge." "They're long gone. You're a pest! Go away! Don't come back!" But I would come back. As soon as she would open the door, I would throw my request at her: "Where is my cousin's violin?" and she would reply: "How should I know?" and go back indoors.

I can't quite remember how the concierge finally managed to get rid of me. It could be that she said—or implied—that Serge's violin might be in a pawn shop, because my next round of obsessive visits was spent window-shopping at all the pawn-shops in my neighborhood and beyond.

And there were indeed quite a few violins displayed in pawnshop windows. So many, in fact, that I soon lost confidence in my memory. I had been so sure that I would recognize my cousin's violin anywhere! But I was wrong. After a few shops, I stood at the window feeling more and more perplexed. Was the violin I was staring at likely to be Serge's or somebody else's?

Did his violin really have that ornamentation or was it totally plain? was it darker or lighter? Why couldn't I remember? Maybe I could ask my mother? No, I had better not: the whole subject—and the most infinitesimal part of it—caused her nothing but grief. She was already having enough trouble, worried by the lack of news from my father in Germany. I couldn't say anything. Anyway, if I began to explain, if I told her of my frequent visits to the Passage des Amendiers, she would surely be angry with me.

But then, suppose this time my memory had served me right and it really was Serge's violin in the window of the pawnshop? What would I do about it? I had no money to buy it. The most important thing, though, was simply to locate it—if I could only know where his violin is, then surely Serge would come back for it. He'd knock at our door. I'd answer and be the first to see him. Even before he'd inquire about my mother, he'd ask about his violin. And I'd say: "Yes of course I know where it is!" The worst scenario was that he would then go to the pawnshop, and either the violin would be gone, just purchased by a stranger, or I had made a mistake: it wasn't his violin. Serge would patiently ask all kinds of questions, all on small details. The sum of my answers would make us face the awful truth: I had let his violin go long ago, thinking at the time that it was the wrong one! So now, to retain some control over the situation and avoid the worst, I had no other option but to make my rounds as often as possible. That way, I could closely monitor the three to four violins I had chosen as finalists, making sure the real one didn't get away, the magical one who had leaned on Serge's shoulder and played lovingly for him—and for me.

If I showed proper respect, the violin would stay put, waiting until Serge would come to ask me where it had gone.

EVERYWHERE, every minute, at home or in the streets, people were readjusting to postwar Paris. It wasn't easy. You had to remember many new facts: this grocery store had changed owners because the prewar ones were deported; your old dentist had been shot in reprisal for an act of partisan sabotage. Among your neighbors and acquaintances: women in black dresses, men with black armbands. You'd have to find out whom they were mourning. You spoke to them very gently, softly. If you were a child, you were warned not to be rowdy around them.

It was as if you carried pages and pages of checklists under various categories: Work, Family, Friends, Acquaintances, Neighbors, Local Businesses, School, Food, Shoes, etc. In dealing with people, you only had three columns to check: 1) dead, 2) alive, and 3) fate unknown. Matters of food, clothing, shoes, or miscellaneous services, were broken down into four major categories: 1) can be purchased for cash, 2) needs ration coupons as well as cash, 3) can only be purchased on the black market, or 4) unless you're rich, forget it.

To make life harder, the winter of 1944–45 was the coldest in years. It was expensive to stay warm indoors and nearly impossible outdoors on the long lines at food stores. And indoors after dark, lighting was a problem. Electricity was on for just a few crucial hours a day (one hoped it was during meal preparation). Food shortages made Madame Marie repeat her comforting thought: "As long as they have apples and potatoes, the poor won't starve." And so we were blessed with a horn of plenty, out of which tumbled kilos of apples and potatoes. Actually, turnips and rutabagas were counted into the potato family as poor country cousins and added "variety." Lentils, rutabagas, stews, and cabbage and onion soups were the most common fare in my neighborhood. As you walked down the streets, it was easy to know what was cooking where: all you had to do was breathe. Poverty's "cuisine" has a staunch smell: there is no mistaking mealtime, anymore than washday, when bleach rolls up its sleeves and beats the shamed linen into mock purity, pretended newness.

WE RECLAIMED our apartment, thanks to Madame Marie. In our absence, she had kept it safe. More than that: she had turned it into a safe house for others, but you wouldn't have guessed this. On our return, my mother found everything just as she had left it, and she joyfully made the rounds of our old and broken-down possessions—those she had remembered as luxury items during our exile in La Basse Clavelière. As for me, I opened the dining room closet and found my box of toys; I had forgotten it. It seemed so childish! Only two objects still claimed my allegiance: a brown rubber ball and a Japanese paper umbrella.

Now that I was two and a half years older, almost ten, I spent less time in our dining area, where I had once played with toys, and more in our bedroom/living area. (In Vendée, such a combination room had been called "La Belle Chambre.") Now, in our "beautiful room," I had three favorite areas: the book cupboard, the armoire, and the window.

The floor-to-ceiling cupboard—where my parents kept books, photo albums, important papers, and documents— housed four volumes of a most extraordinary book: *The Auto-didact's Encyclopedia of Learning*. This was the only thing my father had ever bought on time payments (and he had not finished paying because of the war). You could teach yourself a few foreign languages, astronomy, mathematics, calculus, geome-try, history, geography, and all other subjects formally taught in school. It had copious and fascinating illustrations, charts, and maps, some of which pulled out or popped-up like pictures in my children's book, but the subject matter was serious. My own education was so deficient and fragmented that I looked upon this encyclopedia as the sacred keeper of all useful knowledge. It was very different from the Bible, the *Lives of the Saints*, or even French literature—all of which told stories; interesting, tragic, wonderful stories, but nevertheless just stories. This encyclope-dia, however, could explain to you, if you understood, how the real world is put together absolutely perfectly, with everything right, especially Nature.

I read the introduction. It promised that if you were very disciplined, made a regular study time during which to con-centrate fully, read every word, followed every instruction, you would inevitably master the contents of any course of study you chose. I thought I'd start with astronomy, partly because the map of the sky looked somewhat familiar, though the villagers' had taught me different names for all the constellations, each loaded with quaint bits of folklore. But it was hard to read; it had too many long words that were too difficult to remember. I spent more time staring at the map of the sky than reading difficult words. Still, I was convinced that when I would overcome my laziness and acquire the needed discipline, I would be on my way to becoming a truly educated person! In the meantime, I looked and looked at every drawing, every chart, every table of every volume.

Another area of the room, which through the coming years would increasingly attract my attention, was the armoire—not because of its contents (we had scant and mostly dull pieces of clothing) but because of its full-length mirror. I spent hours in front of it, preening myself, draping my mother's Russian scarves around my head or turning them into a turban and, if she wasn't home, trying her face powder and lipstick (lightly, so I could quickly erase it if I heard the key in the front door.)

Everybody said I was "a big girl," which meant I was on my way out of childhood and heading to womanhood—an endlessly fascinating subject. I just wanted to see how it might look on me.

And, once again, the window. As before the war, I was attracted to the window with its view of the street. Early in the morning, I pushed through the two sets of gauze curtains, unlocked the window, opened the shutters, greeted the day. With my elbows on the balustrade, I leaned over to see what I could see.

It all looked like black-and-white photographs coming to life. (Color didn't immediately return to Paris.) Nuns in long black habits crossed the town square on their way to or from the Catholic school. Looking at their neutral faces framed by large white starched winglike coifs, it was hard to tell if they were thinking, daydreaming, or perpetually praying. Still, there was something awesome, set apart, sacred, superior about them; even in a crowd, they were never shoved; people would make room for them. That old longing came back: oh to be a nun, especially a schoolteacher-nun. . . .

Otherwise, my street had changed a little. Some Jewish businesses were now French. There seemed to be fewer Gypsies; they looked poorer, with more children huddling around the full, long skirts of tired women, keeping to themselves, never speaking to non-Gypsies.

MOTHER HAS FITS of cleanliness. At home, on her day off from work at the knitting factory, she cleans all the floors, all the doors, every wall, every shelf, every piece of furniture. She also wants to wash every sheet, every piece of clothing we have.

We go to the neighborhood public laundry, where you pay to use vats that boil the laundry over steam—a huge room smelling of steam, soap, bleach. When the laundry has gone through its last rinse, we carry it up to the rooftop, to the drying rooms. They are separated by wire fences, so you can see your neighbors. I love the smell of fresh linen; I like stretching my arms to reach the clotheslines, and clipping the hanging sheets with wooden clothespins, the kind you use to make wooden dolls. It's not like climbing trees, but it's nice to be somewhere up high; it's cozy, safe. As we leave, I tell my mother I'll be glad to come and pick up the clothes when they're dry. "It will be heavy," she tells me. "Not for me!" I say out loud. Then, silently to myself, I finish my thought: "Am I not strong like all the girls my age in

St. Fulgent? Can't I carry heavy loads like anyone in the village?"
But I wouldn't say that out loud. Out loud, Vendée is never mentioned, ever.

Mother is a fanatic for anything that requires soapy water.
She obviously enjoys washing dishes in our greystone sink. From
its running cold-water faucet, we also sponge-bathe our bodies
every day, but it is at the public bath-house that we totally im-
merse ourselves in hot-to-warm water every Sunday morning.
Usually, we just rent a shower stall for fifteen minutes. But when
my mother is in a very good mood, or trying to be in a good
mood, she splurges on a private bathroom, with one shower and
one bath. We take turns going from the bathtub to the shower
stall, not wasting a minute, as our allotted time is limited. So
much soapy water! We splash it at each other. Then we indulge
in clear rinse water and dry ourselves heartily with the rough
bathhouse towel. To finish off, we splash cologne all over our
clean bodies.

Though we have to economize on everything, there are moments like these of extravagant splurging, probably when Mother
has just gotten paid, or when a new cache of hidden Yiddish
books has been discovered, or when there is a report that one of
the "disappeared" has been recently sighted.

ONE DAY, as I open the door to our apartment and turn
on the light, something small and alive leaps under the table. I
bend down to see. I can't believe the wonder of it: a kitten, a
real kitten! Sudden pangs of longing for our Basse Clavelière cat,
"Bijou." Life stops. I spend all afternoon persuading this new cat,

still nameless, to acknowledge me, to believe that I am at his service, that I will do everything to make him happy. When my mother arrives from work, she too begins to fuss over the cat. She gives him a piece of ham, some buttered bread—to make him feel welcome, she says. He eats; he feels welcome; he's at home when I return from school. He likes to climb on all the furniture. I pet him, hold him, feed him, show him the window-to-the-world which we open to let in air and light. I'm happy.

But one afternoon I find the house empty. I panic. I ask Madame Marie if she's seen the cat. She hasn't, but she asks if the window is open. It is. "Go look in the street. Maybe he's climbed a tree in the square." I go out, and indeed I do find him climbing the statue on the square, and so I rename him "Tarzan." I adore him, but he causes me a lot of trouble. He keeps jumping out of the window; so far, we've been lucky. He finds his way back into the house, through the lobby, up the stairs, meowing at the door. But Mother complains that someday he won't come back; he'll be run over. She also complains that he refuses to eat plain bread; he wants butter—or something—on it, as if she can afford to feed him in style, like a fat cat in a fancy restaurant. I try to excuse him, but all I hear is that we can't afford his fussiness; he'd better shape up and eat whatever he is given.

My school days are now spent in a relentless state of anxiety; it's hard to concentrate: has my cat behaved? has he jumped out the window? has he run away? is he lying dead in the street? will he anger my mother by refusing her piece of plain bread? I can think of nothing but seeing him again, holding him strongly against my chest, petting him obsessively. Maybe he longs for freedom: he keeps jumping out the window.

One day, my cat disappears. I comb the neighborhood. Tarzan is gone. The next day, when I return from school, he is still gone. And the next day and the next day: still no trace of him; he has joined the ranks of the "disappeared." I am heartbroken. Mother admonishes me not to think of him; he is probably very happy somewhere in a park or a cemetery with lots of other cats to play with. I try to think of him that way, but I miss him and feel terribly lonely.

I wish my cat would come back. I wish Serge would come back. And Sarah. And Henriette. And Charles. And Maurice. And my aunt Miriam. And my uncle Motl. And my father. And all the others who haven't yet come back. Now, my days are lived not in anxiety, but in a dulled and muted hope. Perhaps, if not Tarzan then Serge, if not Serge then Henriette, if not Henriette at least one of my parents' friends, or a neighbor, somebody will come back.

If ever I mention Tarzan, Mother says it's just as well; he must have found another home where they have more money for food, more food for the family, plus some left over for a cat.

A few months later, on my way to school, I see that the front door of a handsome apartment building is wide open for movers to deliver furniture. Mother always talks of that building as very fancy, full of snobbish people. I want to see what it looks like inside, and so I just walk in. And there he is! Tarzan himself—grown bigger, fatter, furrier. He doesn't run or leap; he just walks, in a very dignified way. I can't believe my eyes. My first impulse is to kidnap him and take him back home. But . . . he is obviously thriving on good and plentiful food. We are barely managing. Mother would be upset. He would run away again; I wouldn't know where. At least here I know where he lives and I can see he is well taken care of.

I tell my mother that I have located Tarzan. She gives me a strange, awkward look and says I must be mistaken: it's been a long time; lots of cats look alike. . . . And that is, of course, the last conversation on the subject.

THE WAR WAS still going on outside Paris and with it, talks of battles, of heroism, victories, defeats. I didn't care to follow all that, especially as I'd just been hit by a major civilian disaster: Madame Marie and Monsieur Henri were moving to larger concierges' quarters in a small factory quite a few blocks away. My mother would surely miss her. She was getting on with Madame Marie as well as before the war, talking of recipes for potatoes, tricks to get rid of mice, and how to lengthen my school dress with a border from a remnant: "She's such a big girl. She grows so fast!".

To my own chagrin, I wasn't getting on so well: Madame Marie and I had never regained the closeness we had before I left for Vendée. An awkwardness had come between us: my body had grown too big. I felt guilty when Madame Marie, pinning the hem of a dress or a skirt she was making me, would repeat: "You're such a big girl now!" It was as if I had wronged her, purposefully doing all my growing far from her sight for all of two and a half years. We didn't know how to speak to each other of anything other than practical matters. There were moments when I wanted to tell her all the astonishing things I was learning in school — I wanted to tell her that the earth is really round, but I wasn't sure she would accept this as a verifiable fact. And there were moments when I was on the verge of talking to her about St. Theresa of Avila with her vast castle of the soul, but I always stopped myself in time: Madame Marie didn't go in for castles. I wished she'd at least ask me again what the heart is like, so she could see that I had never forgotten the answer: "The heart is like an apartment, Madame Marie."

But she didn't ask. It made me very lonely.

I DIDN'T LIKE being "a big girl." I didn't see what there was to gain from it. The last time I had been officially treated as a child was at a government-sponsored Christmas party for children of prisoners of war. They had a program with clowns, choirs, jugglers, and acrobats, followed by a distribution of wrapped toys and books. I chose a package that obviously held a toy. Still, we had to listen to a rousing patriotic speech: how brave our fathers were; what sacrifices they had made for France; and how it was that we must never, never forget that we were the bright Future of France, our motherland that would soon be freed from the occupants' cruel boots and would rise from the ashes like a phoenix.

I thought of my Joan of Arc. She was only seventeen when she led France to liberation from the British occupying forces, the same age as many French youth who had fought — and often died — in the Resistance. Such stories were coming out, new ones every day, in the newspapers, on the radio, in newsreels; everyone was talking about these young people — how brave they were and how they made their country proud. As a "big girl", a "Future of France," how many years did I have left till I, too, joyfully offered my life for my country? Enough time, I hoped, to walk through every street and alley in Paris, every square, every outdoor market; to follow every path of every one of its parks; to learn the names of every bridge, every statue, every old monument; to know which subway line to take without looking at a map.

IN THOSE DAYS, everything came in bits and pieces, fragments of a giant puzzle. It was a continuous game of lost and found. Someone had come back; someone had not come back; someone had been heard from, but that was long ago. This theater had re-opened; this one had not. It would take a long time—or forever—to even find all the missing pieces.

For Jews, all of France became a huge Lost and Found. They tried to reclaim their lives from the Gentile world: their children from orphanages, foster homes, convents; their jobs, apartments, businesses; their sewing machines, knitting machines, books, photographs, documents. Some of these were willingly given back by decent people; some were fought over by others, greedy for objects or for Jewish children's souls.

My mother did her part to get books back from their hiding places. It took quite a bit of detective work (and the learning of horror stories along the way), but it was done with zest by a team of volunteers, all from Eastern Europe. Once, to celebrate the discovery of a particularly rich cache of Yiddish books whose owner had not come back, my mother took me out for my first grown-up drink in a Paris café: a glass of green absinthe alongside the Canal St. Martin. She looked as happy as if one of the "disappeared" had suddenly reappeared. And I was ecstatic: absinthe was Verlaine's trademark; photographs showed him drinking absinthe in a Paris café, turning it into lyric poetry.

EUROPE'S Lost & Found Department finally let us know that we Jews could come and claim some authentic concentration-camp human ashes. The Jewish Community of Paris received the ashes with reverence and organized a grand funeral in the Père Lachaise Cemetery. The ceremony would come complete with the unveiling of a memorial statue, and everyone would be invited, Jews and non-Jews alike.

My mother and I went to the gathering place, outside the Père Lachaise Métro stop. We stood on the street island across from the cemetery, waiting to march with our Jewish secular progressive organization. We were grouped by age, my mother with the adults and I with the youth. We had come early, and we saw the very first group arrive to lead the procession; it was made up of the skinniest men and women I had ever seen. Their striped pajamas were mostly too large and too long. As the survivors gathered in the thin rain, they were mainly silent. Their faces were too long, their eyes much too large, and their bones too obvious. They walked strangely, as if they only half remembered how it used to be done or why. Altogether, they looked like amateur actors playing ragged beggars in a medieval passion play or in a silent Charlie Chaplin movie. And yet, there was something untouchable, sacred about them, as with priests and nuns. Like them, in their odd habits, they were set apart from

ordinary mortals. Only one outsider, God Himself, could understand their thoughts and feelings. But unlike nuns and priests,
the camp survivors' vacant stares forbade entry into their segregated world. It had been chosen by Fate, not by them; they
didn't wish it on anyone. We stood in awe. Only the rain ignored
the irreconcilable differences between them and us.

Finally, they disappeared into the cemetery, carrying a
wooden casket smaller than a baby's coffin. Behind them, groups
of normal people—with hidden bones and regular-size eyes—
were forming to join the funeral march. My mother and I found
our separate peer groups. I was glad to be young, delighted to
be with my friends, though we were all so quiet.

We marched slowly, quietly, into the continuing rain, up
the hilly terrain of the lush cemetery. I thought of Madame
Marie: this was where she spent her free Sundays, admiring
trees, tombs, and cats. Here she could mingle with celebrities
and later announce that she had paid her respects to Balzac, or
Molière, or to her all-time favorites: Sarah Bernhard, the great
actress; and Abelard and Héloise, the exemplary lovers of medieval Paris. It gave her much satisfaction "to pay her respects" to
such important people. But she didn't limit herself to them. We
were passing some baroque sepulchral chapels she'd enter on
her rounds, not that she knew the family, or anything about it,
but she just wanted to see that everything was in good order:
the old photographs still in their rusted frames, lined up on the
altar, and the altar free of cobwebs. Monsieur Henri would be
waiting outside, having lent her his huge handkerchief for her
pious housecleaning.

My mother once told me why cemeteries were Madame

Marie's hobby. It was because she lived with Monsieur Henri without being married to him, and so she couldn't go back to her native village in Lorraine. As a result, her mother's tomb remained unattended. That made her sad, so she watched over other people's tombs, especially those that could do with a little housekeeping attention. She was the secret godmother of the dead in the Père Lachaise Cemetery. But there was no chance that I would see her here today, because there were too many people and she always avoided crowds. I suddenly missed her terribly.

As we continued our slow, orderly march—every club, every organization in its turn—unaffiliated adults began to line up on either side, forming stationary borders to the procession. Some of those people tried to control their sobbing. Others couldn't. After a while, I couldn't help it either, and I too started to cry. With deep inner pain, knowing it was in vain, I wished to be little again, sitting on the floor of Madame Marie's loge, listening to her chat with a tenant or a customer, dressing my doll with remnants of an apron-in-progress.

For some reason, it was stop-and-go for both the drizzling rain and the march. Every few minutes we stood in place, waiting for the rain, or the march, or both, to start again. Even my sobbing was on and off. I tried to calm myself by looking beyond the mourners for the familiar tops of famous sepulchers; but today, the tombs just made me envious. Especially those that bore the name of a single family—carved in old stone, with many decorations, in perpetuity, with everlasting love. They were like private mansions in exclusive neighborhoods, sure of themselves, their solid traditions, their past, their future.

Each family chapel, with the names of its dead carved in stone—date and place of birth, date and place of death, each one taking up so much space! But for us, in contrast, all we had for our 75,000 dead French Jews was one spot of ground in which to bury a small box full of anonymous ashes. No individual name; no date of birth, of death; no place of birth—just a collective place and manner of death: Nazi concentration camps.

We have stopped again. The rain is at a low-key drizzle. The crowd surrounding us is getting denser: we must be getting close to the memorial. With so many mourners, maybe we won't even be able to reach it for the ceremony! But no matter: we are all here like a family, for a family funeral. I may be an only child, with a mother and maybe and maybe not a live father, but walking with me are all my buddies, boys and girls my age, some with one or two live parents, some with none. Walking together like this, we are brothers and sisters. So after all, I'm managing to have a very large family—glowing with our bright future in a new world that will never know war; next weekend we're going camping in the forest.

At the thought of it, I feel very cheerful—when suddenly, out of the crowd on the right, a woman about my mother's age rushes straight to me . . . and hugs me till it hurts. I don't know her. I've never seen her. I'm sure she doesn't know me. If she did, she'd call me by my name, tell me hers. But here is this strange woman, hugging me as if she had lost me and found me again.

In pain and joy she cries, over and over again: "I had a daughter like you." I'm so overwhelmed by her physical presence: it's as if all Jewish mothers mourning a child had embraced me at once! I don't know why she picked on me. Was her daughter my age? Did she look that much like me? The mother keeps repeating: "I had a daughter like you!" And all along, to more fully enfold me into her very being, she strokes my hair, presses my face against her chest—until she has crushed all my thinking process. I'm hypnotized by her cryptic refrain and can barely remember why I find her words unsettling.

Within an instant everlastingly carved in my bones, a transfusion of identity changed me forever: this strange woman whose name I didn't know became my mother, I was her daughter; I hugged her and stroked her back as a lost and found daughter would. I could feel her begin to calm down like a child run out of tears. I was every Jewish daughter killed in the mass slaughter of the innocents. She was every Jewish mother orphaned from her daughter. I was a child of History. True, I belonged to my blood mother, and maybe also to my father if he ever returned; and surely to Madame Marie and Monsieur Henri. But all that was secondary. I knew now that I was baptized into a new life, that first of all I belonged to the family of my people— the dead we were burying in the baby coffin as well as the living, the brothers and sisters around me, the mother hugging my live body, and through me feeling the hug of her dead daughter. As they lowered the ashes of my family into the hallowed grounds of Madame Marie's favorite cemetery, anointed by tears into the community of Jews, I was baptized into a new life: a Jewish life.

I T ' S A N O R D I N A R Y school day and the class is quiet. We're all trying to copy a map. I'm sitting in the back when I hear a knock at the door. The teacher opens it; I look up. It's my new concierge; what is she doing here? Although she's old and proper and very skinny, dressed in black, I can't see how she has the nerve to call herself a concierge like Madame Marie. She tries. She's polite and clean and dependable. But she's not Madame Marie. No matter how hard she tries, she will always be oceans apart from my real concierge.

The teacher smiles and summons me to the door. Before I even reach her, she says: "Your concierge brings wonderful news. Your father has come back. He's eager to see you, so you're excused for the day."

I was glad to be excused from map copying, and willing to follow the nice enough make-believe concierge, but I was not eager to see whoever was going to pass as my father.

I worried that his return would affect my social status. Many of my friends were either full- or half-orphans, or waiting to find out which it would be. Since we hadn't had any news from my father for eight months, I fitted into that last category. We shared a silent bond, a suspense about the eventual shape of our family life, once the sands stopped shifting, once everything settled down and went "back to normal".

Now, for me, the sands have suddenly turned into concrete. I am walking on firm ground to meet my father waiting in our apartment. He must be happy to be back, surely ready to stay for good, sleeping in my mother's bed. She will be happy too! It's just me. I don't know if I'm happy. I think I'm happy for them but I'm worried that it will cause me great embarrassment. How can I live in a happy family, a family not mourning a father, a mother, brothers or sisters? That isn't normal. I might lose all my friends! How strange, how solemn a day!

I OPEN THE DOOR. There is no electricity at the moment so the dining area is in semidarkness. Still, it's easy to distinguish a French soldier's silhouette, in full uniform complete with soldier's cap.

I don't know what to do with my body; I put it close to the wall, against the table. He speaks; I must respond with my voice but my voice doesn't cooperate. He keeps trying, very gently, to befriend me (but even German soldiers used to try to befriend children, as long as they didn't know they were Jewish!) My voice comes out very softly with some general nicety. I don't know if he has heard it, but he is encouraged. And now, out of his pocket comes a chocolate bar—just another soldier's trick! What makes him my father if he acts just like any soldier?

"I have a present for you in my knapsack," he says. That is his first interesting sentence. I stare at the knapsack, waiting for my present to be retrieved from it and handed to me. But my father makes no move; instead, he starts to tell me stories. And that is even more interesting. He tells me how his camp was liberated by the Red Army, which quickly moved on to liberate other camps. The prisoners were left to their own devices. Pomerania was far from France, closer to Poland. There were huge forests where you could freeze in winter but which served as good refuges if you were on the run. Still, it was dangerous:

German soldiers, even defeated, might have guns. It was a long way to France, mostly on foot, along bombed out terrain, broken bridges, roads encumbered by ruined tanks, a mess of corpses, passing abandoned houses, sometimes whole villages obviously hastily evacuated. And everywhere, you could hear gunshots but also, worst of all, the pained, interminable mooing of unmilked cows. My father will never forget that, he says. He stayed together with a group of other Jewish prisoners. They would take over an abandoned farmhouse, kill some chickens, pick vegetables from the garden or get preserves from the cellar, make themselves a feast. They'd leave the dishes in the sink — and move on.

Now I was beginning to remember my father the storyteller, my father who read me stories when I was little. He would read me my favorite story, over and over again, about the Old Man who could do no wrong. That Old Man went to the fair to trade his cow; after a series of trades cheerfully negotiated, each one worse than the last, he came home with his final prize, a bag of mostly rotten apples, which his wife cheerfully accepted, praising his wisdom and making applesauce, which they both enjoyed. There was something about the story of this journey of my father the prisoner-of-war and a group of his friends liberated by a "red" army (that must be the color of their uniforms!) wandering on foot through the ruined countryside, listening to cows' complaints, occupying abandoned farmhouses, helping themselves to whatever they liked, eating well and not doing dishes — that was absolutely marvelous storytelling. Now, I wanted more and I was listening most attentively.

Doors to Madame Marie

AND THERE WAS MORE storytelling. We finally reached the important part: about my present waiting in the knapsack, and how my father came to choose it. In one of the abandoned houses, he found a jewelry box. In it was a beautiful pearl necklace, with a single strand of small delicate pearls, obviously made for a young girl. My father thought it would please me, so he put it in his knapsack and resumed his long journey home. (At that point, I was near ecstasy: a pearl necklace of my own, made of real pearls. What a wonderful father I had! in a minute, he'd put it around my neck and tomorrow, I'd show it off to everyone: "Look at my pearl necklace! It's a present from my father. He carried it for eight months in his knapsack because he knew I would love it.")

After more descriptions of journeying through ruin and devastation and having some terribly scary close calls with death, whether by accident or by the hand of a vengeful enemy—all of which were fascinating to follow—I heard my father suddenly make a most astonishing statement: "My knapsack was too heavy. I had to lighten my load, so I threw away the necklace." I must have looked so shocked that he immediately reassured me: "But later on, months later, I found something else for you, something even more wonderful than the pearl necklace." (What a good, thoughtful father I had! But what could he have found that was better—and lighter—than a pearl necklace? maybe a gold ring? or a gold chain?)

At long last, my father reached into his knapsack and, oddly enough, pulled out a small package wrapped in plain paper. It looked much too large to have anything to do with jewelry. I was so curious I could barely breathe. I unwrapped the package, disclosing a leatherbound kind of notebook, diary size, but without the lock and key that French diaries have. I was stunned. It must have weighed as much as ten kilos worth of pearl necklaces! How could all these pieces of empty paper stuck between leather covers possibly be better than one pearl necklace? What was my father thinking of? I was outraged, but I simply asked: "What is this for?" And my father replied very simply: "For you to write in."

Now I couldn't wait to free myself from this disappointing encounter. I asked my father if he wanted to see my mother. He'd be glad to, so glad! (It seemed to me he was also glad to end our awkward reunion.) With renewed energy, I ran to find my mother at the shop. She wasn't there. I suggested we try at his sister's place; my Aunt Georgette. We started walking there, very fast. My mother was in the street, having just come out of my aunt's house. She noticed him, got red in the face, froze in place; he ran to her and they embraced madly. Now my mother was happy; my father was happy. They had each other, and I was free.

The next day, after my mother had gone to work, my father asked me to go with him to a bookstore: he had to get a book of poems by a French Resistance poet named Paul Eluard. I was surprised. I thought he might first want to see his friends, or walk by the Seine, or even do something practical like go to a clinic to see if he was all right (most people who "returned" had something wrong with them and had to see doctors and dentists), but no, he had to get a book of poems. First. Urgently.

He found the bookstore, found the book, held it up reverently as if he were a priest holding up a monstrance. As we walked back home, I tried hard to keep up with his fast pace. I was completely won over by his exuberant mood. It might after all be very nice to have such a father in the house!

"You'll have to read this book," he told me. "This man's poems helped me survive five years of captivity." I was stunned. So it wasn't, as he wrote in letters, the photos and thoughts of me and my mother that had helped him survive; it was poems, words on paper. How strong Poetry must be, stronger than wife and daughter, certainly stronger than hard labor, prison and other hardships—so strong it kept my father alive.

I was eager to read the Poetry book. He let me look through it, pointing out the poems that had been the most important. And of course I read those first. They were easy to understand, but earlier in the book were some curious poems accompanied by odd-looking graphic illustrations. The introduction talked of a strange movement that wasn't the Resistance movement but was something called "Surrealism" which seemed magical and wonderful and incomprehensible, full of tricks like the circus. But I read the poems to myself, and they sang and they gave me strength and hope and they made me happy, and I understood how they kept my father alive. And then I remembered how Poetry had given me back my voice when I had lost it in the village and my mother had tricked me into reading Lamartine out loud before sending the book to my father. I made up my mind to read every word of the Eluard book, including the introduction and the incomprehensible early poems; and to re-read it and re-read it until I learned to draw strength from Poetry as this father of mine (and even I) had done.

WHEN YOU NEEDED outside help and strength, it was important to know where to find it. In Vendée, it was simple: you just turned to God. But God was not here, not in my house, not near my parents. He was across the street with the nuns in the convent school and He was in the nearby church and He was with all Christians and even with some Jews, though it was a different God. Short of God, though, Poetry seemed very potent. And quite accessible: bookstores, libraries were filled with it.

I was happy with my father and Poetry. A few days after his return, however, I was sent away to a summer camp for children of prisoners of war. It felt very sudden. On the train, a girl in my compartment was talking about her father: "He just came back. I hardly got a chance to see him. He was spending all his time with Mother. I think they're lucky it happens to be school vacation: this way they can get us out of their way and just be happy together."

So that was it with my parents, too, and I was in their way!

Maurice, Charles, Sarah, and Serge Melczak in 1935 or 1936

A family portrait. Paris 1930. In front, the Melczak family:
my uncle Motl holding Sarah, my aunt Miriam holding Serge, my
cousins Charles and Maurice. In back, my mother and (l. to r.)
my uncles Moishe and David Gutrajman

Henriette Melczak, almost three, in 1942

Sarah Melczak at age thirteen

Doors to Madame Marie

Charles Melczak

At a Zionist sports camp, just before the war. My cousin Maurice
is in the top row, far right, and my cousin Charles
stands just in front of him, with arms folded.

My cousin Maurice, on the right,
with fellow partisan fighters (Maquisards).

Shmiel Aron Gutrajman, my mother's father,
who died in the Warsaw Ghetto.

My mother's family, the Gutrajmans. Warsaw. 1939. Gita, Sara,
and Tema are in the top row. The little boys are Yosele and Berele.
None survived.

The Gutrajman family on a picnic outing. 1939.

Not one of them survived.

My cousin, Chaim Gutrajman, sensing political trouble,
leaves Warsaw for Lodz. Others, from left, are my cousins Sara, Berele,
and Yosele, and my Uncle Moishe and Aunt Chana.

Aunt Miriam, my mother's sister and the mother of
my five Melczak cousins. None survived.

TWELVE

Strange summer camp. Something dreadfully wrong here.

Not its setting which is just as it was described to our parents: a small, beautiful mountain town in the Pyrénnées, famous for its mineral springs reputed to heal an assortment of illnesses. Residents of the local spas and hotels make their daily pilgrimages to the forest, where they drink the mineral water on the spot or bottle it to take back to their rooms.

All forty of us seven- to fourteen-year-old campers also make our daily visit to the forest. We walk there in rows of twos —two boys or two girls—singing French folk songs, exhorted and escorted by our camp counselors. When we reach our destination, we're made to drink the water. It must somehow be good for us, since wealthy people have come all the way here to drink it, yet it has such a foul taste that we feel we'll choke or throw up. We have no choice, though, but to drink it without protest.

The problem is not in walking to the forest and being forced to drink mineral water. The problem is hunger. It hurts. Mineral water doesn't take away the hurt. Three times a day, we are served one bowl of drab porridge made of wheat chaff. Nothing else. We are always hungry.

THE SUMMER CAMP is in an urban setting. It consists of a two-storey building on one side of a small alley in the very center of town. The building belongs to the camp's director, as do those across the alley, including a popular restaurant at the corner. The whole alley is the director's property. In part of a fenced area next to the restaurant, he raises pigs, while in the other, he grows the feed for them. What the pigs won't eat gets cooked at camp to make up our daily mush. The alley has very little car traffic, so we often get to use it as a courtyard, under strict supervision. It's our entire world. We leave it only under strict escort to the mineral water fountains. On the way there, we speak to no one; we just sing French folk songs to the road and the trees.

Since we are all children of prisoners of war, the camp is subsidized by the government, which makes a weekly delivery of foodstuffs. On the day of the delivery, we are told to stay indoors. A lot of scheming goes on among us to figure out ways of coming out as soon as the truck leaves the alley, having deposited its cartons of food on the pavement. We dream of that food. After the truck leaves, the camp counselors, all men, all ex-prisoners of war, carry the foodstuffs not into the camp kitchen but into the camp director's restaurant. We hope they will drop an apple or a can of sardines. They rarely do, of course, but on those scarce occasions when we succeed in catching a bit of stray food, we get caught and punished.

Punishment is almost as important a subject of camp conversation as food, though it's easy to forget why we get punished:
being caught trying to "glean" after the food truck; whispering
to a neighbor during the long, silent nap times that follow the
porridge breakfast and the porridge lunch; asking for a second
helping of porridge; waking up late; not making up our bed to
army standards; complaining about anything. Worst of all, trying to escape from camp.

The mildest form of punishment is to be forced to kneel
on the floor and "freeze," with elbows up, hands crossed on the
head, in total silence for the remainder of the long nap. Worse is
to be denied one's bowl of porridge for one meal, or for several.
And the most feared punishment of all is to be sent to the infirmary across the alley, at the other end of the restaurant. Older
children admonish the younger ones never to admit to being
sick, no matter what. No matter how much anything hurts, one
does not want to end up in the infirmary, where complainers
or general troublemakers are also sent and are given terrible
whippings. The sick would have to watch, or at least hear, the
screaming.

But food remains our major obsession. Hunger hurts, and
the hurt is easily aggravated: by sounds of revelry coming from
the restaurant; by being forced, as we enter our stark dining
room, to look to our right, where a glassed-off area serves as the
staff's private dining room. There we can see them eating real
restaurant food. We are not allowed not to look. When it has hurt
to look, then we can proceed to our assigned seats on the bench
of a long wooden table and wait patiently to be served our small

portion of unsavory porridge. Memories and thoughts of food hurt. Trying not to remember, not to think, also hurts.

What helps is to sing French folk songs or recite a La Fontaine fable, and so we are eager to learn when our counselors teach us a new song or a new poem. We also enjoy rehearsing skits, dances, choral readings for the weekly show we perform on a small stage set up in the attic. The director and staff have front seats, and when we do well, they applaud. All our performance pieces are cheerful and pleasant.

BUT HUNGER and punishment always came back. Sometimes together. One afternoon, on our orderly march to the forest, we were singing the folk song we had just learned, about a band of brigands, thirty in number, who rob a series of people including the priest. I noticed that Marie-Claude, who was twelve, broke away from the line and slipped into a bakery. I wasn't the only one to notice, but we all made believe we hadn't seen it and sang a bit louder, with slightly anxious zest. It took a while for a counselor to notice her absence. The march stopped. Counselors caucused. One was sent back to camp. The rest of the counselors shepherded us on to the forest, singing the next stanza about the thirty brigands till we had them all hanging for their robberies. We worried about Marie-Claude for the rest of the afternoon.

At supper, we saw Marie-Claude wearing identical signs on her chest and her back: I am a liar! She had to keep standing still in one spot, facing us. One of the "kappos," as we called all our counselors, told us very loudly, pointing to Marie-Claude, that she was a liar who had stolen bread from a bakery. When caught, though, she had tried to cover up her theft by claiming she was not fed properly at camp. Of course, nobody believed her. Nobody would believe a child anyway. And all she got for her troubles was to be punished. She would be deprived of food for the next three meals and would be made to stand during each of those meals wearing her sign. That would teach her to appreciate being fed three times a day. And it would teach us, the kappo insisted, what to expect if we followed her bad example.

TWICE A DAY we had our "appel," the roll call to ascertain we were all present, still at camp. At dawn, we lined up sleepily in the alley and answered to our names. The late afternoon roll call was also in the alley, but that one included mail distribution. A kappo would call our name; if we had a letter or a package, we could come and claim whatever had survived the censorship. During a weekly, censored letter-writing session, we were encouraged to write to our parents asking for cash, ration tickets, and sweets. By the time our parents' letters and packages reached us at mail distribution, they had already been opened. The cash, ration tickets, and sweets had been removed, leaving us with censored letters and tubes of toothpaste or other items undesirable to the camp administration.

The days followed a very strict routine: appel, clean-up, breakfast, a long nap, lunch, another long nap, the singing-march to the forest's mineral springs, appel, supper, rehearsal for Friday performances, clean-up, and bedtime. During what little "free" (though not unsupervised) time we had, we talked mostly of food—specific details of dishes we remembered and fantasies of future meals, all banquet-size feasts. When the kappos left the room, we also fantasized being rescued by our parents, or townspeople, or the Resistance, or the Red Army.

Once, we thought our "liberation" was near. We heard rumors that the Red Cross was going to conduct an on-site visit of the camp. Then, at one supper, we were formally told that it was going to happen on a specific day, at lunch, when we would be served a special meal. We were instructed that whatever the Red Cross staff asked us, we should smile and assure them that we were happy and well fed. Anyone who behaved otherwise would be severely punished as soon as the official visit was over. To be sure we understood, the announcement was repeated twice, and in addition, a couple of children were told to repeat the instructions aloud.

When the Red Cross came, we were indeed served a real meal, with mashed potatoes and ground meat mush. We were eager to eat, but first, the pleasant-looking, gentle-mannered strangers had to be politely introduced and we had politely to greet them, during which time we were not allowed to eat. Then, when the speechmaking was over and we started eating, the Red Cross staff went through the dining room, stopping randomly here and there to ask children how they liked the camp. The children smiled and said they liked it very much. Soon the visit was over. The Red Cross had come and gone and you could hear the van leave the alley. We were concentrating on nothing but the food when, to our horror, the counselors came to collect our unfinished plates.

We ate fast, we begged, we couldn't believe the meal was but a mirage and our wonderful, real food was being taken away, but it was, and we were left powerless and hungry. But something had changed. The close proximity, the smell, the very brief taste of our one real but interrupted meal had shaken us from our passive state. Now, with whatever we had at our disposal, we began to conduct acts of sabotage against our kappos. Someone would steal glue; we'd set it up on their chairs, in their beds, on their notebooks, on their clothes—and then we would position ourselves to watch their expressions. When they would rage and swear to discover the culprit and punish him, we just listened; nothing, no one could have made us point a finger. In any case, we were all in on it. There was a wonderful sense of quiet power in our solidarity. No matter how we were threatened or cajoled, we knew that nothing could weaken our bond. Nothing. No one.

As the staff felt increasingly thwarted, punishments became more arbitrary, frequent, and violent. We responded with our guerrilla tactics. The kappos were subjected to an unrelenting barrage of small acts of annoyance and discomfort. Tension grew. As did hunger, and rage, and fantasies of liberation.

Six of our ten weeks' session had passed since we had become inmates of this camp. We kept losing weight, but not our spirit of resistance. We even had a leader, Pierre, a boy of fourteen.

THE MAJOR BATTLE took place, as did all important events, during a meal. Pierre was seated across from a young boy who was so driven by hunger that he forgot the rules and begged for a second helping of porridge. The kappo on duty gave him a sharp reprimand and took away his empty plate. In a sudden fit of rage, Pierre got up and tripped the kappo, making him fall on his face. Just like that. In full view of everyone. Catastrophe. End of the world, or of the Old Order. Stunned silence. Another kappo attacked our leader and dragged him away. We listened hard for the sounds of a beating. Nothing but eerie silence. We were sent off to an early bedtime.

Over the next couple of days, supervision was so strict we had no chance to speak with one another, no chance really to find out what had happened to Pierre. Rumors flew that he had been confined in a closet, and that one of the youngest boys had been assigned to bring him a bowl of porridge once a day. Furtively, we asked the boy how Pierre was doing. He lowered his eyes and said "O.K." It was not very reassuring. We were worried and lonely, cut off from our leader. Even the folk songs didn't manage to comfort or distract us. These were anxious days.

We remembered how the townspeople had ignored Marie-Claude's plea, but we were so desperate we tried it again—to no avail. Our fate interests no one. It's not a local matter, since all the children are from Paris and the kappos are from anywhere in the country but here. The only local people connected to the camp are the director and the cook. The director is well-respected in town as the owner of a popular restaurant. As to the cook: she is just a woman. She cooks the rough and bland porridge. No one ever sees her.

But one morning, breakfast was inexplicably late, and even though we were hungrier than usual, we found the porridge almost inedible. The kappos looked subdued, preoccupied.

T H A T A F T E R N O O N , a large white van drives into the
alley. Stops.

It's a Red Cross van! Doors open. Out of every van door
come nurses in white uniforms. Just as a kappo wants to keep
them from entering our building, a police car appears. Everything is happening so fast! This is getting to feel like a surprise
attack. The staff is in disarray, waiting for the director to show
up. Meanwhile, we crowd into the alley, still fearful of getting
caught and punished, but at the moment, no one is paying much
attention to us. All that commotion has brought spectators from
the restaurant and the small shops nearby, and everyone seems
to be waiting for an explanation and for the director to appear.

The nurses have gone inside while the police are rounding
up the kappos and searching for the director. We do our best to
help: "Look in the kitchen!" "In the attic!" It doesn't take long,
and they drag him outside.

They're about to take him into the police car when we spontaneously hold hands and trap him inside a circle. The police
have let go of him, lending him to us for a moment. He stands
frightened, frozen in the middle of our circle. We whirl around
him in a diabolical dance. Faster and faster. This is the last show
we'll perform for him. We hurl insults at him as we move faster
and faster. We're getting tired but we'll never stop; we'll go on
dancing around him, faster and faster, forever and ever, throwing insults at him till he shrinks into the ground; then we'll bury
him and dance on his grave, morning and night, all the days of
the week, for months and months. He is stunned, ready to drop
from fear and fatigue. His eyes appeal to the spectators to rescue

him; they show no sympathy. Finally, we too get tired and sur-
render our prey to the police. They take him away.

Now, our white-uniformed liberators take over. They give
us an explanation: the cook had run away the night before and
had taken a train to Paris, where she went straight to the government agency that subsidized our camp. There she told everything
and denounced our director. This time, the Red Cross decided
to come without warning, accompanied by the police. Since the
cook had told them about Pierre, the first thing they did was to
look for him. They found him crouched in a locked armoire.
They immediately transported him to the hospital, where he will
receive medical attention. But he'll be all right, they assure us.
"What about us?" we ask. "When are we going back to Paris?"
"When do we get to eat?" "What are we going to eat?"

To our astonishment, we're told we're not to be released to
our parents for another week, because the doctors are afraid they
would overfeed us and we would get dreadfully ill as a result.
The nurses line us up in the dining hall and examine us. When
they're finished, everything is explained to us, slowly, gently. We
are undernourished, suffering from all kinds of vitamin deficiencies, including scurvy, and a skin disease called scabies. We
may think all we need is a string of banquet meals where we
can eat as much as we want of everything, but that's not the way
it works. When the concentration camps were liberated, some
well-meaning people fed the survivors as much as they wanted.
But their stomachs weren't used to all that food, so many got
terribly sick and died. The nurses won't let that happen to us. We

will have to follow a set of new rules. For a week, we will be fed many times a day, in very small portions. Slowly, our stomachs will be re-introduced to different kinds of food. Little by little, we'll get better.

Our white angels replace the kappos and run the camp. They are very gentle, smile, speak softly, pat our heads. Their first concern, though, is our diet. We don't have large sit-down meals but many very small snacks, just a few hours apart. The alley, in which we are free to play most of the day, becomes our outdoor dining room. We rush to read the cheerful-looking menus posted on the doors, announcing the next snack. When nurses call a halt to our play, we line up to choose a small food offering from the trays they are holding. They tell us to eat slowly, as slowly as we can. Then we all have a quiet activity before being allowed to play freely again.

The week is happy and uneventful, as it must be in Paradise.

THE TRAIN ENTERED the Paris Métro station welcomed by a flock of nervous parents waiting on the platform. I was wondering if I would recognize my father, but he materialized near me as I came down the steps. He looked terribly shocked at how thin I had become and he immediately relieved me of my backpack. I was chatty and giggly, very happy to recount all our ordeals. My father was less of a stranger to me now that I had learned what it was like to live in a camp, oppressed by kappos, ignored by townspeople, and then finally liberated by people in uniforms.

Within days we were sent to Hôpital Saint Louis, where

they treated us for scabies. We had to undress, then walk down a hall that was lined on both sides with nurses, each holding a bucket and a brush. Their mission was to get our bodies fully painted with a medicated lotion. But the brushed lotion delivered a painful sting and we tried to run away from the nurses. They ran after us and painted us the best they could, on the run. As we ran, other nurses lay in wait for us and they, too, painted us as best they could, wherever they could. We cried and hollered. There was no mercy till we reached the end of the hall, when we were shepherded back to the dressing room.

We also had to get shots of iron and vitamins, but that wasn't so bad, though it was to go on for a couple of years.

Meanwhile, summer vacation wasn't yet over. So my parents sent me to another camp, a Jewish camp this time, located in an old mansion outside Paris and run by an organization to which my parents belonged. I was glad to hear it wasn't far from Paris and that, in fact, one could get a view of Paris from the mansion's tower.

IT TURNED OUT to be idyllic. The camp counselors were told which children, for one reason or another, had just gone through traumas, and the cook was told who had suffered from malnutrition. As a result, I was treated with enormous patience and indulgence and was fed a lot of protein. I spent my days most pleasantly: playing with others or daydreaming by myself, walking on the lush grounds of the mansion or lying in the grass listening to wind and cow-bells.

I made a memorable discovery: comic strips for children. Perhaps this was during an after lunch "quiet time."

I found myself in a room with a couple of other children who were looking through a thick bound copy of the *Katzenjammer Kids*. Up to that point, I had only seen mostly incomprehensible political cartoons in grown-up newspapers. I couldn't believe there were cartoons designed for children! Here, it took only a few pages to get totally familiar with the characters, which from there on were easy to follow as they bumbled their way through the book, one page of mischief at a time. I couldn't get enough. When the other children went off to play, I stayed and read the playful collection several times over.

Summer ended up very pleasantly.

Back in Paris. Like other Jewish children, I am fussed over more than ever, not only by my parents, but by all their surviving relatives, neighbors, friends. For us, there is no lack of cookies, sweets, chocolates. The women have learned so many tricks of substitution that, even though food is still rationed, they can make some of the old prewar baked goods reappear on the table, especially for sweet-toothed children. Pleased with themselves, they stare at us as we gobble up the desserts that took them so long to make.

They talk about us and to us. The subject is the same: getting back to normal after the terrible years "from which these children, thank goodness, were spared." We have been the lucky ones. How then can we ever complain about anything? We have one duty: to get "back to normal." For those of us, like me, who are too young to remember much of "normal" prewar times, it is hard to figure out what it all means. For instance, did children never complain before the war?

But yes, we are aware of our good luck. We weren't taken into the camps (none of those children seems to be coming back!) Once, with my Jewish youth group, I went on an "outing" to see the now-emptied Drancy detention camp. My cousins were taken there during the July 1942 roundups, as was my mother's friend Berthe a year later, when she was denounced by her Gentile husband's relatives. My cousins went on to Auschwitz and haven't come back; the train convoy that Berthe Moulin rode on her way to camp was derailed by partisans, and so she has come back, frail but alive.

We wander around the abandoned camp. It is eerie. A counselor points to a large room—concrete walls, concrete floors—and tells us the inmates had to sleep on the cold floor. It looks so desolate! It's hard to imagine how they could fall asleep: especially parents worrying about their children who were either in the children's section of the camp or, one hoped, in hiding somewhere in the outside world.

Outdoors, an outside wall has a graffito that still howls in my soul: in a small child's handwriting, one word: "Mama." To recover my bearings, I stare at the ground, but in the dirt I see a used toothbrush. My first instinct is to pick it up: maybe it was Serge's or Henriette's or Sarah's toothbrush. I try to remember what their toothbrushes looked like, but I can't. So it wouldn't be right to pick up somebody else's toothbrush. The more I stare at it, the more forbidding an object that toothbrush becomes. Who am I to touch it? I wasn't incarcerated here; I didn't share the fate of my cousins. I have no right to touch it. I didn't end up riding in a cattle train, with people screaming, crying, and dying under and over and all around me. I have seen the photographs.

I have seen the movies. While that was happening to them, I was free, safe, fed, and sheltered in Chavagnes-en-Paillers. If I hadn't been saved, I could have died in Drancy, or in the cattle train. If I had reached the camp alive, I would soon have faced the gas chamber, like all children under fourteen. But no, I didn't die at any one of those points. Instead, I went on living. I became eight, then nine, then ten. I have reached this moment, when I am still alive to stare at a child's toothbrush.

Maybe the owner of the toothbrush, in the cattle train or in Auschwitz, remembered it with nostalgia and wondered what had happened to it; did somebody else pick it up, make good use of it? Did the child get a new toothbrush at camp? The tooth-brush stands its dusty ground. I don't dare touch it. I imagine that it will stay where it is and, perhaps, when nobody is look-ing, it will grow into a giant monument, a memorial to those who will never return.

THE LIVING RETURNED. The Dead didn't. With time, fewer and fewer of the Living returned. More and more names of the "deported," the "disappeared," made it to the list of the never returning Dead.

But, now and then, relatives taken for dead would miracu-lously be located. They were usually in such a terrible state that they barely had the strength to pronounce their own names, let alone make any effort to be reunited with their family. That happened to some very close friends of my family. Like my par-ents, and almost everyone we knew, they were immigrants from Poland. The father, a businessman and editor of the Yiddish progressive newspaper *Die Neie Press*, had been shot to death by the Nazi occupants in 1941 along with other Jewish political activists and community leaders. His widow, a tough woman, fed herself and two teenage sons by selling old clothes at the Flea Market, and she fought the Nazis through her Resistance work. Eventually, like all foreign-born Jews, she had to go into hiding. Despite her heavy Yiddish accent, she swore and cursed fearlessly and became a successful smuggler of arms for the underground army.

Both of her sons joined the partisans. Léon was arrested and sent to concentration camp; his younger brother, Maurice, was not caught, continued to fight, and survived. After the war, he came back to Paris with his mother. Their rented apartment had been taken over by Gentiles, who refused to give it back to them. The landlord let them occupy an attic apartment in the building across the courtyard from their old one. Even as war heroes, it would take years of bureaucratic litigation before they would be allowed to reclaim their prewar apartment. In the meantime, they kept looking through the lists of survivors in the hopes of finding Léon. Finally, his name appeared on the list! They inquired at the Red Cross. Yes, they were told, he had survived the camp and the long Death March, but barely. They did not expect him to live much longer. It was decided that Maurice would go fetch Léon and bring him home, even if it were only to die.

EVERY DAY after school, on my way home, I visited Léon. He lived in a very old building. Before the war, I used to love to enter its courtyard, go up the old staircase on the left, just one flight of spiraled stairs, then knock on the tall door on the right. As soon as the door opened, I felt at home. I would be offered something to eat and drink. Léon would tease me affectionately or would teach me to play dominoes and checkers.

But now I passed through the dark and musty entrance hall and came out in the noisy courtyard with its large carpentry shop. Instead of turning left to the old apartment, I now had to turn right and go up the stairs to the attic floor, where the family had been forced to relocate.

Everything was dark and sparse. When I came in, Léon was alone; his mother and brother were at work. The first thing I saw was Léon's single bed, its foot in front of a window. Then the question was: did the thin body in the bed still have the breath of life in it? You had first to look at the cover, to see if it had any slight movements, then at the eyes staring at the ceiling or turned toward you. He was so weak, he barely moved and could only talk in a very low voice; you had to stand quite close to hear him. He didn't say much. His daily quota for me was one question and one gesture. The gesture came first. It invited me to gently lift a corner of his pillow and pull out a stick of American chewing gum from a pack someone had put there for him. I would do so and thank him, then sit down on a chair by his side and wait for the ritual question that shaped my every day: "What did you learn in school today?"

I hadn't particularly liked school until Léon's return. Now, I entered my classroom feeling as I did back in Vendée, when I entered the forest to forage for natural foodstuff—blackberries, mushrooms, wild greens—wondering what I would find and how much of it to take home. All day, I was on the lookout for what would be of most interest to Léon. He liked history and geography, and even science, which I had so much trouble learning. I tried to remember exactly what the teacher said, and I would check the textbook during recess so I could remember everything and explain it clearly to Léon.

At first, I had been surprised by his question. But I couldn't ask him why he asked it and why he was so interested in the answer: he was too weak, and one question was all he could manage. Yet, each time I came, the fact that he still had the strength to ask the question was a triumph. But that's all he could say with his voice. For any further question, any further comment, he had to depend on his eyes. They were dark brown, large, intense. I consulted them to see if something I reported was particularly interesting to him. That's how I learned his taste in Poetry. I would recite a poem. I could tell from the way he looked at me that he didn't care for any of the Romantic poets. It was obvious, though, that he loved Paul Eluard, Louis Aragon, and Jacques Prévert, whom we didn't learn about at school; so I cheated and lied, learning their Poetry at home but pretending I was learning it at school.

I KNEW he was much too weak to recover. He had been one of my prewar heroes. I remembered him as being tall, of course, and quiet and full of sweetness. When I was very little and he lifted me on his shoulders, I pretended he was my big brother; he acted as if he were. He was always ready to play with me, make me laugh, give me a compliment on the slightest of my childish accomplishments. And now that I was a big girl, I knew my big brother was going to die, that it was just a matter of time. I wondered how one died without being shot or gassed.

If you knew Death would soon come for you in your own bed, how did you prepare for it at eighteen?

The thought haunted me. I figured that if it were I in that bed, I'd be furious with the Nazis, the collaborators, the people who took over my old apartment. But Léon showed not the slightest sign of anger. I remember when he was brought back home as a live skeleton, how his huge eyes were filled only with pride: he had survived to die at home, in his own bed. True, he was in his own bed, but that bed was not in his old apartment, which he could see from his window when someone lifted his head. It made me angry. It was different with him: he didn't seem to be angry at anyone. Maybe anger was too heavy for his slight frame, his light breath. Simple gentleness was all he was able to carry.

One day, in school, I had a Surrealist experience. The geography teacher was trying to explain the relationship between the sun and the earth. To illustrate, she had an apple and an orange. Since oranges were still an expensive luxury, she thus caught the attention of the entire class. It was wonderful to see her rotate the orange! It reminded me of that other, mesmerizing orange, Marshal Pétain's gift to the children of French soldiers in captivity, which I had received during the first year I attended this school. Now, Marshal Pétain had been tried and sentenced. He was in exiled captivity on a small island near the Coast of Vendée. As for me, I was completing my last year in elementary school, and my ex-soldier father had introduced me to Surrealist Poetry and leftist politics.

I still had the geography orange in mind when, later that

day, in perfect illustration of Surrealist coincidence, I was reading Paul Eluard's poems and came across the magical line: "The earth is blue like an orange." Something of radical freshness, of childhood magic, something of unexplainable exhilarating truth . . . and I went joyfully to Léon's house to bring him my day's good find.

On the way, I passed the Church of St. Joseph, our neighborhood church. It necessitated a slight detour, but I had gotten in the habit of coming at it from the back by Avenue Parmentier, then going alongside the church to the front, to its impressive Gothic façade on rue St. Maur. I had made a deal with God: since I could no longer be a practicing Catholic, I would show my devotion by this personal daily walk. If I couldn't go inside the church, I would at least come close to its outside walls. That was the best I could do for the time being.

It was a strange feeling. It reminded me of those days when it was against the law for Jews to enter any public building: we were not to mingle with the pure French, not infect them with our uncleanness, our corruption. Yet the war was over. Anti-Semitism was officially forbidden, and Jews could go everywhere—to movies, theaters, museums, parks, restaurants, concert halls, anywhere they wished. But, although there were no signs to that effect, I, a Jewish child, could not enter this Catholic Church because I was Jewish, and because I was still secretly Catholic.

As a Jew, I could not betray my people: they had been killed simply for being Jews (and not Catholics or Protestants). In my

Jewish youth group, I learned how the church had spawned European anti-Semitism. So, as a Jew, I could not enter the church.

I could not enter it as a Christian either, though that was more complicated. Like all good Catholics, I was duty-bound to attend church regularly, for Mass, Communion, confession—the way I did in Vendée in my church of St. Fulgent. But now that I was back in a secular Jewish home, there was no question of my attending church. It would be worse than attending synagogue services, although that too, was bad. In my parents' view, religion was simply organized superstition, a refuge for the weak of heart and mind. I would have died with shame if my father had found out that his daughter was a believer, and a Christian one at that! On the other hand, I was mortified by my situation: how would I ever be worthy of salvation if my life were totally lacking in any Christian rite, if I didn't sit, or stand, or kneel at the very same time as a church full of other Christians? If only I could enter the church, just once, to let God know, in His own House, that I still believed in the Holy Trinity and in all the precepts of the Catholic faith as I had learned them in catechism. If God heard me in His own House, after I had crossed myself with Holy Water, He would let me know what to do, how to furnish Him proof of my faith and devotion. Just once—I was sure just once would be enough. God was good and merciful. He would understand the urgency of my petition. He would show me the way to remain a good Christian, even in a Jewish secular home.

But every time I began to go up the front steps of the church, the words of my anti-Semitic Vendéen priest still rang in my mind. He had made it clear that if a Jew so much as entered a Catholic Church, it caused such spiritual chaos that the parishioners' prayers were derouted from their heavenward course and did not reach the throne of God, who was awaiting them. Truly, it would be un-Christian of me to prevent prayers from reaching God! So I could not enter the church as a Christian anymore than I could as a Jew.

The huge wooden doors of the church opened wide enough to accommodate a small herd of elephants but when I came close, they shut me out with a double padlock: "You're a bad Catholic because you're a Jew" "You're a bad Jew because you're a Catholic".

O N M Y W A Y to see Léon, the dying Jew, doing my Catholic outsider's devotional routine, soul caressing the walls of the church, I heard weeping and chanting. When I reached the outside of the church entrance, I happened upon a funeral cortège. Everyone had stopped in their tracks, even strangers on their way to work or to shop. Men took off their hats; everyone bowed. Almost everyone made the sign of the cross. Those who didn't were probably Jews. Before I could think, I had automatically crossed myself. I was afraid to look at anyone, Jew or Christian. Then a disturbing thought came to me: "What if Léon's funeral procession took place in the streets of our neighborhood, just like this one? Would people stop, cross themselves, stay still and silent for a full minute? Would they do that for a Jew? A single Jew? A neighborhood Jew, who as a boy used to play with the other children in the town square? Or would they do it only for a mass funeral of Jews in the formal setting of the Père Lachaise Cemetery?"

This time as I entered Léon's room, I was hit by an air so somber, a stillness so eerie that I thought I'd actually see Death sitting at Léon's bedside, beckoning me with his scythe. But no, there was no one else in the room but me entering and Léon still breathing under his blanket. Yet I immediately sensed that something was different, solemnly irrevocable. It was as awesome as if I had at last been allowed to enter St. Joseph Church, or summoned by God to enter His private church. I moved around more softly and quietly than ever. Léon's body was perfectly still. Only his eyes moved. They were exceedingly large, more than usual, of a deeper, more urgent brown. On the path of their stare, they traveled at top speed, found my eyes, locked my soul in their embrace. They wanted to say something, something of terrible importance. And I wanted to ask them what I had not dared ask Léon's ears: "What was it like at camp? What is it like dying? Is this what being a Jew means? Are Christians right when they pair Jews and Death as an ancient couple married at the Crucifixion? Is it better not to be a Jew? Would it be better to be a Catholic?"

I can't remember if I actually told Léon about the earth being blue as an orange. If I did, the words to tell of that wonder weren't as loud as the intense silent dialogue we carried on with our eyes, Léon and I. His eyes read mine and answered: "The horror at camp was worse than any description of Hell by your anti-Semitic village priest. Dying in bed with dignity in a world at peace is a privilege. Being a Jew is to know Death and to love Life. It takes more courage to love Life in spite of horrible persecution than to go to Mass every Sunday. Be a Jew like me. Remember me, always remember me if you are tempted to run away from your Jewishness." It was impossible not to hear him: his eyes spoke with complete clarity, absolute lucidity, utter conviction. They told my eyes to carry his Holocaust eyes forever. To remember not only the horror of the Nazi persecution but also the culture of the dead: Jewish devotion to life, family, learning, and social justice. Léon's eyes said: "Be a proud Jew. Like your father and mother. Like your relatives murdered by Nazis. Like other ancestors who died in ordinary ways. All Jews. Like you. Like me." My eyes must have answered: Yes, Yes, and Yes, and I promise, on my heart I promise, forever I promise . . . because after a while his stare loosened its grip, softened, his eyelids closed and all was still.

I left. This had been our very last conversation.

LÉON HAD left me an unexpected legacy. I had worked so hard at school in order to report to him that the principal talked to my parents to encourage them to send me on to high school. There were two problems: money, and my deficiencies in math and science. I was eleven; at twelve I could get a work permit and, like other girls of working-class families, could start earning money to contribute to the family income. My attending high school would place a financial burden on my parents. The principal had remedies for both problems: as a child of an ex-prisoner of war, I should be eligible for a government scholarship, and, to amend my deficiencies, my parents should take on the expense of a private tutor to give me weekly remedial lessons in math and science.

It was arranged that the tutor should give me lessons at the home of my father's sister, Aunt Georgette. This is where I spent whatever part of my Thursdays free of school were not claimed by my parents to send me on errands.

The tenement building came with the usual heavy smell —that mix of urine, bleach, rotting garbage. But when you entered my aunt's and uncle's apartment, you were greeted with a comforting aroma. It came straight at you from a kitchen that doubled as a garment shop: a hefty iron being pressed on an ironing board against the inside of a jacket sleeve in progress. Competing with that smell, but equally comforting, beckoning you to turn to the dining room on your right, was the smell of furniture polish lovingly spread over the imposing dining room set with its matching buffet.

After the war, when my aunt Georgette and uncle Henri and my cousin Sarah came out of hiding at the farm of my uncle's Gentile relatives, their apartment was totally bare. Every nail had been pulled out. But they felt lucky to have the apartment back at all, and to be alive, all three of them. They were very good-natured. My uncle Henri loved to sing, for any occasion or none at all. And my aunt sang along. My aunt Georgette always went along with anything my uncle or my cousin wanted. She would cater to me, too. Mostly, I wanted her to open her cupboard and give me what I called "eating paper," the matzoth treat I was denied at home. My father would not tolerate matzoth because of its association with religious observance. Other Jewish food was all right, but it wasn't the usual fare in our family, whose Jewishness centered around Yiddish language and culture, not religion or food. My aunt and uncle were not religious either, but they were not as political as my parents, and so they kept matzoth simply because they liked the taste of it.

My home was dominated by the daily newspaper. My father started the day with the early-morning edition and ended it with the late-evening edition. In between those two editions, he carried on intense and elaborate interpretations of events, followed by prophecies of doom. My mother tried to counteract with whatever optimistic remarks she could muster, which only drove my father to cite historical precedents for all the misfortunes that can befall nations. Any unlearned lessons, any mistakes, could lead to a repeat of the Holocaust, of that he was certain. If my mother tried to persist in interjecting some upbeat thoughts, my father invoked the difference of their wartime experiences: he had spent five years in captivity, four of them in a punitive hard-labor Jewish prisoners' camp, while she had remained free. How, then, could she ever understand?

Following that logic, it was evident that I, who had been sheltered and taken care of during the entire wartime, not having any responsibilities, any worries, would understand even less. All I knew was that, as the father, he must be right. He read every word of the newspaper. Most puzzling, because I literally could not see it, but he claimed he could always read "between the lines." There was no question but that the way my father understood world events was the correct way. After all, aside from being my father and so well-read, he was also the ex-soldier who knew what fighting a war was like, and the ex–prisoner of war who had experienced long captivity on enemy territory. But how I wished his view of the world and its future weren't quite so dark and ominous!

In the Schwartz household, on the contrary, my aunt and uncle took each day as it came, paying little attention to long-range politics. It made for a more tolerant, more cheerful home than mine. My uncle sat at the Singer sewing machine, singing French and Yiddish songs; on the wall facing him were yellow paper patterns of men's suit jackets, scissors, notes with measurements, notes of deadlines for each order. Behind him stood my aunt, in the small kitchen corner with its greystone sink, its cold running water, its little gas stove, and the curtained-off cupboards under and over the sink, under and over the stove. She would be stirring a stew or ironing the sleeves of a jacket, or sometimes both, steaming up the room with a strong and hearty smell. She sang along with my uncle or laughed at his jokes. Two long work tables, each against a wall filled with patterns and tailor's tools, occupied the greater space of the room. For their meals, unless they had company, which of course called for dining room splendor, they would clear part of the shop table and eat right there in the kitchen in the midst of unfinished suit jackets. They always greeted me warmly, prepared to let me do what I liked: eat a piece of matzoth, marvel at the very loud tick-tack of the alarm clock set on the table, wash my hands with a rough pumice stone, and use a tailor's chalk to draw on remnants.

I felt warmly sheltered and comfortable in that room, as I

used to in Madame Marie's loge when I was little. Though her sewing space was also in a small room that served as living quarters, she had much less equipment than my uncle. All she had was a sewing machine with drawers for needles, pins, spools of thread, as well as a large basket filled with remnants, and a dress form. I wondered why flower-print dresses were less serious and required less space than men's double-breasted striped suits!

My uncle Henri carried his professional authority into the streets, which to him were peopled most importantly by those men wearing suits. He would stare at them in passing, and if the suit happened to be on someone he knew, he would stop the man most cordially, get very close to him, check the cut of the jacket, the shape of the collar, the buttonholes; he would then take a few steps back, to see how it looked at a little distance. When he had completed his examination of the jacket (the pants held little interest to him except for the precision of the length of its legs in relation to the shoes), he would pass judgment, whether or not it had been solicited.

He was indeed a very gifted, skillful tailor. His wife and daughter had only to point out a coat or a jacket on a store-window mannequin; he would stare at it for half an hour, and later, back in his home shop, he would make a close copy of the original.

It was a robust, earthy, practical family. When my aunt Georgette made cookies, they were "mendelbroit" or any other kind that could be packed in tin cans. This way, they could last a long time in the cupboard, for home use or to serve as gifts when needed. Whenever my uncle came back home from the outside world, he always brought cheerful news of the neighborhood, or of friends and acquaintances he had run into: prewar products were re-appearing in the butcher shop, the dairy store, the hardware shop, or on market stalls; a friend had gotten a better job; someone else had opened up a notions shop; a neighbor was about to marry off his oldest daughter to the corner shoemaker. My aunt proudly greeted every bit of good news as if her husband himself had made it happen. Pleased with her approval, my uncle would burst into a whistle or a song.

My cousin Sarah, their only child, was also a good-natured optimist. At nearly fourteen, she could have had a work permit and made her own living in a garment shop, but her parents had made sure she had the chance to learn to be a bookkeeper. Soon she would be able to earn a good living in decent, clean working conditions. Now, at seventeen, she knew how to dress in tailored clothes, to get her hair done just like our mothers, and to put on makeup without smudging her face or her hands. She managed quite easily to please both her parents and herself. By becoming a bookkeeper, she would not only escape the sweatshop world of her parents, but would also be better positioned to marry eventually into additional comfort and security. In the meantime, when Sarah wasn't working, she was out enjoying herself with friends, or flirting with a neighbor boy, or off on a camping trip with the older group of our Jewish youth organization. I looked up to her. All was well in the best of worlds.

The only time when my aunt and uncle refrained from singing or joking or making any but the most necessary conversation was when my tutor would come in. The two of us would settle at the dining room table, where he would help me prepare for the extremely difficult entrance exams to a girls' academic high school in Paris.

My parents were paying the university student to tutor me. My aunt and uncle provided the place and the supervision. My part was to concentrate, to make full use of my teacher's time, to do whatever assignments he gave me. For the occasion, my aunt would have freshly applied a double dose of polish on the dark wood of the heavy dining table, which was the pride of the family. Its chairs were large and imposing. Displayed on the matching buffet was a set of translucent Limoges painted with scenes of eighteenth-century gallantry—aristocrats caught in the act of dancing, embracing, or bowing to each other. At night, this splendid dining room doubled as my cousin's bedroom. For that purpose, a wine-colored stuffed chair opened up into a single bed. I envied my cousin. Her parents slept in the small bedroom and she had the dining room to herself every night, while I was still sleeping in my parents' bedroom. But the luxury item I envied most was a radio that, instead of blurting out news all day as in some homes, was tuned in to popular music—songs of Edith Piaf, Charles Trenet, "Les petits chanteurs de la croix de bois", a famous teenage boys' choir. It was, of course, turned off during tutoring lessons.

Surely, I reasoned, with that impressive dining-room set, including the radio, my aunt and uncle must be rich, even though their apartment only had three small rooms, counting the kitchen/shop. On one structural point, though, we were better off. We had a small toiletroom in our apartment. They, however, had to share the Turkish toilet outside in the hall with three other families.

WITH A SERENE SENSE OF WELL-BEING, sitting at the elegant dining room table I let myself be instructed in math and science. My tutor was a good teacher, patient, soft-spoken, always ready with clear explanations. I was happy learning.

In the course of one Thursday's lesson, my uncle suddenly announced that he had seen my aunt through the window and he was going to go down to help her carry heavy bundles of materials up the stairs. They'd both be back soon.

The door closes. Footsteps are gone. My tutor stops the lesson, bends his head, whispers: "I have a secret to tell you. Can you keep secrets?" "Oh yes!" I assure him. "In the village during the war, I never told anyone I was Jewish. I can keep any kind of secret." But he is still hesitant and radiates a floating anxiety that comes my way and settles into my throat. "Oh God," I pray. "Please keep him from asking me anything: I couldn't answer; I'm not fit to speak!" God is good and my tutor keeps an awkward silence. In that silence, I hear all the noises from the street below: a peddler chanting Old rags for sale!; a mother yelling at her oldest child; girls singing jump rope rhymes, a fireman's siren at a distance. What does my tutor mean to say? For the first time, I look at him as if he weren't a tutor. He must be the same age as Léon, but he wasn't in a camp and you can't see his bones. He even has, as the womenfolk love to notice, some color in his cheeks—or is he blushing? In his shyness, he seems a much nicer person. He gets closer to my ear to whisper the secret; now I'm the one to get shy. Suddenly, as we hear footsteps coming up the stairs toward the landing, he blurts it out: "When they say that Man evolved from monkeys, don't believe them! The truth is: Man evolved from mice." With that, he straightens himself, re-opens the textbook and resumes the lesson. My whole world has changed: I have been trusted with a weighty secret, dealing with the very origin of Man. It is a theory that contradicts both my Christian teachings and my secular ones (which, in fact, did claim that Man evolved from monkeys). I am flabbergasted by the importance of this secret revelation. From that point on, I would become a more attentive student than ever.

A YEAR of private tutoring had helped! The entrance exams for scholarship students were exceedingly difficult. On my first day of exams, my mother woke me up at dawn, and had me sit and review my notes with my feet in a bucket of very cold water and my head covered with a cold-water compress—the better to sharpen my thinking.

Following tradition, the list of students who passed the entrance exams was posted outside the lycée's entrance doors. As my mother pulled my hand and dragged me to the list, I could see other mother-and-daughter sets coming to the bulletin board, the mother looking for the only name that mattered, the daughter frozen in fear, looking at the floor or across the street. Strange how all those who walked away dejected looked so fine and intelligent! I didn't have a shadow of a chance. I would surely share their fate. In preparation, I had already begun the process of feeling and looking equally dejected when my mother gave a triumphant cry: "There! There it is! Look!" She was pointing to a name. I thought it was just a familiar name, that of someone in her circle of friends, but no, it was actually mine, my own strange name of Melszpajz! It was hard to believe I was among the chosen few to earn a scholarship to that elite high school.

My mother took me to my favorite ice-cream store back in our neighborhood and soon proceeded to make sure everyone we knew had learned of my academic feat. I was congratulated and got gifts of fancy chocolates, books of French literature, and a wooden pencil box.

I *WENT TO SEE* Madame Marie, so she could be proud of me.

She was sitting at her old sewing machine in her new lodging, which was relatively more spacious. Aside from giving her more floor space, her new apartment offered her something she didn't have before: wall space on which to hang pictures. So now the wall clock of my childhood had company. One picture fascinated me, almost lost in the sea of sentimental greeting cards and old calendars with bucolic landscapes. It showed a rosy-cheeked adolescent girl, double cherries hanging from her ears, standing in front of a bowl of cherries. She was holding one very bright cherry, about to pop it into her half-open mouth. What fascinated me was the caption, which I found incongruous: "Life is not a bowl of cherries." It was as difficult to comprehend as René Magritte's realistic picture of a man's pipe, entitled "This is not a pipe." In fact, there was something about it that seemed to fit right in with Surrealism, but I didn't yet know what it was. What did Madame Marie mean by it? Did she choose the picture or did someone give it to her? If I had the money, would I have bought her such a present?

The picture was very distracting, but I did manage to tell her how difficult the exams had been, how I had gotten up at five o'clock in the morning, how my mother had me sit with my feet in a bucket of ice water so I could wake up and think clearly in preparation for the grueling set of examinations (here Madame Marie nodded her approval of such maternal strategy!), and how it turned out finally that my name was on the list of those allowed through the pearly gates of a quality second-ary education. Madame Marie froze halfway through a turn of the machine's wheel. Half the cloth of a quarter of a dress lay limp on my onlooker's side of the sewing machine: Her foot stopped pedaling. She just beamed at me in a huge embrace of a smile and, for an instant, she stared at me as though she could see something new and wonderful bloom inside me. Finally she said, "You'll make your parents proud," sealing the remark with a look of great satisfaction. She returned to her work; everything got back into motion—the wheel, the pedal, the cloth.

She had made me exceedingly happy. I now felt ready to take on the lycée, then the university, and eventually to become a well-loved teacher and a well-read short-story writer. Noth-ing would stop me; I would overcome whatever obstacles Fate would place in my way. If God wanted to test me, He could. I was ready. I would prevail.

Before I left, I looked up at the girl with the bowl of cher-ries. She seemed so engrossed by the sheer joy of being young and pretty with her dangling earrings of double cherries, savoring the pleasure of having a bowl of cherries all to herself, of holding up a red ripe cherry destined for her eating delight. Why then did it say: "Life is not a bowl of cherries"? Was it a warning to her? to me?

THIRTEEN

IN OCTOBER 1946 I became a scholarship student at
the most prestigious girls' academic high school in Paris, from
which, if I successfully completed six years of demanding course
work, I could enter a university. Two and a half years later, in
early May of 1949, I reluctantly left Paris with my family to mi-
grate to the United States. By then, I was about to be suspended
from a pre-vocational two-year high school for working-class
girls. It was a "terminal" post-elementary school, terminal because the completion of its study course would not lead to entry
or re-entry into an academic secondary or university education.
Between those two dates, I had at times agonized over several in-
compatible identities and visions of my future, and had at times
enjoyed friends, Paris, books, and the attention of some teenage boys.

After the Liberation, in the privacy of one's inner life, everyone more or less efficiently operated a complex switchboard
of emotions. Publicly, though, a curious simplicity dominated
most conversations. For adults, those conversations were struc-

tured around references to three points in time: "Before the War," "During the War," and "Since the Liberation." Young teenagers like me charted our talk by more immediate points of reference: "last summer vacation," "this coming vacation," "this Thursday," "last Thursday," "next recess," "when school lets out."

If only I had a clear label for those crucial years—dramatic and banal, volcanic and idyllic in turn!

In politics, those years had a name—and often even more than one.

For the government, that period saw the eventual phasing out of *épuration* (shoving the skeleton of collaboration into a dusty corner of the basement of national consciousness), and of the patriotic *reconstruction* (talking workers and employers into a united workaholic binge to rebuild France's economy). For the Communists, whose popularity had hit an all-time high, soon to be slowly eroded, the Resistance slogan of "singing tomorrows" was still a rallying cry for the People, the long-suffering and deserving People who, in the meantime, were absolutely wild about Edith Piaf's sad love songs and Yves Montand's mellow live-and-let-live exuberance.

In my Jewish world, this was a time when certain ghostly words—normally pronounced either tonelessly or with heart-rending grief—became more ghostly: "disappeared," "deported," "Auschwitz," "Death March." They were to be replaced by strong and proud words: "A Jewish State," "Kibbutz," "Aliyah," "Hagannah."

As the Yiddish language sought refuge in the conversations

of the older remnant of Eastern European Jews, Hebrew became the language of choice among young Zionists. But there
were also other words, pragmatic negotiators of personal lives
in reconstruction: "a sweet deal," "a good lead," "a useful contact." And there were exotic words: "New York," "Buenos Aires,"
"Cuba," "Palestine," "California."

With those words dancing around them, circles of families
and friends were reconstituting themselves as best they could.
The war dead—killed at camp, in prison, in battle, in ghettos,
in Polish forests—had resisted all resurrection wishes and en-
treaties from their loved ones; they had refused to come back
home, where photographs continued to substitute for them—
on dressers, walls, bedside tables. As time went on, the photographs became them, exclusively, for all eternity.

A new person entering our lives would soon be shown
these one-dimensional relatives smiling their most photogenic
prewar smiles. They helped to complete the family history.
Names were named: "This is my Uncle Shmuel, the shoemaker."
"This is my sister Sarah, after whom Suzanne is named." The ultimate compliment from the guest was: "Of course, such obvious
resemblance!" Then would come brief sighs quickly absorbed
by silent stares. They too were typical of adults in those days.

On a couple of occasions when I was home alone with my
mother, I saw her suddenly stop to stare at a family photo on
the wall. I could see by her lips and fingers that she was counting. She then announced the results of her calculations and told
me how old the relatives in the picture would be were they

alive today—if by some miracle they had managed to jump off a cattle train to Auschwitz and to proceed somehow to the safe, far reaches of Siberia.

With the photo ghosts looking on, attacks on family poverty were attempted daily, obsessively, and semiclandestinely through private guerrilla warfare. The "fighting forces" all belonged to the Black Market; some were officers, who took the greatest risks (and made the largest profits); some were simply private-first-class soldiers.

Before the war, the garment trade had depended on the inexpensive labor of mostly illegal Eastern European Jewish immigrants. Since by far the greatest number of French Jews killed in the war were stateless immigrants from Eastern Europe, those who survived were in great demand. A cousin of my father reopened his men's clothing store and guaranteed him some regular work.

My father could now work for himself, with my mother as a helper, ten to twelve hours a day, in a little apartment turned into a shop. Only as an adult would I learn to my astonishment that he, too, had dabbled in the Black Market, although very peripherally and as an ordinary foot soldier. At the time, of course, we the children were not told—wartime secrecy had found new outlets. Indeed, had I been told, would I have been capable of understanding, or of accepting, my father's reasoning? Probably not. My Jewish youth group had too thoroughly indoctrinated me and my peers with the ethics of the Labor Struggle. Yet today, that parental reasoning strikes me as so simple, so justified!

My father had come back from five years of captivity with

two strong wishes—never again to be subjected to authority, and to treat himself to two packs of cigarettes a day. If he took a regular job as a machine operator in a union shop, he would earn union wages: 40 francs an hour. Since a pack of cigarettes cost 200 francs on the black market, he would have to work ten to twelve hours in the shop, answering to a boss, for nothing more than his daily quota of cigarettes. And what of food, clothes, and other necessities? My mother could provide for those, of course, through her job as a knitting-machine spool-winder, but what of my father's pride? So he really had no choice but to participate in the underground economy based on the Black Market.

My mother gave up her job in the machine knitting trade to join my father in his workshop apartment situated in the bustling working-class street of the rue du Faubourg St. Martin. I knew nothing then of the Black Market involvement. All I was told was that my parents wanted to be alone together through their long work hours as freelance garment workers. It made sense to me, even romantic sense.

I loved going to my parents' workplace on school-free Thursdays. My father would give me my job assignment: materials to pick up in a sewing supplies store, or a bundle of completed men's jackets to deliver to the shop of the tailor who had commissioned the work. Once my chores were done, I was free to do whatever I wished.

What I most wished to do, especially after I began to have troubles at school, was to wander for hours through Paris, which was remarkably generous in free street spectacles: fairs, strong men, fire swallowers, hurdy-gurdy players, pimps and prostitutes soliciting business, Black Market vendors quick to vanish at the sight of policemen, drunken GI's easily drawn into fights, young seamstresses and hatmakers modeling new fashions of their own creation . . .

What I hated most was to be confined for the better part of the day, from eight to six, within the walls of a schoolhouse.

It had not always been that way. Before my high school days, I was obsessed with learning, pure learning, with catching up on my interrupted education. I loved being in the classroom during my last year of elementary school, or at my Aunt Georgette's dining room with my private tutor, or sitting by our one window, leafing through my father's autodidact's encyclopedia, or at the Jewish youth after-school club, where I volunteered as a librarian—whenever I could. But as my high-school days began, so did my troubles, and as my troubles increased, so did the hours I spent wandering the streets after school—and even during school.

MY FIRST DAY at the Lycée Hélène Boucher had been the start of a new era.

Since I was clearly out of my normal working-class element, my first challenge was to look the part of a proper student of an upper-class high school. In the lobby, I joined the other girls lining up for the daily grooming inspection. Two middle-age women dressed in navy-blue suits with starched white blouses were checking each of us, one by one. First they saw if we were clean, with our hair duly combed. Then they checked for possible infractions of the dress code, which clearly ruled out nylon stockings, makeup, and nail polish. After inspection, we went to the locker room. From our assigned lockers, we took out the smocks we were to wear over our clothes. Mine was beige, the color of the freshman class.

THE CLASSROOM is spacious and, to my astonishment, everyone has her own, very pretty pastel-colored desk. For the time being, we are ranked by alphabetical order. But this will soon change. By the results of the first test, we are told, we will be ranked according to our scores, the best students in the front row, near the teacher, and the worst ones in the last row, against the wall. Right now, though, I've landed in the middle of the classroom, at a light-turquoise desk. I feel like a rich girl, the kind who has her own room with a real bed, a dresser, a radio.

At roll call, we are to stand when we hear our name. When it comes to mine, I feel sorry for the teacher struggling with its irrational spelling, so I stand up anyway and pronounce it for her: Mademoiselle Melszpajz ("Melsh-pies"). I notice a girl staring at me. She is short and wears a gold cross on a gold chain. For the rest of class time, she keeps an eye on me, then befriends me during recess. As the bell rings and we are to resume classes, she whispers firmly: "When school is over, follow me!"

That first day is very long but finally ends. Outside, the girl with the cross is waiting for me. I follow her. We take a subway train and end up by her home. We've only exchanged a few casual words, and I still don't know why she has asked me to follow her home.

We reach her apartment building and go up a flight of stairs. She opens the door to her home and ushers me into the traditional small entrance room. Its central piece of furniture is a dresser topped by a framed mirror, flanked on one side by a wooden coat-and-hat rack, and on the other by a ceramic umbrella stand. In this purely conventional picture, however, there is one incongruous object. Displayed on the dresser and reflected in the mirror is a brass menorah. To my astonishment, my classmate silently takes off her golden chain with its pretty little cross and places it at the foot of the menorah. I finally understand: she's really Jewish! But why then is she passing as a Catholic at school? I thought the war was over and nobody had to do that anymore. Not in the fall of 1946!

I'm invited to sit in the meticulously maintained, heavily curtained living room. As soon as I'm seated, the girl, surely knowing the answer to her question, nevertheless asks me: "You're Jewish too, aren't you?" "Why, yes, but I thought you were Catholic!" I answer, although noticing that, without the cross, she looks reasonably Jewish. "Look, I wanted to catch you right away while you still have the chance to pass as Catholic." "Why should I do that?" "Because otherwise you might not get through this school. It's very strict and difficult, but it's got a great academic reputation, so if you get through the six years and pass the final year's exams, you're sure to get into the university." "What's that got to do with passing as Catholic?" "It's simple: all it takes is one anti-Semitic teacher to give you low grades, and at the end of the year, your report card shows you're below standards and . . . but you go, dropped from the school forever." "Can't you complain?" "No, that would get you into more trouble. The only thing that works is to pass as Catholic. It's very easy: you wear a cross; you hang out at your local church and learn everything about it—memorize the names of the parish priest, his assistants, the order of nuns or monks connected with that church, the kinds of missions they have, the hours of daily and Sunday Mass, of confession, which saints are particularly honored, the name of the youth group and what they do. Make sure to take note of the calendar for all Catholic holy days. Also, check it every morning to see whose saint's day it is; then be sure to give saints' day good wishes to anyone bearing that saint's name. So when girls at school talk about church or other Catholic things, you can act like you know all about it: it's your world, too! It's not hard; it doesn't take long. Then at least, that way, you don't have to worry about anti-Semitism! Just worry about getting good grades in class and good marks in behavior."

I am stunned. I tell her I'll think about it. She says I don't have much time; of course, it is up to me; if I decide not to pass as Catholic, at least she won't have to blame herself, because she has indeed warned me that I am taking great risks in being openly Jewish at school. I'll think about it, I repeat. Then I go home.

I DIDN'T THINK; I agonized all during the subway ride. Then when I came out at my neighborhood exit, Couronnes, I was too restless to walk down the street to my home. Too restless to be confined indoors. Walking, whether on country roads and forest paths, or on city streets and alleys, was the way I did my "thinking through" on any difficult subject. So I started walking very slowly the long series of wide boulevards (Madame Marie's favorite Sunday walk) that stretched from Belleville to the Cemetery of Père Lachaise. I walked for hours, stopping at every jewelry shop, every religious bookstore, looking at rosaries and at wooden, silver, or gold crosses with their coordinated chains. I imagined how one would look around my neck, how it would feel to run my fingers on the cross itself. I imagined I was a Catholic girl of eleven, born and raised in St. Fulgent; this cross had been given me by my godfather on my first Communion, and I treasured it. I wanted to savor that simple feeling, and so I spent half my allowance on two pistachio ice-cream cones in a row.

By then, I was at the foot of the Church of St. Ménilmontant, with its picturesque set of hill-climbing steps so favored by photographers of weddings and first Communions. I went up three-quarters of those steps, ardently praying for divinely manifested advice. More than ever, I longed to enter a church, burn a candle on the altar of the Virgin Mary, kneel at her feet, and beg for her assistance in this grave matter.

I also thought of going to consult Madame Marie, but I knew exactly what she would say: "The war is over. You are a Jewish child of Jewish parents. It is as good as being a Catholic child of Catholic parents. In the eyes of God and of upright folks, the main thing, anyway, is to be a decent person who lives by her heart." In my mind's scenario, I could hear the silent echo of the question that had shaped my childhood: What did I tell you the heart is like? And I could remember my answer: The heart is like an apartment that needs the tenant's constant dusting and general housework. My heart was indeed a mess at the moment. I had to put everything back in its right place.

To do so, I had to keep walking the wide boulevards, from Belleville to Ménilmontant to Père Lachaise, where the high wall of the cemetery and all the thick old trees on its bordering sidewalk stood as the guardians of solemn answers to grave questions.

On the way, the cityscape of storefronts gradually changed from pawnshops to mortuary shops, and crosses in the shop windows changed from delicate gold jewelry, destined to lie lightly on a human chest, to heavy marble crosses that nailed down the dead in their tombstones. I thought of Jesus carrying the cross on which he would be forced to die such a cruel and public death, still young, still unmarried, with no children to survive him. To the end of time, all Christians would bear the cross of Jesus's death themselves, by periodically walking along the church's inner walls, contemplating the whole set of the Stations of the Cross that portray Jesus on the Road to Calvary. And Christians would identify themselves by making the sign of the cross in church, in passing a funeral, and in private prayer. For good measure, wearing a gold cross would let others know you as a Catholic, even if they didn't see you at prayer or at church.

But then again, not every Catholic wore a cross. So if I didn't, why would I automatically be taken as a Jew? How indeed could people distinguish Jews from non-Jews if they weren't wearing a cloth yellow star stitched over their hearts? True, some religious Jews wore a gold or silver Star of David as a piece of jewelry. But other Jews, like those in my parents' world, wouldn't be caught dead with any religious symbol, on their person or in their house.

My wanderings had brought me inside the Père Lachaise Cemetery, on its uneven hilly terrain. Crosses were everywhere. A single large cross for one Christian dead, or one Christian family. Multiply that hundreds and hundreds of time: one cross per body or per family of bodies. Eventually, though, I came across the symbolic mass burial place of the French Jews murdered in camps, where all the 75,000 Jewish dead are under the protection of a single Star of David. Nearby were other Jewish graves, private ones, some of them family crypts, nearly all bearing small marble stabs inscribed "We shall never forget!" often accompanied by a prewar photograph of the dead, obviously taken in a photographer's studio. Something solemn, poignant, dignified.

And what about me? Could I forget? Could I forget that woman who had hugged me during the mass funeral procession, crying "I had a daughter like you!" transfusing me with a puzzling identity from which no cross could protect me?

What would it be like to try again, in this postwar period, to pass as one of those who really belonged, in this world and in the world to come, one of those followers of a personalized God who died on a cross to guarantee individual salvation of every single Christian?

In my Jewish youth group, I'd been learning how my people tend to come about in groups, to huddle or to be huddled in ghettos, shtetls, cattle cars, detention camps, concentration camps in this life, and in mass graves in the afterlife. I remembered a girl who said her grandmother told her that Jews have been persecuted since early Christian times for stubbornly believing the Messiah will come only when all Jews are living a proper, pious life—salvation will be collective or will simply not be!

A S I W A L K out of the cemetery, my people's dead follow me—invisible honor guard—in the hundreds and thousands. I try to shoo them back. I didn't mean to draw a crowd into my decision-making process! If I can only convince one of them, surely they'll all go back. But no, they're not in a hurry: the dead have no deadlines to meet. They take their haunting leisurely, in an open-ended manner.

All right, all right, I'll bury the cross! I promise. I can't stand it anymore. It's getting to weigh a ton, anyway! Still, it seems awful to risk not surviving my first year of high school. What a comedown that will be—after having being admired for getting a scholarship, to end up wasting the year and closing myself off from an academic career!

In the end, the dead exerted their influence in a purely existential manner. They knew that Maybe is a temporary word, a witness to the duel-to-the-death between Yes and No. The duel ends with only one survivor: Yes, or No. The Maybe witness has served its purpose and fades into nothingness. Should I wear the cross, yes or no?

How would I feel as a Catholic, if I wore it? Impure, because of being Jewish. How would I feel as a Jew, if I wore it? Disloyal to my people. Could I live with myself, feeling impure and disloyal? No. So how could I wear the cross? But what if it then meant that I wouldn't survive this year of high school? That would be a terrible defeat, a great embarrassment, a dreadful prospect, but not as distressing as a permanent state of moral uncleanness. So, here we go. Decision made; risk taken. Come what may, I will not wear the cross! So be it. Amen!

At last, the apartment of my heart seemed to be in good order: swept and dusted, linen changed, cupboards cleaned. The dead were satisfied. They re-entered the cemetery, heading for their segregated mass grave, to remain eternally huddled.

I was free to go home.

IN SHORT ORDER, everything happened at school just as I had been forewarned.

No matter what I did, my grades were low and I was relegated to the back row—an ominous sign. If this were to go on for the entire school year, I would not be promoted to the next grade. As I kept hugging the back wall, month after month, I became more and more discouraged. Before totally giving up, though, I found a foolproof way to test my literature teacher's ill will toward me. For the all-important composition assignment, we were always given two well-defined subjects and a third which was a "free choice", literally anything we wanted to write about. I decided to take the subject-of-choice option and submitted a description of autumn for which I had recently won a prize in a citywide contest during my last year of elementary school. That should at least have given me the equivalent of a C. Instead, it got me a failing grade. That's when I gave up. At which point, a number of things happened to me, good and bad, in no clearly sequential order. Hotchpotch, stirred all together, they made up the stew that somehow nourished me during the schoolyear of 1946–47.

I'm troubled by nervous tics that I take great pains to hide from my parents. Involuntary eye twitches feel hugely noticeable; sudden difficulty in swallowing is scary but passes quickly enough, though each time it feels like a close call. Surely next time I'll be unable to catch my breath and will die of lack of air and saliva.

Worst of all are the fits I get only at school which land me in the infirmary. These are most embarrassing: they start with inexplicable, uncontrollable laughter that will not stop until it's turned into uncontrollable and noisy sobbing. I have to be placed in the nurse's care, and she of course does everything to quiet and comfort me. She's so nice. I'd like to please her and turn into a model of serenity, or at least stop all that noise that comes out of me. But I can't. I hear the nurse explain to someone: "It's hysteria. It will take its course and pass. By then, she'll be worn out, and we'll get her to rest till school is out." Everything comes to pass just as she says. I feel like a defective specimen of young humanity, a faulty "second." Thank goodness my mother is pregnant. I can hope my parents will manage to make another child who, unlike me, will come out just right.

I'VE BEEN ACCEPTED by the "bad girls," those who make it a point of honor to break school rules. It takes imagination, creativity, courage. I love it! While the teacher is making an example of the star student, we mentally refine the plans of a prank intended to bring her to the point of rage. For instance, we could get hold of her grade book, leave the list of names, but tear off the recorded grades.

When school is out, we run to forbidden territory: the boys' high school, for a bit of blatant flirting with the seniors; or the "Fair of the Throne," a major seasonal fair near our lycée. That fair is strictly forbidden. It is considered not only a distraction from homework but also a den of impropriety. The swinging cages lift one's skirts as they fly up to dizzy heights, then down close to the ground again, around and around, faster and faster. Also considered dangerous to adolescent females: the rowdy language of sideshow barkers, the strange lonely men gawking at groups of giggling schoolgirls.

Knowing we're forbidden to wander the fair makes doing so all the more delicious. We run from one booth to the other. We'd love to see the bearded lady and the midget family, but, with limited money, we go for a gingerbread man or a taffy.

SINCE MADAME MARIE has moved away, my parents have found me a new seamstress.

I'm sent to her tenement, up a slippery musty-smelling spiral staircase, with instructions to tell her the following: my name; the name of the client who recommended her to my parents; how my parents have heard she can make me, for a reasonable price, a plain navy-blue gaberdine dress, gathered softly at the waist. (I hate navy blue; I hate gaberdine; I can't stand gathered skirts!)

She looks at me and sighs: "Girls your age have no waist! But I'll do it." She then proceeds to wrap a measuring tape loosely around my hypothetical waist, looking for the spot where my waist should be. Not only am I too big, not only am I generally defective, but now it turns out I have no waist: how mortifying! I wish this seamstress, her mouth a live pincushion, would stop making me turn this way and that. She has such a disgruntled look! She's still complaining about my ill-defined waist which gets more stubbornly elusive. In her thimbled hands, my body grows more awkward. I can't stand this. I must talk my mother into buying me a ready-made dress like my classmates have. I know why she doesn't: the piece of gaberdine is leftover material from one of my parents' commissioned jobs; it must be used. Even with the seamstress's pay, it will come out cheaper than a ready-made dress. There is no question of taste in the matter, certainly not of my taste. The dress will be dull and dowdy, and I'm going to be embarrassed to wear it outside of home, and especially at school! I wish Madame Marie still made all my clothes! They were so much nicer looking, fanciful, full of useless buttons that gave them character. Why did she have to move and I to grow big and awkward, unworthy of her time at the sewing machine?

My waist is unsatisfactory. I'm too old to sit at Madame Marie's feet picking up pins and needles with a magnet. I'm too young to leave school and go to work, though only by a few months, as one can get a work permit at twelve. I'll have to hang out till then; in the meantime, as long as my scholarship holds, I'm contributing some money to the family. My choices are limited: a higher education, with a course of study on scholarship; or a job in a factory. In my schooling, I seem to be heading for a crash, and I can't stand the thought of being cooped up in a noisy factory, exiled from my beloved daytime Paris streets. Whatever will become of me?

Oh the joy of being alone, walking wherever I please, stopping at storewindows to fantasize wild purchases, looking up at people taking their ease leaning on windowsills, or sitting on a bench in a little park to eat an apple and listen to the alluring sound of the carousel! Nobody to judge me inadequate in any number of ways, or to intimidate me with their elegance or efficiency. Alone among strangers, on benevolent boulevards or in friendly alleys, I can indulge in all the daydreams I wish.

I go to the City Hall, which has my favorite library. In front of the bulletin board by the entrance, I stop as always to read the current list of couples publicly announcing their intention to marry. Someday, I too will publish my (our! how strange it sounds!) wedding banns. One of the two names will read: Odette Sarah Melszpajz. What will the other be? I look through the list and try on the men's names for size, one by one. None of them quite fits.

When I'm finished, I go up to the library.

I generally head straight to the section of literary classics. Today, though, still hurting from the recent slight to my waistline, and my consequent longing for those wonderful prewar days spent within whispering distance of Madame Marie's sewing machine, I go to a section I've long admired from afar: the children's section. I haven't been back since the day Cousin Sarah took Henriette and me to that little basement library one unpleasant wartime afternoon, when the magic of storybooks made all the unpleasantness disappear.

I'd like to see the children's picture books again; go to the shelves, pick the largest, the thickest, those most filled with pictures, then sit with them at a table and read for hours. I look around the room: what if someone I know comes in, recognizes me, laughs and calls me a dunce for reading children's books?

I know what to do: I'll pretend to be checking out books for a little brother. No, that won't work for people who know I'm an only child. Then I'll pretend it's for my little neighbor; everyone can have a little neighbor. I babysit him, I'll explain, and I've read him all his books; I have to look for something new. He's begged me to. I put on my best "big sister/good neighbor" look and head for the oversize picture-book section, where I spend hours of pure pleasure making up for years of precocious reading.

This is a wondrous, forbidden feast!

As the library is about to close, I quickly check out a Zola novel I haven't yet read.

MILK IS STILL rationed. We have a clay pitcher, light yellow, country-style. I love that pitcher; it goes back to my earliest memories. It's yellow like the baby blanket Madame Marie made for me and which is still on my bed, a bit worn, and without the religious medals, which my father took off when he returned from Germany. Yellow like a fresh daisy, brighter than butter. I dangle it by its handle, our beautiful pitcher off to the dairy store to be filled with milk. I stand in line; when my turn comes, I hand out the proper ration tickets and the right amount of money. In return, milk is ladled out of a huge tin pail. I leave the store, holding the pitcher very carefully. Turning the corner by the horsemeat store, I stare at a drunk's antics on the plaza. He's singing a bawdy song and gesticulating wildly. People are moving out of his way. Someone rushes out of the store to see what's happening—and knocks the pitcher out of my hand. I'm horrified. There's our beautiful pitcher, broken up in yellow bits and pieces, floating in spilled milk on the sidewalk! The butcher's wife sees me frozen in horror and embarrassment, on the verge of tears; she cleans up the mess on the sidewalk till all traces of daisy-yellow clay have disappeared, and she tries to comfort me by telling me it's not so serious, it's not the end of the world.

I go back home emptyhanded with a wrenching feeling of abandonment. I remember the time I lost the birthday doll Madame Marie had given me, and my mother scrimped for the money to purchase an identical doll so that Madame Marie wouldn't learn of the loss. I wish I could replace the yellow pitcher with an identical one, put it back in the kitchen, and just get scolded for having "forgotten" to buy milk! But it is a useless wish: the yellow pitcher was one of those prewar objects adults sighed over, nostalgically remembering the "prewar quality" they apparently expected would never, never again be duplicated!

"Prewar quality" is a catch phrase that evokes bygone times when everything was better: food and wine, clothing, furniture, kitchenware and other household objects, newspapers and magazines, weddings and all forms of partying.

On the other hand, Paris is buzzing with celebrities whose reputations were built during or after the war. People read Resistance poets and writers, such as Vercors, Camus, Sartre, Eluard, Aragon, Char, and many others. They turn their radios to the songs of Edith Piaf and Yves Montand, and they flock to the many re-opened stage theaters to see their favorite actors—Jean-Louis Barrault, Simone Signoret, Louis Jouvet.

Since I remember so little of prewar days, nothing qualifies me as a critic of quality-of-life except that in my private life as a small child, Madame Marie was perfectly there, perfectly mine; and my mother, my father, family, friends, were exactly right, exactly where they should be, and whatever they did was exactly as it should be. But otherwise, as to the world-at-large, "prewar quality" was difficult for me to imagine—until I broke our yellow pitcher. I knew it to be irreplaceable, indeed of pre-war quality.

DOMONT WAS a short train ride North of Paris. My parents loved to spend their free time there at the home of good friends, the Moulins, a childless couple who lived in a two-storey house with an attached garden. The sleepy little town had a small eleventh-century church, blatantly lacking in charm or symmetry; a covered market, lively as a bazaar, outside the train station every Tuesday; a monument to the war dead in front of the post office; and tying it all together on sets of narrow streets were congregations of modestly quaint houses, set behind flower gardens protected by wrought-iron gates and bells activated by pulling a string.

I particularly enjoyed going there alone, on school days off, when I would have Berthe and Edmond to myself. The friendship between Berthe Moulin and my mother dated back to their youth in Warsaw, and she had been the only person from our Paris world to have visited us in Vendée. My mother had then tried to talk her into hiding with us, but she had refused, feeling she should remain with her French husband. Soon after she had returned to Domont, however, her husband's Catholic family had denounced her to the Gestapo and she was sent to camp at Drancy, the same dreadful detention camp from which my

cousins' family was deported to Auschwitz. My mother loved
to retell the story of her friend's survival. A miracle: the train
taking her and a whole transport from Drancy to Auschwitz was
derailed by partisans and the inmates were thus liberated.

After her camp experience and her dramatic liberation,
Berthe returned to Domont, where her husband held a tenured
position as inspector for the government-owned gas company. A
civil servant, he had the free use of a house, part of which func-
tioned as the gas company's local customer-service office. A sign
to that effect was posted on the glassed porch, clearly visible
from the street. The house, the office, the garden, the dog —
everything was there, just as before. Berthe's husband, his family,
neighbors, friends, and acquaintances acted as though she had
been away for a while visiting relatives, so she resumed her previous life, exactly as it had been and as everyone expected her to
do. There was nothing in her appearance — her dignified beauty,
her simple elegance, graceful posture, courteous manner — nothing at all, not even a trace of a foreign accent, that could make
anyone doubt her origin as other than pure French. Thus, in our
world, she was the only one who truly succeeded in "getting
back to normal," to that prewar normalcy that so eluded us.

To me, prewar normalcy was first and foremost represented
by thoroughbred French Domont and by Berthe's house. It had
the nice smell of fragrant soaps and colognes. In clean and peaceful rooms, antique or Art Deco wooden furniture was set against
wallpapers of subtle shades of blue, pink, or beige, with a design
of either thin stripes or small flowers. Down the stairs, in the
dim and dank cellar, lined up on cellar shelves: sleeping bottles

of old wine, upright glass jars full of jams or preserves, ceramic bowls of dried fruit, mushrooms.

Prewar normalcy *was* Domont. There, just as before the war, I was treated as if I were the couple's child, or niece, or god-daughter—with tenderness, solicitous care, strict discipline, and dependable criticism. Edmond called me "glue pot" because I was always behind or near him. Berthe found me good-hearted but slow-moving and lacking in good manners. As for me, I loved, admired, and idealized both of them.

THE GARDEN is divided by narrow paths, on either side of which flourish distinct little colonies of well-mannered flowers or vegetables. Along the path, Edmond is walking slowly, his back solicitously half bent, surveying his territory. Behind him, an old shepherd dog named Diane, and behind her, me. The air is light and fresh. I mustn't chat. Edmond is concentrating on the garden, looking for vegetables and flowers precisely ready to be picked and taken into the house. If his hands get too full, he might hand me something to hold. With full or empty hands, I'll follow him into the house. He'll deposit his pickings in the kitchen and disappear into his office. I'll stay with Berthe, who will give me peas to shell or string beans to trim. Then we'll chat, she and I, mostly about Domont, clothes, jewelry, Diane and her blind cat-friend; we'll chat like ladies at tea.

I follow Berthe on errands up a slight hill to a cluster of shops. She lets me hold the fresh loaf of white bread she's just bought, but admonishes me not to nibble on the crust. It's bad manners, she says. Unlike my parents, real French people know about good manners, especially if they live in a house with a garden and if they dress well. Manners have apparently something to do with holding off on certain small pleasures.

In the delicatessen she reviews with the butcher, point by point, the comparative quality of the various types of displayed hams, holds a pensive pause, then decides on "Paris Ham."

We cross the street to a store that radiates the very essence of French femininity. In the shop window, skeins of variegated wool partly unravel over stuffed toy cats stiffened in playful poses; silky embroidery threads of every color hang over the edges of an end table on a brightly embroidered small cloth. Knitting needles of all sizes, fanciful pinchushions, sewing and knitting magazines evoke a dizzying array of activities fit for la femme au foyer, that woman who stays home and whose only duty is to make that home as beautiful as those pictured in glossy homemakers' journals. Berthe looks, frowns in concentration, then buys several skeins of lavender angora wool—for a sweater to match the winter suit she has just sewn, she explains. If there is any leftover wool, she promises to save it for me if I do well on my scarf project.

Berthe is now my ideal: self-assuredly perfumed and fashionably dressed, serenely polite, skilled at all the arts of homemaking, and very beautiful. I follow her every move in the house or at the market place. At night, before falling asleep between freshly ironed sheets on the large bed in the attic guestroom, I imagine myself as a thirty-year-old woman, soft-spoken, poised and capable, very French.

Just as Berthe was a model homemaker, her husband was well suited to his tenured civil service job. Aside from running an office in his home (with Berthe's help) and giving out information on services offered by the gas company, Edmond's major task was to perform a safety inspection whenever a resident of his service area had a new gas heater installed. Since he knew everybody, the inspection visit generally entailed a good deal of socializing, with his client opening a bottle of wine to accompany a bit of chat, or a game of chess or cards.

Sometimes, weeks passed when hardly anyone needed an inspection. That gave Edmond more time for his hobbies: playing classical music on his violin, gardening, motorcycling, or playing chess.

The motorcycling was a recent development. Besides tenure, with a modest but livable salary, the gas company provided free housing and transportation. Before the war, that meant a car, but after the war, it additionally meant a motorcycle.

Edmond couldn't persuade Berthe to ride with him on the motorcycle; she found it too noisy, much too fast a means of getting around the town and the surrounding countryside. "How could anyone enjoy the sights?" she complained. But I was very eager to get on the strange, noisy, speedy machine! And finally, Edmond let me.

Holding on tightly to Edmond's broad back, my hair violently blowing as we sped down country roads, creating wind and raising dust, I was so happy I only feared the moment we'd stop. I could close my eyes and feel something of the motor-

cycle's enormous power. I could share its triumph. It didn't matter where it was going, or how far, or if it were safe; all that
mattered was that it shouldn't stop.

On our return, Berthe was horrified at my happily agitated
state: "The child is overexcited," she complained, much as one
might say: "The child has a 105° fever!" Edmond affectionately
teased her to calm her down. Berthe gave him a forgiving smile
and, as she took me into the kitchen, shrugged her shoulders
and muttered something about men and their incurable love of
danger.

I knew what awaited me when I was "overexcited": a small
snack and a couple of hours of absolute quiet, preferably in
my room, so as to regain my equilibrium. Berthe was keen on
cleanliness and serenity. Sometimes, if whatever had caused my
overexcitement had not been fully my fault, I could succeed in
negotiating to spend my quiet time in another room—the dining room, the sewing room, the music room, or the office—with
the solemn promise not to say a word but just to read or knit.

This time I won the right to stay in the dining room while
Berthe worked in her sewing room. For an overexcited child to
return to normal, solitude was as essential as silence and a clean
and peaceful room.

As soon as I heard the Singer sewing machine hard at work,
I carefully opened the photograph album. No photographs of
either Berthe or Edmond as children, but lots of them as young
adults. Some brown-toned ones, very solemn: portraits of Berthe
with her girlfriends from Warsaw, including my mother, all with
bobbed hair; a small black-and-white photo of Berthe on a city
street talking to a man with a long black coat, hat, a long beard.

My mother had once explained that this was Berthe on her last visit to Warsaw in 1938, and that the man with the beard was her father, a respected rabbi. She never saw him again, my mother had added. He died in the ghetto. Those photos of her past were the only ones of their kind in the album. The others, the ones I loved to look at, were the ones of Berthe and Edmond in their early days together, mostly with their bicycles on deserted country roads. Such a handsome, capable, energetic couple — so sure of themselves, so in love! They had met at a bicycle club. How romantic to bicycle together on a day's outing till you ended it staring at the sunset together! But that was long ago, an old-fashioned romance. When I'd meet my future husband, I hoped he'd have a fast motorcycle, and that he'd take me riding with him wherever he went!

Once back to Paris from Domont, looking through a collection of Vogue patterns at a neighbor's, I fantasized all sorts of outlandish or extremely elegant clothes, that of course I'd wear with the right perfume, shoes, jewelry, and makeup. I would then be transformed from a frog into a princess, or at least into a "chic Parisienne," like the department-store mannequins.

In real life, though, I wore a pleated skirt in dull navy-blue gaberdine, and a white cotton blouse, plain but for a white lace collar, so I had to remain a frog.

I HARDLY EVER see my parents not working. Father stays in the shop till late in the evening. Mother stops work at seven, but by the time she gets home from shopping and other errands, cooks dinner and cleans up, the only dependable "conversation" we manage to have is her verbal checklist: did I do this, did I remember to do that, and so on, to which I answer yes, no, and oh, I forgot, I'll do it tomorrow. We conclude with a few of my mother's basic criticisms: that I'm slow, disorganized, forgetful, that my head's always in the clouds, that I'll have to come down to earth someday, and so on. And I present my basic set of excuses: I have so much homework, I was about to do my house chores when I suddenly remembered that I had a test coming, and so on.

After school and on weekends I spend most of my time not on homework but with friends. Our apartments are so small and there is nothing to do there, so we're always out, out in our neighborhood or a nearby one, window-shopping on the boulevards, eating French fries in white paper cones, stopping to look at a strong man breaking out of iron chains or at an acrobat standing on his hands on top of a stack of chairs at a café terrace. We chat about cosmetics, boys, movie actors, high-heeled shoes. We sing a popular song, practice the lyrics of the latest hit. Someone tells a joke; we laugh. Life is good!

Once, our little group passes a movie house. There's a film about concentration camps. "Oh, let's go in! Everybody says it's a must!" says one of the girls, whose mother but not her father came back from Auschwitz. I don't dare admit that I'd rather not see it. I hate the subject. But if she's going into the theater, how can I not go, since neither of my parents was in a camp?

We all go in. We chat. Finally, after the newsreel, the feature movie starts. A lugubrious musical background shows a group of living skeletons in striped camp pajamas standing behind barbed wire; their eyes are enormous. Some are smiling; some look stunned; some are teenagers. This is their "liberation photo." We then get flashbacks of their stories — roundup, deportation, cattle-car ride, arrival at camp, selection, roll call, hard labor, watching relatives or friends or comrades-in-Hell die of either "natural death" by exhaustion, sickness, starvation, or in the gas chamber. Nothing is spared us. The survivors even have names, as do all those doomed to die. We're trapped in a torture chamber with strict orders to keep on staring at the screen until the words "The End" appear and the music begins to wind down. We must not get distracted for a second. We must not cover our eyes or even close them. All the images have a passport to our innermost selves. Not one of them can be turned away. They must all enter us. As they do, I feel them pile up in my chest, in my stomach; they fill me with lead; I'm so heavy I think I'll never be able to stand up again, not even to leave the chamber of tortures.

We must have been "liberated": we're in the street again, shellshocked. We're standing on a sidewalk; people are passing in both directions; there is much talking, laughing, taxi traffic, horn-blowing, policeman's whistle. We've been ejected back to normal life, but that seems so strange, so alien, so shallow. I have the unsettling feeling that we don't belong in normal life; we belong in the other, the horrible life in the film, peopled with our people.

We have to move: we're in the way of others lining up to see the film. So we start walking, slowly, not knowing where, absolutely silent, each in our own set of thoughts, our individual daydreams.

Maybe the names of my relatives will after all never come

up on the survivors' lists we still check periodically. I call them to mind. From Paris: my aunt Miriam, my uncle Motl, my cousins Charles, Sarah, Serge, and little Henriette. (Their brother Maurice, the partisan, was spared the camps and had a war hero's burial.) From Warsaw, my mother's hometown: my grandfather, aunts, uncles, and cousins (though a second cousin, who had fought in the Ghetto uprising, had managed to escape through a tunnel). From Tomashov-Mazowiecki: my father's relatives.

What I just saw, is that what happened to them? And if so, why to them and not to me? Why am I here, safe and healthy? Why me and not Serge or Henriette? I didn't play the violin beautifully like Serge; I wasn't three years old like Henriette. Here I am, with both my parents alive yet! Neither one went to a camp. I'm not any kind of orphan, not full or even half, like the girl whose idea it was to see the film.

I don't know how long we were walking, in such eerie silence, when someone suggested walking to a fair. That broke the ice. Energy returned to us all at once and totally. We walked faster, full of purpose, taking every shortcut we knew.

At the fair, we rushed onto the caterpillar ride, crowded into one four-seat wagon, giggled in fear and hung on to one another as we were flung down near the ground and without pause thrown back up again in a continuous circle of joyful fear.

I'm getting old enough to learn Paris by heart, by foot. I can see with my own eyes that it is indeed everything they say in books — the City of Lights, a Lovers' Paradise, and the Capital of Fashion.

It's wonderful outside: covered markets, street entertainers, lovers everywhere, pushcart vendors, sidewalk chalk artists, prostitutes and thieves (just like before the war, says my mother). But lately, tourists are replacing soldiers. Signs of war have diminished, except for some monuments and plaques honoring war heroes or remembering local victims, or for celebrities being introduced as having fought in the Resistance, or in titles of books or films . . .

Horror's new name is Auschwitz, the laboratory of the "final solution to the Jewish Problem." And even in a party-mood Paris —filled with smiles, flowers, lovers, and baby carriages—the words "Auschwitz" and "final solution" still find their way into books, newspapers, magazines, films, photo exhibits, and conversations. At unexpected moments, like scorned vampires, they suddenly catch up with you, pierce your heart with fragments of survivors' memoirs—and run off, leaving you drained of blood.

You recover with a stutter: But why? How could it be? Who let it happen? Did my family die right away? Did they suffer long? Did any of them escape? How could it happen? Why didn't somebody stop it? Whose fault was it?

The reasoning in my parents' milieu was simple. There were two culprits. One was ignorance. If more Europeans had been politically enlightened, they would have united in effective protest, effective action; they would have prevented the worst.

The other culprit was Religion, on both sides of the Auschwitz box of horrors. On one side, Christianity, which created European anti-Semitism. Nazi ideology had then exploited that anti-Semitism to its fatal conclusion; the wartime Pope had failed to protest it. On the other side, the religious Jewish establishment had encouraged Jews to leave their fate up to God, who, it turned out, in my parents' view, couldn't care less about them. They would have been better off forging an alliance with secular Jews. Together, they could have fought back more effectively.

As I saw it, Christian anti-Semitism was a given. It came with being born Gentile, though some good Gentiles were inexplicably free of it. Something, however, puzzled me about my parents' strong dislike of religious Jews. To be a religious Jew in modern Europe was to my parents an archaic aberration; it meant one was unforgivably weak, ignorant, and passive. My parents' own, very religious relatives, though, were always portrayed as kind, loving, and upright, qualities that seemed utterly Christian to me.

I thought about my parents' reasoning and, (silently of course) of the Passion of Christ. I couldn't remember anyone on any of the Stations of the Cross in a posture of protest or political action against the impending Crucifixion. Here and there, someone offered to help Jesus carry the cross or to get up when he fell, and surely all his followers must have prayed. Nothing, however, resembled insurrection or armed resistance. Nobody stopped the Crucifixion.

My report cards have gotten worse, the teachers' negative comments more negative, and my parents more disappointed in me. They warn that if I carry on this way, I'm doomed to be kicked out of school. They're shocked, unable to understand how I can waste a scholarship in the best girls' high school in Paris. How they, who had no formal education, oh how they would value every minute of every lecture! And what would Madame Marie think of it? Have I told her how I am doing? (No, I haven't; in fact, I've been so ashamed that I hadn't even visited her in a long time.)

Feeling that all is lost anyway, I talk back to the teachers, fail to turn in homework, daydream and doodle during class, and, during after-school study sessions, I hide a "real book" behind a Latin textbook. Once school is out, I run off with my buddies to have a good time and, if need be, to break a few school rules.

The school year ends with the expected catastrophe: I'm not promoted to the next grade. I'm just "dumped." Judged to have insufficient quality of both intellect and moral fiber. Returned to my neighborhood as a faulty product, damaging to the good name of the school.

My parents are crushed. My father, when I do see him, hardly speaks to me. He hides behind the screen of an unfolded newspaper held wide open. He must be reading the same page for the third time. My mother, however, is humbled. Eager somehow to find a next-best school situation so that I can get a bit more education, she drags me to a two-year post-elementary school for working-class girls in our neighborhood. Here one can graduate with the lowest of secondary school degrees that can lead to an entry job in the lowest echelons of commerce and industry—although most often the girls simply take up the same trade as their mothers.

My mother explains to the principal that my education was disrupted by the war; she begs, she solemnly promises that I will totally reform and be a model student. I stare at the floor. There goes any chance of an academic future! On the other hand, I hope they'll let me in. If not, I'm twelve, so I can get a work permit, but I'm not eager to be cooped up all day in a garment sweatshop, a fate worse than being cooped up in a classroom.

My mother has won me entry into this school: we're both relieved. What a contrast, though, with that moment of glory just a year ago when I was allowed to start a climb to an academic Mt. Olympus! Too ashamed to look up, I stare at the pavement. My mother, as she used to do when I was smaller, pulls me by the hand: "Don't drag your feet! Walk faster!"

I've just had horrible news: my mother has had a miscarriage. My father says it's my fault: a pregnant woman needs her rest and I gave my mother so much trouble, so many headaches that she couldn't sleep, and now she's lost her baby. Actually, my mother didn't seem to take it so badly, I thought. She bottled the boy fetus in alcohol and showed it to me when I woke up one morning. It took me a while to comprehend what it was she was showing me. I thought it was the ugliest thing I'd ever seen, but I just couldn't tell her: she was so proud of having made a boy! On the other hand, my father was very upset to have lost a son.

It was my fault.

I took stock. I had had happy walks through Paris, good times with friends, peaceful moments in Domont, exhilarating rides on Edmond's motorcycle. But on balance, I had accumulated failing grades, nervous tics, and a variety of character deficiencies. Madame Marie found me too big. The new seamstress still couldn't locate my waistline. My hair didn't grow long enough for braids. No matter how much time I spent in front of the mirror, I still looked very plain, so plain in fact that in my Jewish youth group, my nickname was "potato"; my reputation: good-natured, verging on the simple-minded. Berthe thought I was sweet but awkward and prone to overexcitation. My mother found me too slow, too forgetful, given to too much daydreaming. Edmond called me a glue pot.

And my father, what did my father think of me? My father thought I had come out all wrong because he had not been around to raise me right. He had had high hopes for me, though, when I earned the high school scholarship; it proved I had the intelligence, the ability to get a fine education. And look what I did with such a golden opportunity! Causing grief, shame, disappointment. Worse than that, causing a miscarriage.

I didn't know what to do with myself. I was worthless, ugly. Uglier than that bottled fetus my mother passed off to me as a failed attempt at a baby brother. It was my fault. I could have had a brother, a full one, a complete one, if only I had done well at school and moved up to the next grade.

Gradually, the thought that I had killed my brother, that I was a murderer, that I would in due time be fully punished for it, that thought obsessed me, causing my nervous tics to increase in intensity and frequency. I panicked that I wouldn't be able to swallow, catch the next breath, keep my eyelid still. I was embarrassed to be in public, stayed home as much as possible. I could sense that, even though I was such a monster, my parents worried about me.

Then I developed a quantity of warts on my fingers. I was

sent to have them burned off at a hospital across town. I went by myself. When the doctor examined my fingers, he asked me if I were Jewish. Yes. That confirmed his diagnosis: this kind of wart was typical of Jews and Negroes. It was a relief to me: I thought I was the only one with such deformities!

With no other explanation than the racial origin of my problem, the doctor tied me in a high, huge leather chair. I panicked: surely this was an electric chair, this was the sentence agreed upon by my judges. The doctor was annoyed at my agitation, told me to calm down and not move my fingers. He would burn the warts one by one, and Oh Lord did I have many, sometimes three on one finger. If I didn't stop wiggling and making faces, his hand would accidentally slip and the fingers themselves would get burned. I tried, I tried to control myself, to look else-where—and found the window. The chair was high enough for me to see through the window—right into the cemetery! The pain was horrendous and I couldn't help screaming. But when the doctor was finished and had bandaged my fingers, I figured the ordeal might serve as partial penance for my sins, especially for the murder of my never-alive baby brother.

After I left the doctor's electrical chair, and went down the hall, I passed a ward of elderly patients. The door was open; they called me in. To my surprise, they sympathized, filled my pockets with chocolates. I was so moved that I stayed a while and chatted. Through their one window, I could see the same cemetery I saw from the office.

SUMMER HAS COME. Children should not be in Paris in the summer. I usually go to a summer camp. But this year, I'm a mess. Berthe has an idea: "The child is overly agitated. She needs to calm down. She shouldn't be in crowds of rowdy children. She should go to a very quiet place, a private home in the country where she'll get good food, fresh air, and a lot of rest. I know just the place. My neighbor across the street has a grandson who often visits her on school holidays; he and Odette like each other, they play for hours together. His parents are caretakers of an aristocrat's country home with which they share a beautiful garden and live in a small cottage on the premises. Just the mother, father, and the boy. Simple, good people. An ideally quiet place to board Odette for the summer."

My parents take their friend's advice and send me to spend the summer at my playmate's home.

This aristocrat's country home is quite nice. My friend's mother, Madame Grangier, goes in once a week, opens all the windows, sweeps, dusts and generally freshens up every room of the two-storey house. The owners, she tells me, come very seldom but may do so unexpectedly. My friend André and I are allowed in the house only during the weekly cleaning. We take advantage of it by playing baron and baroness, putting on airs. Madame Grangier laughs, says the owners aren't really like that; they're not stuck up.

The cottage is surrounded by shrubbery. When you go in, you feel you're entering a den. It's dim, the ceiling is low. As with rustic Vendée houses, there is only one door from the outside, and it goes right into the "main room" with its centerpiece of a wooden table and two benches. In one corner, a simple kitchen area. In another, on a little table, a statue of the Virgin Mary. At its feet, a small cot with a mattress has been set up for me. Here and there, some wooden chairs, including a rocker. On the wall, a crucifix and a decorative wooden clock. The door on the right side of the main room leads to the parents' bedroom, and on the left, to André's bedroom. There, kitty-corner: two small mattresses on the floor, one for him and the other for a male guest, or a small child. The rest of the room's contents reflect André's two obsessions: Tarzan and the Virgin Mary.

André knows everything about his two heroes and delights in answering my questions.

He has piles of Tarzan comic books, and he remembers the origin of each one he lends me: this one was for his last birthday, that one for a Christmas present two years ago, and those two his mother gave him when he had the chickenpox. I read them eagerly. Whenever I finish one batch, he provides me with another. I can't have enough of them.

As for the Virgin Mary, André has lovingly set her on an altar to the right of his door. It's covered with a white cloth embroidered by his grandmother in tiny blue flowers, forget-me-nots. At the center of the altar: a little replica of the Virgin Mary of Lourdes, where he went once with his father and grandfather. Also from Lourdes: a few tiny bottles filled with Holy Water, souvenirs brought back by various relatives. Around the little statue, André has placed many of his treasures. His first Communion rosary, a number of holy pictures depicting the Virgin at various stages of her life—as a girl, a young woman with an old husband, as a new mother with a naked baby, and finally as an old-looking woman without a husband (widowed?), fainting with grief at the sight of her son nailed to the cross. Similar to those pictures, also with gilded edges, are cards of text: prayers, litanies, all related to the Holy Virgin.

I WAS EQUALLY attracted to Tarzan and to the Virgin Mary.

The Virgin never left her indoor shrine. All the special rites and devotions took place right there in André's room, but Tarzan was best played outdoors where he leaped out of the remembered comic strips. Around mealtimes, we played Tarzan and Jane in the garden, but at other times we could wander away into the woods.

André was surprised at how well I did outdoors even though I came from the big city. I explained St. Fulgent to him, how the trees were not so delicate as here, but how it came naturally to climb up to the highest branch, look for birds' nests, fall to the ground without getting hurt.

My legs, my arms, my eyes remembered; my body felt strong, confident. When we found a soft grassed area in a clearing by a brook, we rolled on it like puppies till André suddenly challenged me to wrestle him. I didn't hesitate. I was strong enough. I could wrestle anyone, even a boy. We wrestled for a long time. I fought with all my strength—and to my immense pride, André claimed defeat. From then on, I was eager to get into a wrestling match with him and sometimes provoked him into one and, oddly, I always came out the winner. But André didn't look unhappy at all in his defeats! Maybe because he was such a good, disciplined Christian boy!

As for the Virgin: my soul remembered to be awed by her quiet compassion and dignity, my lips remembered long-forgotten prayers, even parts of a litany, and my hands searched for flowers to bring her.

Life was wonderful again! As long as we were on time for every meal, André and I were free to play all day—in his room, in the garden, or out in the woods. His parents left the cottage only to go on errands. Otherwise, we could see them through-out the day—both of them moving slowly. His father gardened or fixed tools; his mother kept house, cooked, chatted with us, her husband, her neighbors. On Thursdays, we all gathered at the big, always-vacant house, to help André's mother with the weekly cleaning.

The only problem came up on Sundays, when the family went to church and I was left home alone. They were devout Catholics and so spent most of their Sunday in the church. Memories of my Catholic years in Vendée came back to me, pos-sessed me, reclaimed me. I could visualize being there with my host family, starting the Sunday at the early, abbreviated Mass, staying for the gloriously complete ten o'clock Mass, then taking a few hours break for a picnic lunch with friends and relatives and returning to church for Vespers in the early afternoon. Then back home—cleansed, pure, at home with family, community, the Body of the Church, the Body of Christ, and with one's own heart and soul, facing the coming week with renewed calm, energy, faith.

André didn't like to leave me behind. "I'll be with you in spirit," I assured him. But as the family left, I would go through the loneliest day of the week, the only one which forced me to remember that I came from Paris, from a passionately Jewish but antireligious home, and that at the end of the summer I would return to that home in Paris.

My whole being revolted at the thought. Here I felt good: no one criticized me for anything. It was as if no one here knew that I had failed my first year of high school, murdered my unborn baby brother, wasn't even a half-orphan, had an undefined waistline, was plain looking and plainspoken, moved too slowly, was forgetful, disorganized, messy, undisciplined — and deeply disappointing to my family and my teachers. All that in spite of having been so lucky: protected, sheltered, fed during the war; not once taken away by the Germans or the French police; spared the camps, the ghettos, brutal death; even spared orphanhood. Then, after the war, given special privileges — a private tutor to help me catch up in my education, a scholarship at an excellent school. But there I went, bringing ruin upon myself, shame and dishonor to my family!

I didn't know what to do: I was beyond repair. Surely, a tragic mistake had been made — by God or the German authorities or the Vichy government (whoever was really in charge). Instead of me, any of my cousins should have been spared. Not one of them would have made such a mess of their lives and so disappointed their parents!

Sundays were so lonely and depressing I couldn't face going through another one, so I asked Madame Grangier to take me with them to church the following Sunday. I expected her to quickly say yes, but instead she told me she'd have to talk it over with her brother, a local priest who had already expressed a special interest in the well-being of my soul.

He was a kind soft-spoken man who loved his sister's cooking. She made special dishes when he ate with us. In the privacy of his room, André had explained in a whisper that his uncle had only half of his stomach left.

When the priest shared our meal, he always managed to turn the conversation to religious subjects. After he finished saying anything, he allowed a long pause, long enough for me to overcome my shyness and question him on Christian beliefs, Christian rites. To my relief, he never treated me as if I were stupid or simpleminded. He answered kindly, clearly. Then he would stop again for an inviting silence. So I would ask another question, and another.

Before going back to the presbytery, he would leave me little gifts: a rosary, holy pictures, catechism and Sunday School leaflets on various subjects—the life of Jesus Christ, the list of sacraments, of sins and of virtues. I cherished every one of those gifts; they helped me reclaim what I had known in Vendée but had since forgotten.

Now that I was older, though, I could understand much more than in my days in Vendée! For instance, that it was all right, especially for a girl, to be shy and plain-looking, withdrawn and dreamy. It was my soul, my inner life that mattered, not my waistline, nor my academic future.

What a miracle it was that so many of my secular Parisian sins tended to turn into Catholic virtues! As for the remaining sins, they could be redeemed by prayers and good deeds. In my memory, the worst sins were greed or lust, but the priest said that wasn't so: the very worst of sins, the deadliest, was lack of faith, or despair. Of that I was indeed guilty, especially on those lonely Sundays in the cottage.

That Wednesday, when the priest came to visit, Madame Grangier sent André and me out to buy a loaf of bread at a bakery on the other side of town. Later, we all sat down to lunch for a delicious lamb stew, and the conversation as usual, wandered from chitchat to religious matters. "Father," I asked, "what can I do about a temptation to despair? It comes upon me every Sunday when I'm left alone here." This time, the priest took the initiative: "My sister hasn't let you go to church because your parents are nonbelievers. But if it's so difficult for you to resist temptation when you're alone in the house while the others are in church, then you'd better go with them." I almost choked on my food from excitement.

AND AT LAST it's Sunday. The long-awaited Sunday when I have a priest's blessings to reenter a church.

Cheered by the joyful church bells, I'm leisurely walking to church with my host family, admiring the fields, the houses, every flower along the way. As we get closer, we run into more little groups of churchgoers merging from the main road and from narrow streets.

Now we go up the steps, then through the giant wooden

doors. Like a sleepwalker, I turn to my left, reach for the Holy Water basin, dip my fingers in, make the sign of the cross, follow André down the center aisle to the family pews, sit down next to him. He puts a missal on my lap. The organ music starts. While people are finding their seats, I look around. Though it isn't St. Fulgent, everything is in the same basic order. On either side of the main altar, so generously surrounded by space, the more intimate, sheltered spaces go to St. Joseph and to the Virgin Mary. The baptismal font is behind me, near the front entrance, and before me, to the right, stands the door of the vestry, through which the priest appears in glorious robes of various colors—white, purple, yellow—depending on the time of the liturgical calendar. Along the walls, a series of paintings marks the Stations of the Cross, irrevocable, oppressive. In dim alcoves, below stained glass windows, I see the statues of gentle saints; and near the side-door entrance, a pair of confessional booths, those tall and narrow dark-wood cabins where crimes of the soul enter and exit.

Such an ingenious, multipurpose design—God's mansion can accommodate everyone! The sanctuary for large crowds facing the High Altar; the baptistery for a family circle; the recessed chapels to Mary, Joseph, St. Theresa, and others for individuals or little groups at personal prayers; and the privacy of confessionals for mild to heavy sinners. The church has everything anyone could want, including the grand show of solemn Mass!

The service continues along its meticulously ordered path. The costumed priest and his assistants stand apart on a carefully prepared stage with elegant flower arrangements and tall candles.

Their backs turned to us, slow and reverent, they stand or kneel by the High Altar with its cover of spacious white linen cloth. The focus of everyone's attention, they bemoan human frailty and chant the praises of God. In chanted responses and songs: the choir boys, the organ player, the chorus of nuns, and nearly everyone in the pews accompany the priest. Leafing through the missal, I stumble along on half-whispered half-remembered fragments of phrases. I look up very often to see if it's time to change position, stand, or kneel.

LIKE AN EXILE on his first visit back to his childhood home, I'm attacked by memories, the past invading, obliterating the present. How could I have survived so long away from the church? It had been my haven, my refuge in Vendée, my art gallery, theater, and concert hall, my meditation chamber, my "Father's Mansion"—such a large high-ceilinged, splendid place! In the Vendéen church of my memory, the front door was always open. God was always home; so were all the saints: Joseph and Mary, Little St. Theresa of the Christ Child, St. Francis and his birds. But the true host was Jesus. There were pictures of him everywhere—from the time he was a swaddled baby cradled in his mother's arms to the moment of his resurrection when he walked out of his sepulcher. The well-decorated home is conscientiously maintained. Madame Marie would approve: the heart of the Parish is well swept, dusted, polished; there are candles and flowers and it smells good of incense. God is holding open house, accepting praises and gifts from his guests. Alleluia, I am one of His guests!

On the way to address the assembled worshippers in the

name of God, the priest ascends his pulpit. We sit up and look up. He is quoting from the Prophet Isaiah. I'm straining to understand. I think it means that God does everything. When He's angry with people, He gets violent, crushes the earth and scatters its inhabitants. He makes life so difficult that most people die, but He leaves a few to wallow hopelessly in an oppressive, mournful, lonely silence. Then, for some inexplicable reason, those few survivors start to sing His praises, lift their voices in joy. Very loudly, they proclaim the majesty and glory of the Heavenly Lord! And, as they do—Terror strikes again, and there are pits and snares to swallow up or trap any fleeing people. The Heavens open up, the earth trembles, shakes, "staggers like a drunken man." God punishes the sinners. Everyone left sings His praises. He throws a great banquet at which He does away with Death, wipes tears from the weary survivors, and forgives them their transgression. Mercifully, just as I'm getting dizzy trying to follow the mercurial Deity, the priest stops quoting the heady poetry of the ancient prophet—beauty to get drunk on, or lose your mind over, abandoning all hope or all despair— and he now breaks into the more ordinary speech of a mortal clergyman. He exhorts us to get back to the true Christian path, the path of righteousness. The most dependable, the most experienced, the best helper along that path is the Church. There, we will be cleansed, nourished, and strengthened by Mass and confession. We must bear in mind, as the Prophet Isaiah pointed out, that it is in God's power to punish and reward, as will be most evident on that awesome Judgment Day which will herald the Reign of the Lord in Jerusalem. On that day, the evil ones will suffer unspeakable punishments, while the dead victims of the evil ones shall rise, put on their body of worldly flesh like clothes taken off for the long sleep, wake up, regain their voice and sing for joy. . . . And the trumpets will blow. . . .

SUDDENLY (was it the sound of those trumpets blowing in my mind?) I am hit by a ghastly vision—a concentration camp where dead inmates, just reawakened in their mass graves, are putting on their cadaverous bodies of rotten flesh, pushing and shoving one another to emerge from the broken ground, in a deafening tumult of moans and groans, terrified shrieks, moribund whispers. But just as details of that pandemonium seem to be on the verge of becoming clearer, the entire campsite is overwhelmed by a noxious smoke that hovers over the crowds of resurrecting corpses. Like clouds taking on the shape of famous saints, the floating smoke keeps slipping in and out of silhouettes of anonymous Jews, losing the outline, trying again and moving on—If only I can keep focusing on a shape, it will pause long enough for me to recognize someone. I must do it. I am condemned to stare until the shape reveals itself to me, even if, in the end, the smoke will roll over me and reduce me to a cloud floating with the rest over the camp, the surrounding countryside, the entire . . . there! there! my little cousin Henriette with her curly hair, seated, holding her doll, waiting for something, someone . . . "Henriette! Henriette! it's me, Odette, I'll take you home!" . . . but she doesn't hear: she's still as a photograph on a fading screen of moving smoke.

I wake up in full daylight on my cot. Bent over me, looking

greatly relieved—André, his parents, and his uncle the priest. "What happened?" I ask. "You fainted. You fainted in church during the sermon," answers Madame Grangier, in the kindest voice.

FROM THEN ON, I was treated with exquisite solicitude. Much was made of my having fainted in church. Like dreams and visions, it was a sign God visited upon girls my age to point them toward a religious vocation. Tenderly phrased questions tested my interest in becoming a nun. I was flattered at the importance given my responses, really quite monotonous in content as I said over and over yes indeed! oh yes and how! I redoubled my devotions to the Virgin. Monsieur Grangier let me pick flowers from his garden whenever I wanted to bring a bouquet to the statue of Little St. Theresa of the Christ Child in the tiny chapel on the edge of the estate. I was given a book about her with passages of her autobiography. She had become a nun at fifteen. She made it sound simple and natural, something anyone could do. I stared most attentively at all the nuns I passed, in pairs, in groups, and I visualized myself walking in a graceful, flowing white novice habit and soft white coif, chatting pleasantly, treated courteously, on my way back home to the dependably quiet, orderly life of the convent.

No one would yell at me. No one would pull my hand, complaining I was too slow. It wouldn't matter that I had survived the war when my cousins didn't. It wouldn't matter that I wasn't even a half-orphan. As to the location of my waistline, that would become totally irrelevant. And best of all, my future would be all worked out for me, step by step, from the novitiate to the retirement home for nuns. All I had to do was to follow instructions, rules and regulations, all given with loving gentleness. Nothing was simpler, nothing more satisfying.

By the end of summer vacation, André had resigned himself to seeing me abandon the Tarzan comic books for the *Lives of the Saints* and other religious books provided by his uncle, who now came almost every day to oversee my reeducation as a Catholic.

I didn't want to return to Paris, that modern Babylon, nor to my pagan parents, my new pagan school. The priest said I had to, but he assured me it wouldn't be for long. He had a plan. The mother superior of a convent had agreed to take me in as a boarder in the convent school, where my vocation would be carefully monitored. As to my parents' opposition to such a plan, it wouldn't come into play, as they simply would not know my whereabouts. All I had to do was to keep up a correspondence with him. His letters would instruct me as to precisely when and how I was discreetly to leave my parents' home to meet with him, so he could secretly escort me to the convent.

IN THE MEANTIME, it couldn't be helped: I had to get back to Paris. I did so, smuggling presents from my host family. André had given me one of his tiny bottles of Holy Water from Lourdes, and his parents had bought me a wooden rosary. Back home, I hid the gifts under my pillow and otherwise quickly resumed my former life. Secretly, though, I recited the rosary when no one was home, sometimes took the subway to faraway neighborhoods where no one knew me, so I could however briefly and gingerly enter a church, and at all times I dreamed of my future in the convent. Whenever I received a letter from André's uncle, I read it several times to make sure I didn't miss a single instruction. To my disappointment, each letter still advised patience: plans had to be made carefully so nothing would go wrong. Aside from patience, prayers and good deeds were highly recommended to help advance my cause. And in my prayers, I should not forget to pray for the souls of my parents, those nonbelievers who, as such, played into the hands of Satan.

I hid the letters under my pillow, along with the bottle of Holy Water and the wooden rosary.

ONE WEEKDAY EVENING, much to my surprise, both my parents came home early. I wondered what the occasion was. "We want to talk to you," my mother said sternly, setting up three chairs in the dining area. Two were side by side, and the third chair stood at a polite distance across from them. My father had gone into the bedroom and, as he came back, I could see him slip something into his pants pocket. He sat down on one of the two chairs, the one closer to the table, with my mother next to him closer to the kitchen, and he motioned to me to sit down on the third chair. Formalities between us in our own home? It did not bode well! I sat silently, waiting anxiously for the next move from my parents.

As usual my mother was the one to break the silence. She was furious: "How can you? After all we did for you! For this, we got through the war?" I didn't understand. She made herself clearer, though she nearly choked on the words: "How can you? How can you have a correspondence with that priest? He says we're under the spell of Satan! How can you go along with such slander? About your own mother, your own father? How can you? How?"

If she had thrown a bucket of ice water at my face, it would have had the same effect: I would have awakened with sudden realizations. She had discovered my "Catholic" hiding place; she was reading my letters; I had no privacy. Why did she pick on that one phrase about Satan? Why didn't she see how important it was for me to become a nun? Why?

My father then took my rosary out of his pocket, held it up contemptuously, and asked me if I realized the true symbolism of that object. I was going to answer, but he told me to be quiet, he was doing the talking. And he did, going into an elaborate analysis of how the Catholic Church's treatment of Jews had led to vicious anti-Semitism, which had led to genocide at Auschwitz and elsewhere. And how could I, a Jewish daughter, so betray my own people? How could I? Everyone had put themselves out to save me, and I had survived, and I even had both my parents alive. They were working hard for me.

I wanted to try to defend myself, to explain how orderly and peaceful life would be in a nunnery, how it wouldn't cost them anything, how I would never be a burden to them, how I would pray for them and for every single Jew, dead or alive. But I was too slow. My parents were taking turns speaking angrily, accusingly, asking questions of me but not waiting for an answer. Their duo performance picked up speed; they interrupted each other; they spoke faster, louder. I turned my head to one, then the other. I was getting dizzy. They were going too fast. I was rapidly falling behind in my understanding till finally I lost it.

Their words had a sound to them, but it was as if I had become deaf to what was inside, or behind, or around those words. I just turned my head from one parent to the other and back again as if I were shaking my head no, no, no.

When the meaning of the words no longer reached me, I turned and turned to the source of the sound, looking at the face that went with it, first one, then the other. And I was increasingly overcome with immense affection for those familiar faces, those proud, passionate Jewish faces of my mother, my father, both so dear to me! It was so wonderful to sit across from them, to have them together, like this, all to myself! It was even better than the occasional meal eaten together: here we were not distracted by food. There wasn't even a table between us. Just empty space. Formal space. Oh but it hurt, that space between us! I wished their chairs would slide forward of their own volition so my parents could be within touching distance. They were still making a lot of gestures, but as time went on, they spoke more softly. Maybe it was fatigue, or maybe they had said everything they wanted to say — very quickly at first, then slower, as one eats too fast when one is too hungry. As they softened, so did my love for them, my mother, my father. I could cover them with a feather quilt of love. At the same time, my longing for their love grew more urgent: I wished they would get up, right then, each in turn, breach that formal space between us to stand by my chair, then bend down to kiss me on both cheeks with an endearing word in between. I couldn't bear that space between us.

SOMETHING VERY STRANGE has just happened: there is a silence. Why? Where am I? What am I supposed to be doing? I must have stared at my parents in bewilderment because my mother was asking me very kindly: "Do you understand now?" I said yes because her voice was so kind, though I wasn't sure what I was supposed to understand: I had missed so much of the explanation.

My father then asked me if I would answer any more letters from the Grangier family, and I could see him hold his breath with solemn anxiety. I said no, because I didn't want him to be anxious.

By then the space between us was no longer so forbidding. Soon, I had one of those brief moments of absolute happiness, that taste of eternal bliss: I was with both my mother and my father; I had their complete attention. They must have forgiven me all my transgressions. They were desperate for me not to leave them for the nunnery but to stay with them. My little family!

Again, my father was dangling my rosary. Now I stared at it as at an enemy. I was furious with myself. I had let it happen: I was taken in. I had lost my bearings. I had betrayed my secular upbringing. Worst of all, I had almost let them take me away from my parents and hide me in a convent without their knowledge! What would my parents have done when they discovered my absence? I hadn't thought of it before. Surely they would have called the police. Surely they would have been hysterical with grief and they would have cried: "For that we survived the war?" Didn't the priest think of all this? What kind of religion did he represent? Separating children from their parents! He was evil. I was seized by a hard hatred of that priest—Satan in disguise. Nobody, not that man, not anyone, ever would separate me from my mother, my father. No one.

My father got up, still holding my rosary. "All right," he said. "That's settled." And he motioned for me to follow him. I did just that. He led me to the tiny toiletroom, opened the door, gave me the rosary and ordered me to throw it in the toilet. I did. Then, on cue from him, I pulled the cord to flush it down.

My class photograph, 1948, at the "Terminal School" in Paris,

a nonacademic school for working-class girls.

I am seated in the front row, extreme left.

Place de la Rèpublique, Paris. Rallies, demonstrations, and marches
start here. It was also a meeting place for my friends and me.

Edmond and Berthe Moulin

Berthe Moulin holding my baby sister, Anne-Marie,

born April 24, 1949.

My mother and father on holiday in the
French countryside after the war.

My parents and I with my aunt Georgette, uncle Henri,
and cousin Sarah in Paris, 1949, shortly before
we took the boat to the United States.

In southern California, a new immigrant at age fifteen, with a new
American name: Odette Melszpajz has become Odette Miller.

FOURTEEN

1948: I'M THIRTEEN, Paris is cheerful again and I have a best friend!

In a partying mood, the city tries on its new fashion collection, dresses up all its shop windows, opens up new cafés, small theaters, night clubs. Musicians, acrobats, strong men, fortune tellers, ice-cream vendors, newspaper sellers—everyone's out in the street. And so am I. . . . at least as often as I can be.

Too much of the time, though, and much against my will, I have to be indoors. Cooped up in the drab convent long ago taken over by my new high school, I take comfort in how easy it is to make friends with classmates whose parents, like mine, are workers.

Esther, for instance, always wants to know what book I'm reading. Whichever it is, it's guaranteed to be unrelated to school assignments. She is fascinated. One day, to her great delight, I invite her home to look at my family's books. I eagerly lend her some which she eagerly returns for more a few days later. Since she has so many chores, we discuss the books while she's doing her round of food shopping, walking our neighborhood, standing in line at shops, crowding around pushcarts, crossing streets, passing flea markets, newspaper sellers — talking, talking passionately.

We seem mostly to be of the same mind. This is odd, since our temperaments and our settings are so different. As I am slow and dreamy; Esther is fast and efficient. My home has books. Hers has a stack of records, popular and folk music, which she plays on her phonograph, singing along. She also has a small violin which has survived the war and which, of course, fascinates me.

We become the best of friends, bosom friends pledged to eternal-friendship-all-secrets-shared.

ESTHER IS TWO YEARS older than I am. She lives with her mother, a little sister, and two brothers in a dreary-looking crowded tenement in the upper part of rue du Faubourg du Temple, not far from the Belleville Métro station. To reach the entrance of her building, you need to push your way through the sidewalk crowds of housewives shopping at pushcarts. Once you're in, you quickly pass the cranky concierge's loge on your left, then you take the staircase between the two courtyards, go up just one grimy flight of stairs, and knock at the first door.

If she's not home, you try the leather gloves shop where she works in nearby Passage Jules Verne. She's there every Thursday and sometimes, if there is a rush order, even for a few hours at the end of a school day.

When I have something urgent to tell her and she's at work, I wait outside the shop till she comes out, and then I follow her on her errands. She works hard, to supplement her brothers' meager take at the lower level of the black-market trade in American cigarettes. The family struggles for sheer sustenance. So, no matter how involved in conversation we may get, Esther stays on the lookout for any bargains loudly vaunted by pushcart merchants or street hawkers.

Before the war, Esther's life was easier, of course, and her family was different—and larger. There were five children in all. The three who would be spared the camps, plus an older sister and an older brother who would die in Auschwitz, as would her father.

After the war, her mother had come back from Auschwitz without her husband and without her two eldest children. For a while she was half-crazed, trying to resume her life with the remnants of her family. The three surviving children, two boys and a girl, had each been placed with a separate foster family during the war, each raised in different religions. During that confusing first postwar year of trying to get her children back to an orderly Jewish life in a kosher home, she got pregnant and gave birth to a baby girl of uncertain origin who became the joy of her life and whose care she shared with Esther.

All this went on under the gaze of the whole family, the ghost family of prewar configuration, staring at a photographer who had also disappeared into ghosthood. Displayed in solemn photographs on the buffet of the main room, there they were, the full group—two parents and five children squeezed into faded, ornate frames. It reminded me of the altars in the sepulchral chapels of the Père Lachaise Cemetery.

Not in any photograph, but with the livelier gaze of a some-what of a sometimes housemate, was the mother's man-friend, mostly unemployed but always on the verge of a "promising" small business that required hardly any capital investment. At the time, he had crowded a tiny room with dilapidated barbershop chairs which he had talked someone into giving him, first with the thought of patching and selling them, then with the idea of setting up a little business by undercutting the local barber.

The three small rooms plus a Pullman kitchen had to ac-commodate up to six people, including one baby, plus an at-tempt at a barbershop. And whatever the season or time of day and night, everyone had to go up to the Turkish toilet located on the next floor's landing.

MY FRIEND AND I spend very little time in each other's apartments, as we much prefer being outdoors. The problem is that Esther doesn't have as much free time as I do, since she works at the shop on Thursdays and sometimes after school, and she also helps run her large household because she's the only girl except for the baby. My only obligation is to run errands for my parents on Thursdays. Also, as an only child, I have no one else to look after.

But at last, luck is on our side and we gain one day a week to spend together as we wish!

At the start of a new term, we find out that our regular teacher will absent herself every Monday and will leave us in the care of a home economics teacher. That day's whole program, she explains, will be of a practical nature, the better to prepare us for our future daily lives. We will learn housekeeping skills such as sewing, mending, taking out stains, shopping for bargains, cooking, and making preserves.

We've assessed our situation and are taking a chance. We simply won't show up at school on Mondays. We'll surely be taxed for our fits of stolen freedom at the end of the school year, when grades will be reported to headquarters, but that is far into the future. In the meantime, Mondays will be entirely our own, every single week.

M O N D A Y I S indeed the most beautiful day of the week!

We meet at a subway station and go off exploring our vast and wonderful city. What a feast! We set goals for ourselves: we are to discover all the private gardens in Montmartre, walk by the shop windows of the Galleries Lafayette, locate used-book stores new to us, watch the barges go down the Canal St. Martin, climb all the steps up to and inside the Church of the Sacré Coeur and end up with a good look at the spread of Paris below; or catch a Monday morning open-air market at closing time when the merchants are packing up and might sell us some of their overripe, unsold fruit for very little, or, if they are gracious, simply give it to us.

Monday—our sweet secret!—a day of leisurely exploration in the togetherness of our friendship, as Paris good-naturedly unrolls it street spectacles while we pass through its neighborhoods. We've prepared for it all week, collecting whatever small change has come our way, now using it for bargain books and ice-cream cones.

The other days, except on Thursday, I stay anchored in my immediate neighborhood, going from home to school and back, stopping in local shops along the way for whatever is needed in the house.

Esther admires my home. There are no tenements on my block, only very modest but well-maintained and clean apartment houses. The pleasant rectangular plaza has trees and benches, a water fountain, and a pissoir with urinals for men and boys.

The apartment itself has its own private toilet, with a water tank and flushing chain and, above that, a storage shelf full to the ceiling with stored goods.

But my friend is also in awe of the paintings on the walls, the books on the shelves of the bedroom cupboard, the double set of curtains on the window which you can push open for a good view of the square. Every time she admires it, my apartment becomes more luxurious.

My favorite room is still the bedroom, made even more pleasant to me since an important change that took place when I was twelve.

Up to that year, I had still slept in my original crib, with its footboard sawn off to let my feet rest on a pillowed chair put up each night, blocking the door. When an adult cousin from Argentina had a three-months' visa to stay in Paris, we literally didn't have floor space for her to sleep, but our friend Mrs. Burstzyn, Léon's mother, offered space for a mattress on the floor of her apartment. My parents were to provide the mattress. But what would we do with it after she left? The plan was to replace my crib with a folding bed. When my cousin would leave,

I would inherit the mattress and place it on my bed. I was so excited at the thought that I talked my parents into buying both at once and letting me begin to use the folding bed, even with my old crib mattress and foot pillow. Folded, it was covered by a dark, thick bedspread. I was very proud of it.

I enjoyed giving my cousin informal tours of Paris, found her cheerful and pleasant, but I couldn't help counting the time she had left till her visa expired. As it happened, she loved Paris so much that I ended up accompanying her to consulates and embassies to help her get an extension of her visa. We were successful; she stayed six months. Finally, though, she left for Marseilles, where she caught a boat to Haifa. From there, she settled on a kibbutz.

My father was going to come from work early—meaning in the early part of the evening—to carry the mattress home, but I was too excited and couldn't wait that many hours. So, immediately after school Esther helped me, and the two of us carried the mattress out of our friend's apartment, down the dark spiral stairs, through the cobblestone courtyard to the sidewalk, crossing two streets and the lobby of my apartment house, then going up one flight of stairs, and through our dark dining room and the tiny hall. At last we were in the family bedroom.

I opened my folding bed, threw the crib mattress and the pillow wherever, into the other room, and replaced them with the new mattress. Then Esther and I joyfully took turns throwing ourselves down the whole length of it, stretching limbs in every direction, and generally bouncing on it till it felt alive.

A T   T W E L V E , I got a grown-up bed, and at thirteen, my grown-up soul.

Maybe it was because our street was then still known by its two names, the old one and the new one. Its old name, rue d'Angoulême, was that of a provincial Catholic town and its aristocratic family. The convent, of course, fitted that name perfectly. But the street's new name, rue Jean-Pierre Timbaud, honored one of the three major figures of the French Communist Resistance. His funeral procession through the neighborhood had naturally originated from the headquarters of the steelworkers' union (the CGT) on my side of the square, facing the convent.

In the inner square of my moral life, the convent and the CGT played tug-of-war for my soul's allegiance.

These are intense days of stocktaking, recorded on a set of double sheets of paper detached from a school notebook. The left page is headed "I believe in God"; the right page, "I believe in Man." Each entry has its corollary on the facing page, such as "God created Man" with "Man created God". I carry the double-column list in my pocket, taking it out and studying it several times a day. The project is awesome, demands a quality of attention I have never before accorded to the world of ideas. My soul, the course of my life, my very destiny depend on it. I'm about to come into my own, take sides as a Catholic or an atheist. At thirteen, this is my rite of passage into adulthood.

After exhausting days of playing both sides of this spiritual tug-of-war, I declare Man to be the winner and God, his folkloric creation.

At last, my long-festering conflict is resolved. Now I fit into my life as simply and comfortably as in a well-made dress with the waistline exactly at the waist, and I can move on, without disrespect to Madame Marie, to follow my father's path.

MY FATHER'S PATH points to a world that takes me into account equally with others.

From my father's reasonings, I draw my own conclusions. If the world, as he suggests, rightfully belongs to the working class which created it, though it is still waiting for its title deed, it follows that I no longer have to aspire to be as meek as those nuns across the street who were promised the Kingdom of God after they died. Instead, as a daughter of the working class, I have an imminent birthright. I can inherit, in the here-and-now, a human world organically evolving (if reactionaries don't block the way) toward peace, harmony, equality, and justice.

Not only did my father give me a key to a better world to come (a more useful gift than the looted German notebook!), but we had the good luck to be located practically next door to an institution devoted precisely to the bringing about of such a fair and tolerant world. Our apartment house neighbored the Café de la Baleine, where my father met his buddies for passionate political discussions. Next to that was the headquarters of the Steelworkers' Union which also housed the Workers' University. I took courage from the sight of those strong, burly union men coming in and out of meeting rooms or evening classes in labor studies. Sometimes, I recognized them from the Café de la Baleine.

It felt good to now be at peace not only with my father's world but also with him. The trick had been to get the nuns to stay on their side of the street, to stay within their starched coifs and their convent or, when they did venture out, never to dare cross my stare, my thoughts, my memories, my dreams.

And my father's path now merged with all my other paths.

Even where, as in Esther's case, the family practiced Judaism, social consciousness was a given.

One day, from my window, I watch as at last the long-distance buses are unloading on our square the children of striking miners. They will get room and board in workers' apartments for the duration of the strike. The CGT is coordinating this act of solidarity. I feel deprived as we won't be able to take in any child because there is no adult to assume daytime guardianship; my parents instead have contributed to a fund to pay for their stay. But in Esther's family there is generally someone home, so they will take in one boy. I wonder which one it will be. Although he'll sleep at Esther's, we'll share him in the daytime, of course.

MICHEL, OUR MINER BOY, it turns out, is well meaning but he gets into all kinds of trouble because of money he doesn't have. He looks at our local dime store as if everything on display is his for the taking. Without the slightest attempt at dissimulation, he takes whatever strikes his fancy. We try to explain that he shouldn't do that. Everyone is supposed to pay, we tell him; he could get caught. That only makes him indignant. He protests that it's not fair to tease people and have all those goods just lying there, making you want them, if in truth it's only for those who have money. It isn't fair! he complains. We worry about him, though we suspect the salespeople are pretending not to notice his peculiar way of shopping, and we try to plan more of his activities.

In spite of other problems with our eleven-year-old Michel —such as his finding daily toothbrushing too prissy a habit, and eating vegetables and salad basically effeminate—we really like him. Chronically curious and easily overexcited, he still doesn't mind answering all our questions about his life in the mining town. Miners, for us, are as exotic as sailors: they also leave their women and children and go off every day to face danger from fickle Nature (though sailors sing in chorus in wide-open seascapes while miners just hammer laconically in dark, subterranean caves).

Michel is proud to belong to a family of generations of miners and relishes our admiration. But when we talk politics with him and try to get him to go with us to a solidarity rally for the miners' strike, he laughs: oh no, that's not for him; people walk too slowly on a march and all for what? to get a platform of speakers who deliver boring speeches! No, thank you! Besides, this is his first time away from home, and there's so much to see in Paris, and the strike could be over any day, then he'd have to go home.

All right, we understand, so we go to the rally without him.

Their children safe and well fed, the strikers carry their strike for a record-breaking fifty days. At that point, the government, afraid any further neglect of the mines it owns will jeopardize life and property, has to give in to the miners' demands for better wages and improved safety. This is a victory for miners and an object lesson in workers' solidarity. Trainloads of foodstuffs from all over Europe had reached the Northeast mining country. Now, the miners' children, including ours, get back into the buses in better clothes, well-nourished and full of stories to tell their parents about how well off and generous Parisian workers are!

Current events, such as the miners' strike, are a field of study that Esther and I take seriously. We conscientiously clip news articles and arrange them by subjects in our scrapbook. Sometimes events are close to home.

I wonder, for instance, why I haven't seen one of Esther's brothers for quite a while. Last I saw him, he was obsessed with boxing—he let me try on his boxing gloves. My friend won't tell me what has happened, but I can tell she's nervous. "He's gone away," she says. I don't like the term; I can't stand the vagueness; would she at least tell me where he's gone? She tells me: to Marseilles. "But why?" She can't say: she's sworn to secrecy. I'll have to figure it out for myself.

In time, I hear of other young Jewish men who have made their way to Marseilles, and I remember how my girl cousin from Argentina ended her visit in France by taking a boat from Marseilles to Palestine. Now I can put all that information together and guess Esther's brother's destination. Jews with boxing gloves and guns are fighting for a Jewish state. Will there really be an official Jewish army, a Jewish flag, Jewish post offices, a Jewish agriculture department, a national Jewish orchestra? Or before any such miracles can happen, will the British and the Arabs kill all the Jews in Palestine, including Esther's brother? These are anxious times.

But the first miracle happens and it's Independence Day—Jewish Independence Day! Jews have a state and its name is Israel! The pride, the wonder of it: we will never be the same! In no time, our scrapbook testifies to an Israeli flag, an Israeli Parliament, an Israeli Department of Agriculture, and to the Old Testament coming back to life as thousands of Jews live in huge tents and learn to speak Hebrew in the land of their ancestors. But in no time we also paste articles on how Jews are divided about Israeli politics and their effect on the Diaspora.

My father sides with those who consider Zionism just another dangerous form of nationalism, and he believes that only a truly internationalist approach can lead to a world free of anti-Semitism.

While boats of Jewish refugees were at last welcomed in Haifa, the streets of our neighborhood were restless with strikers and demonstrators. Esther and I did our best not to miss a single public protest, especially if our local boys were there, having learned of it by word of mouth or from graffiti on tenement walls.

A demonstration is gathering at Place de la République. When we get there, the police are out in greater force than usual. The rumor is they are expecting the tough guys from Belleville and Ménilmontant. We greet the news with anticipation. After waiting quite a while, we see a small group finally arrive. How few they are, but how handsomely they swagger down rue du Faubourg du Temple! When they reach the police academy at the corner, they are met by gendarmes in full riot gear. Luckily, the battle limits itself to verbal taunts, and our boys are the crowd's favored predicted winners as they unleash their arsenal of man-to-man insults in what they pride themselves to be the purest slang in town.

While this is going on, we notice that more of our boys are coming to the central plaza to join the march in formation. This is going to be good, we know, but we're not about to make a public show of interest in macho Gentile boys, so I look for the secular Jewish youth group I belong to (too secular, too liberal to be approved by my friend's mother), and Esther joins me there. The march was to be peaceful, but along the way some men of draftable age (including a few of our boys) grow angry about the war in season. They half-yell, half-chant "Get out of Indochina!" and are attacked by patriots sitting with beer mugs at a passing café. The police intervene, make some arrests; the crowd gets angry. By the end of the day, many police arrests have been made and our neighborhood is heavily patrolled.

I didn't want to go home: the excitement was in the streets or in the jails. But I didn't know what I wanted most: to stay out all night in solidarity with the jailed comrades, or to get arrested and thrown in jail to share their cell, or to catch the eyes of a local tough on his way home—and pretend not to notice.

Esther went for the boys and said she had to go home—her

mother would worry. I should stay if I wanted to but under no circumstances should I wander alone, she warned with the voice of an older sister. There were little clans of acquaintances I could hook up with; for instance, she pointed to one that was coming toward us on the boulevard right then. I went in that direction but quickly turned back to see Esther crossing an arched canal bridge, swinging her hips and her hair like an actress in a movie. A couple of boys looked up at her from the quay, whistled their admiration, and walked away. Away? My feelings were hurt. But maybe, maybe they were just walking over to the other side of the bridge and would welcome her with those boy-to-girl remarks you had to pretend not to hear, no matter how much you really liked hearing them.

But no, I was not to see the outcome of that probable encounter. Recognized by a classmate, I was drawn into her group of girls and joined them.

We were all determined to follow the police and taunt them till they arrested us, which they seemed determined to avoid doing. We hounded them while they did their best to shake us off or escort us home. But home had no appeal. We didn't want to go home. We wanted to get arrested. Why couldn't we get arrested? We could chant the same slogans, hurl the same insults as the boys who did get arrested! The police said we were too young and we were girls; girls shouldn't be in prison. "They should if their boyfriends are there!" said a girl I didn't know had a boyfriend. We persisted, though with fatigue we became less articulate, and in the end we were whining that it wasn't fair of them not to arrest us! We tried and tried, following them down the boulevard all the way into night-life, neon-lights, sex-town Pigalle, where our quixotic quest was mocked by stationed prostitutes who humiliated us by calling us "kids." In that setting, the policemen suddenly looked professional and formally distanced themselves from us. Defeated, we dispersed and went home.

On the way home I solemnly promised myself that someday I'd be old enough to do something illegal and get arrested! Then, at last I'd get to see for myself what a jail cell (if not a prison cell) looked like. And I'd be brave, and no matter what they did to me, they would never, never get me to say the name of any of my comrades. I'd serve my time with dignity: recite French poems to myself, keep an inner calendar, talk to my next-cell neighbors in a secret language of coded knocks. And when I'd walk out of prison at last, all my friends would be waiting outside, holding flowers.

SINCE THE NIGHT I was not arrested, Esther's interests switched from reading about love to flirting her way around it. Instead of bargain-hunting for used books at flea markets, she now preferred going to a skating rink or a ballroom. She took me along at first, but it soon became clear that this was her territory, not mine. I was too young and awkward to attract boys as she did; but then again I feared that if one of them would by error or boredom single me out for elementary courtship, he would only find me extraordinary dull from shyness. It didn't take long before I found it too painful to stand there as a spectator, and so I let my friend go by herself. She didn't seem to mind. And though we still pledged eternal-friendship-all-secrets-shared, we didn't see each other quite as often as before.

In a way, it was something of a relief. In the hierarchy of our working-class milieu, I belonged to the privileged elite and Esther didn't.

To blur this inequality, I had to make light of all the pleasures taken away from her, especially during my frequent outings to Domont where I slept over in a beautiful attic room that I had all to myself. From its window, I could look out on the garden, the train station, and the outdoor market. I got to go with Berthe to her dressmaker, and to ride with Edmond on his motorcycle.

And what's more, I got to go to good children's camps —summer, Easter and Christmas—at the seaside or in the mountains.

Now that I didn't see Esther as often, I could relish my privileges more openly.

Once, when I came back from a summer camp in a Basque Country seaside resort, I was startled to discover that Esther had never seen the sea and that her greatest desire was to see it. A winning lottery ticket would make it possible, she assured me. Should that not happen and she remained confined to Paris, she hoped that someday she would have her own studio apartment near her mother's home. She would paint the walls ocean-blue and then brush in high rising waves complete with foam. "That would be nice," she said dreamily. "It would tide me over till I could see the sea in person!"

She had the boys and I had the sea, and there was no way for us to pool our possessions and redistribute them equally between us.

AS LONG AS I stayed on home turf, in the streets and shops and movie theaters of my neighborhood with its mixed population of Jews, Algerians, Gypsies, and poor French, I felt quite sure of myself. My view of the future was upbeat: I would surely grow up to be admired by everyone as a poised, capable, and quick-witted woman, a cultured, intimate friend of proletarian and Surrealist writers and artists. My parents would be proud of me, although they'd worry about the financial insecurity that was part of hanging out with artists and political activists. I would reassure them that if you're needed to make the world better, and if you have many friends, you come out all right: they only had to remember their own youth.

But should I accidentally wander off by myself to one of those neighborhood preserves of patriotic monuments and baby carriages pushed by uniformed Breton nannies, I was struck with panic. The perfumed adults, the starched servants, even the babies and the miniature dogs were French, totally French, of pure French blood. Nothing foreign, nothing Jewish in the air! It made me terribly ill at ease. Walking steadily and as fast as I could, feeling doom and danger, I was careful to catch no one's eye. Looking ahead and on both sides for a boulevard, a plaza, a large open space, I desperately yearned for a Métro entrance into which I could rush to safety and the way home.

In my friend's company, or with my family, I would have enjoyed the exotic quality of those fancy neighborhoods. Alone,

I felt prey to shadows of doom and danger following me. As I tried to escape, it seemed that the whole neighborhood said yes! go! as if I had just activated a mysterious magnetic force that would throw me onto the conveyor belt designed to eject all undesirable elements from the protected grounds.

I would promise myself to pay more attention to where I was going, but it was difficult, as I tended to daydream full force whenever I was alone.

Home alone was still wonderful, especially for dreaming and reading. It was particularly delicious to pillow myself in a comfortable position on my parents' bed and get lost reading books.

My favorites were works of Surrealism, which stood rereading any number of times. Mysterious, erotic, and religious, they combined everything I liked: poetic images, absurdist humor, random structure. And they dealt with subjects of great interest to me: Paris streets, anti-bourgeois pranks, chance encounters, flea market outings, mad love, great friendships.

ESTHER DOESN'T CARE for Surrealism. She thinks it's just weird, some kind of idle boys' play.

Posters all over town are advertising a panel discussion on Sergei Maïakovsky, featuring Louis Aragon, Elsa Triolet, and Paul Eluard, and sponsored by a left-wing cultural committee—nothing to do with Surrealism. I wonder about Eluard's presence on the panel, if it means he's back to normal, if he will really speak on Maïakovsky. Everybody knows that Eluard is still mourning his wife, Nush. Her death was announced on the front page of newspapers. Trying to distract him, his friends took him on a trip to Russia. Maybe it worked, and now he's better and ready to speak on the wild young Russian poet!

I tell Esther about it. She screams with excitement: Aragon! Aragon's wife! Aragon's friend Eluard! Talking about Maïakovski! Was it true? Was it possible? Did it cost money? Could we go?

It's as if the famous movie actor Jean Gabin had given us a private invitation to a rehearsal. How easy it had been to interest her in attending the lecture!

Now she complains she doesn't know the work of those writers well enough; do I have anything to give her to read?

Oh yes, I do! There's *The Peasant of Paris* by Aragon, one of the two major books that popularized the Surrealist movement. I could lend it to her. In it, three poets, on the spur of the moment, decide to explore the Buttes-Chaumont at night in the mid-twenties. "Our Buttes-Chaumont?" she asks. "Absolutely!" I tell her.

A couple of days later, she brings back the book. She loved it; she absolutely, totally loved it! She can't get over the fact that such a classic, in all the bookstores and libraries, is half about the Buttes-Chaumont, our park. She marvels: "Imagine that! The bridge of suicides, the temple of meditation on top of the grotto, the lake and its ferries, the guignols and the merry-go-round, it's all there! I didn't realize Surrealism could be so close to home. Do you have something else as exciting?"

I lend her André Breton's *Nadja*, telling her this one is the romantic story of the poet's encounter with a poor young kept-woman, who lures him on the most magical walks through

Paris, some in our neighborhood, some in other, nearby ones. She borrows the book.

A few days later, she returns it with a bonus: her enthusiastic revelations of Surrealism's relevance. "Hey, Odette. Do you realize we've been doing Surrealist things? Like our Mondays off from school—that's freeing ourselves from established routine, isn't it? And we spend our time in the streets—walking, looking for interesting books, going to the flea market, checking out quaint old prewar objects and prewar books—that's Surrealist, too! And do you remember the night we wanted to stay in the streets, get arrested, then I got tired and walked home? A man followed me, and I was very tempted. He was so handsome, but I didn't sleep with him and I regretted it and kept looking for him in the streets. I never found him, but I found others. That's Surrealist—it has to do with sexual desire, with street encounters. Who would have thought that that's what Surrealism is all about?"

I HAD ALWAYS HOPED Esther would come around and develop at least a lukewarm interest in Surrealism. Instead, she was so astonished at how familiar it all seemed that she now acted as though Surrealism had been created for the likes of us— Jewish working-class girls from Belleville.

At her suggestion, we began to haunt bookstores again, looking for any material on Surrealism. I was glad we were spending more time together, as we used to.

Esther discovered that Surrealists invented games they played together. We came up with two of our own.

One took place in the subway. We called it an "observation game." It required that as soon as we entered a coach, we would both "spontaneously" stare at some part of the side or back of a person facing us, as if we were discreetly noticing something absurd or ludicrous. That person never failed to get nervous. The fun of the game was to see how our targeted victims would react—would they try to position themselves so as to see their backs mirrored in the windows? would they smooth out their pants, their skirts? or would they, on the contrary, do their best to melt into the crowd, to get their backs blocked by another body? We always got to see the results of our experiments, and as soon as the subject of our study in social behavior would leave, we would burst out laughing.

Our other game in a public setting was a one-time-only event of irreverence.

As planned, we wandered the streets after a late movie until the early hours of the morning, at which point we could assume that everyone was asleep in bed, their own or someone else's. Starting north of the Canal St. Martin, we each positioned ourselves on either side of the rue Faubourg du Temple. "One, two, three, set, go!" We ran up the street from doorway to doorway ringing the house bells. It didn't take long before we began to hear angry concierges awakened by the prank, yelling every insult they had ever yelled at anyone. We looked back in midrun and burst out laughing at the ridiculous sight. Some of the concierges were shaking their brooms at us. We ran faster, still ringing new doorbells. It felt like a chase in a silent comedy. Luckily, the street was poorly lit, and the concierges were in their nightclothes and eager to get back to bed; so no one chased us.

Doors to Madame Marie

THE GREAT DAY of the lecture has finally come. As novice Surrealists, we are naturally awed; tonight we will see Aragon, Eluard, and Triolet! While Breton lost status when he migrated to New York in 1940, Aragon and Eluard, now star poets of French Communism, still remain living legends of Surrealism and the French Resistance. As for Triolet, she is a famous novelist married to a famous poet—an exemplary pair!

In honor of Surrealism, we will not take the subway to the reading hall. We'll walk across town, in a roundabout, random, leisurely manner, stopping to look at whatever pleases or mystifies us. We'll leave ourselves a long time to get there—the more so to relish the night.

Along the way, in a spirit of Surrealist observation, we point to architectural oddities, quaint displays in shop windows, incongruously positioned statues, overzealous water fountains, old-fashioned street lamps, antique umbrellas, a furtive view of a pair of lovers kissing good-bye outside a front door.

Nadja and *The Peasant of Paris* of twenty years ago are coming to life for us.

It occurs to me that those books were written about the Paris to which my parents had migrated. I find the thought very poignant. Both of them young, poor, and idealistic, they still practiced the Jewish-Polish principle that "Life is with People"— at the shop; at home; at the park; at the club with its meeting rooms, libraries, bulletin boards, and Yiddish newspapers; or walking the boulevards in hopes of running into people they knew, then stopping with them in a crowded café.

The Paris they lived in then was a major focus of the twenties Surrealists, who favored the most modest neighborhoods and the haunts of the poor—the Buttes-Chaumont, the flea markets—this was the very Paris that our prewar families had known! We both grew wistful at the thought, because Esther's folks also had left Poland, fleeing poverty and anti-Semitism, for the chance to blossom as full human beings in the open-minded City of Lights.

"Imagine that!" I said. "This was here in the thirties, and it's here today. Paris as our parents first saw it: still here! all around us!" This is our hometown, our tradition, our ancestry, our roots—going back to at least the late twenties! As to the Poland of our parents and grandparents, it's our more ancient, ancestral home, but it has nothing left to offer us. If we ever visited, we'd only get to see the ghost towns of shtetls and ghettos.

Both of us felt nostalgic for that bygone Paris we barely remembered. It wasn't quite ours, it was really "theirs"—our parents' young adulthood. But it was the only past we had a chance to inherit in real life, since their other past—the one of their Polish childhood—was destined to remain but an immense family graveyard in some ghetto of our mind. The choice was clear: Paris was better than a giant ghostly cemetery for three million Jews!

WE WALK the rest of the way in a solemn mood. As we get closer, I predict that something wonderfully Surrealist will happen at the lecture, but only if (how well I know my Breton!) we are in a state of receptiveness—something like the Catholic "state of grace," or Madame Marie's just-cleaned apartment of the heart. Esther is game!

We finally get to the lecture hall. We can't believe our eyes — only seven other people in the audience, a couple of whom look like truck drivers. On the platform, seated from left to right: Aragon, Eluard, Triolet. We find ourselves two choice aisle seats in center rows, behind the scattered few other people.

The lecture begins. Elsa Triolet, so pretty with her braided crown hairdo, presents a vivid, entertaining memoir of Maïakovski, whom she knew in her native Russia when he was courting her sister. She tells the following story: it's her sister's birthday. Maïakovski comes calling. The poet, all smiles, pleased with himself, is hiding something behind his back, which he then abruptly delivers with a flourish to his fiancée as she enters the room. It's a freshly picked carrot, well formed, well fleshed out, with a beautiful head of dark green leaves. She's charmed; her parents are scandalized.

Esther and I look at each other — apparently with the same thought: this is a perfect Surrealist story. We must indeed be in a state of grace.

Eluard has said not a word, and probably not listened to one either; he's just sitting between his two friends, totally absent, most likely with Nush somewhere in his memory. He looks like a sad, kind uncle.

Questions are asked of Triolet and Aragon, but not a single one of Eluard. As if by tacit agreement, everyone leaves him alone as he continues to stare at the back of the room right into his dreamworld.

One of the truck-driver types stands up. "Comrade Aragon!" he shouts, scandalizing me. How did he dare call "comrade" one of the greatest French poets of the twentieth century! To my surprise and relief, though, Aragon doesn't at all look shocked. In fact, he is thoughtful and answers the truck driver, who, truly grateful, says in a now soft voice: "Thanks, Comrade Aragon!"

From Esther's home to mine, I carried on a silent soliloquy, as buoyantly as Candide, that I was living in the best of all possible worlds. That I was, in every way, on the "right side" of politics, poetry, even geography, since Paris was the capital of the nation with the greatest artistic innovations, the most important philosophies of modern times—the cultural capital of the world.

EVERYTHING WAS RIGHT with my world. Even being Jewish had been simplified. When Gentiles held certain suspicions and would ask: "What church do you go to?" they knew better than to expect the only answer to be: "I don't go to church because I'm Jewish, so I go to synagogue." It was also all right to say: "I don't go to church or synagogue: I'm a secular Jew." Everyone knew there were two kinds of Jews: religious and secular. And even though France was an overwhelmingly Catholic country, secularism sounded almost patriotic, since the public schools of the Republic had endowed it with civic dignity.

ONE AREA OF LIFE in which I was not yet on the same level as my peers, my girlfriends and classmates, was that of menstruation. All my classmates, Esther of course, and nearly all the girls my age at the Jewish youth group had already had their periods. But it hadn't yet happened to me.

My mother had told me what to do. She had shown me what she did for herself: how she made washable sanitary napkins by cutting up strips of old torn-up towels, filling them in the center with a bit more towel, then pinning them into her panties with safety pins.

You knew when a girl had her period because, as the French put it, she was "indisposed." It was a privilege to be indisposed; you could be excused from anything stressful. I kept dreaming of the day when I, too, could say that I was indisposed. I wondered why it was taking so long. My mother repeated her old assessment of me: "You're slow, you're late. You were always that way. You were born late." This was not of great comfort. In the meantime, I longed to be indisposed. There were moments when I thought I felt something odd going on in my body. Maybe this was it! I'd look for the blood; but no, no blood. Not yet.

And one Thursday, it happened. I woke up, got dressed, ate breakfast and, as I got up from the table, I knew it had happened. At last, for the first time, like the others, I was indisposed! I went straight to the wardrobe drawer to the neat pile of home-made sanitary napkins and took one. My first sanitary napkin! I held it against my cheek, just to feel it was real, it was mine—white, ready to be drenched in blood, my blood. Proof of my being indisposed. Suddenly, I remembered my village in Vendée—how the girls sat in a circle by the well where the bloody proof of menstruation was passed around, and how the first-timer was officially treated as a full-fledged woman needing instructions on how to avoid unwanted sex and pregnancy.

I followed my mother's instructions, wishing today were a schoolday so I could just announce, very casually, on the first possible excuse, that I was sorry but I was indisposed.

As every Thursday, Esther was at her shop and I had to go help my parents. Yet, everything felt different. The day had a new flavor. People were going about the regular business of their daily lives. But for me, it was the day of Creation. Everything was new. I was new. Now I was to be an apprentice woman, a novice woman, a beginning woman. There was much to learn, I knew, but I was one of "them." I looked at every woman who passed, especially the younger ones, and the thought that I belonged to their kind filled me with pleasure and pride.

As I was slowly dreaming my way down rue du Faubourg du Temple to the Métro station of Place de la République, I was noticed by a classmate walking across the street in the other direction. She called to greet me. I shouted that I had great news; she came over, and when I told her, she jumped up, embraced me, and with a grand gesture said this must be celebrated this very minute, without delay. Arms around each other's waist, we walked to a famous ice-cream store down the street on the other side of the Canal, where my school chum bought me a double ice-cream, in a double sugar cone—one side filled with vanilla and the other with chocolate. Now I felt properly "baptized." All was well and would only get better. Boys gravitated to girls who were indisposed once a month; so they would come to me too.

ONE GOOD THING brings another. Luck begets luck.

My parents' long hours of hard work and frugal habits have paid off and they have bought a small house of their own in Domont. It has two side-by-side rooms, both facing the front garden with its double-blossom lilac bushes outside the windows, and a kitchen in the back, set up in what used to be a covered porch. The yard has a garden, a shed, and an outhouse.

We're ecstatic about having our very own house. Under Edmond's guidance, my father has become a successful weekend gardener. At the flea market, he bought a wooden glassed bookcase which, also under Edmond's guidance, he has refinished. It locks with a key. Now the books my father loves, his most precious possessions, have a handsome home.

The living room doubles up as my parents' bedroom; by one door it is attached to the kitchen in the back, and by the other, to the dining room that also houses my bed and my father's glassed bookcase.

I have my own wooden bed that fits in a corner and is a cleverly self-contained unit. The sideboard has a cabinet in which to store bedclothes, a towel, and a pair of slippers, and the headboard has a simple bookshelf above the pillow with room for an alarm clock and books. I don't have to fold my bed; it stays open all day. I just need to pull up the sheets and blankets in the morning, fluff the pillows, cover the whole thing with a bedspread, and put my pajamas neatly away in the sideboard cabinet. Then, from the bookshelf, I can take the book I'm currently reading and go sit outdoors on the back patio under the cherry tree.

My father comes in from the garden to put his freshly

picked vegetables on the kitchen table. My mother will wash them right away and prepare them for cooking.

Our weekend house even has a radio and we listen to Radio Luxembourg, which has very classy cultural programs, concerts, plays, book readings, and children's programs.

Although Edmond affectionately mocks my parents' Yiddish accent and mannerisms, here my parents are the closest they've ever been to being French, with their cherry tree, lilac bushes, and outhouse. We have great pride of proprietorship.

On Sunday night, we take the train back home, carrying flowers from our garden. Life is good.

NOVEMBER 11TH, Armistice Day, a holiday. Tomorrow I'm supposed to be fourteen. The age of my Cousin Sarah Melczak when she was taken to the Drancy camp, and from there, as we now know, to Auschwitz in a cattle car—and from there . . . nowhere but up in smoke into the sky.

How can I be fourteen? How can I usurp my cousin's age? We had the same name, Sarah, after our grandmother, except that she used it as her first name and I as my middle name. I thought of my cousin each time I wrote out my full name: Odette Sarah Melszpajz. Sarah, my hidden Jewish name, was the name we shared. That was all right. That was comforting. But how could I take on her age, which I never had before? Fourteen was her age, not mine. It was, in fact, her last age. She was fourteen, and then from fourteen she went not to fifteen but to nothing at all.

It was so strange! I knew, in all my being I knew, that I

could not casually go from thirteen to fourteen, that somehow I would simply not become fourteen. There was nothing upsetting about it. It just was. This was my last day and that was that. I had reached the end of my Destiny. I could not cross over to November 12, as I was used to doing. There would be no November 12, 1948, for me. There would be no *me* on November 12. Everything else would be the same. All this could not be helped: this was just the way it was meant to happen.

A solemn peace flowed through my veins. I fell asleep.

To my astonishment, I woke up on November twelfth. I was fourteen years old, like my Cousin Sarah on her last year. The daylight had an acutely fresh sweetness. It had all happened exactly as on the eve and the morning of my thirteenth birthday, when, contrary to what I had expected, I had awakened as an thirteen-year-old, the age of my Cousin Serge on his last year.

MY SCHOOLWORK has been totally erratic. I do well in French literature and French composition, and I love history, but I find life sciences, mathematics, and especially civics impenetrably boring. As to home economics, I've not even been there to try. My scholastic score card has a negative total; since we are graded in points, I owe the Department of Education a terribly important sum.

I refuse to take my debt seriously. I clown around and often, as punishment, get sent out of the classroom into the hall. But I don't mind; I just daydream, or fantasize, or make up stories.

But I do get nervous when the principal calls me in, as I'm

still intimidated by seldom-seen authorities. On one of my visits to her office, she announces a new form of punishment which she obviously perceives as a humiliation: from now on, whenever I give my teacher a hard time, she has the authority to send me for the rest of the day to the primary-grade classroom. Actually, I find it to be a pleasant experience, and though I pretend to be unhappy when the teacher hands out her punishment, I'm delighted the minute I get into the classroom and a few of the small girls signal for me to sit next to them, though I can't do it and I have to wait for their teacher to assign my seat. I like it in that class: it's restful, the material studied is easy, the girls look up to me because I'm older, I help them and I'm liked, and the teacher is very sweet.

ASTONISHING NEWS: we have visas for America! We can't leave, though, until my mother, pregnant again, gives birth, which is expected in late April. But I'll be out of the country before the school year ends in mid-July 1949; so it doesn't matter how well I do or even what I do for the rest of the term. Still, I don't want the school to know about it. I'll keep the news to myself, and share it as a sworn secret only with the most carefully selected friends.

Life takes on another tone since we'll be leaving in just a few months. There is so much to do in so little time! My future sibling is threatening to burst through my mother's pleated navy-blue maternity dress, and my family's social and cultural calendar is getting so full I have less time for my own circle of friends, which has been growing ever since I first became "indisposed."

Suddenly, everything my parents had postponed to do or see has to be done this very week.

We start on a dizzying round of parties; all our friends and relatives want to say good-bye to us with much eating and drinking. We go to theaters I had only read about. What a luxury to see stage plays with famous actors like Louis Jouvet! We even go to the opera, where, with my aunt Georgette, uncle Henri, and their daughter Sarah, we rent a box and hear Bizet's *L'Arlesienne*. Since it's Christmas, the management distributes a small tin pin in the shape of wooden clogs. I'll keep it as a souvenir.

Everyone seems to take me for a walk or to a museum—those inexpensive pleasures. I had gone to museums before, of course, but only occasionally. Suddenly I think Paris has been taken over by museums. Some of them are very large, like the Louvre, where they say it takes a week to visit all its rooms. I focus on every painting, every statue: I want to remember everything. Once in America, especially in Los Angeles, where we're headed, there will be none of that, I'm sure. They say there is no culture in America except for Hemingway, and no arts except for Jazz.

I think my parents are getting nostalgic for their own past in the city. We even walk the fancy Champs Elysées. I'm not sure why, but it's okay as long as I'm in company. And we visit all the tourist spots: the Eiffel Tower, where we take the huge elevator to the first level; the vast expanse of well-manicured grass at the Champ de Mars, going up to the Trocadero and the anthropological Palais de l'Homme, with strategically placed statues and fountains on the way up.

Montmartre: either up the hill, to the wedding-cake Sacré Coeur; or staying at the foot of the hill, all the fabric stores and the famous Marché St. Pierre — so many sets of window curtains! (I can't even daydream about curtains, as we're not going to take any to America; besides, American's rooms and windows are so enormous, they probably only use drapes.) Then we go on up to the Sacré Coeur. My mother, big as she is, is still full of energy. My father and I just follow her. We even picnic in the Bois de Vincennes by the romantic lake, and under aristocratic trees in the Bois de Boulognes. We stop in cafés for a drink, where my parents invite their friends or relatives, and, with a grand gesture, my father says to the waiter: "This round is on me." I wish the rounds would go on and on, now that I'm discovering Paris in style.

NEW YEAR'S DAY 1949: I won't see this year in Paris to its calendar conclusion. In a bit more than four months, we'll be leaving. The countdown is getting more dramatic: we've seen these places, these people; we still need to visit this forest, that museum; go to dinner with those cousins, these friends. My father is limiting his gardening to what is already in the ground and its future harvest, but he can't plant for next year. It seems so strange, all this stopping in midcourse. And then, too, there are new chores. We have to get passports, pack the belongings we'll take with us, sell the rest, find a new tenant for our apartment and a buyer for the house.

Increasingly, everything has a "last time" or "maybe last time" tag on it.

In this round of good-byes, this putting the past behind, monument by monument, along with all the memories and all the people of my Paris childhood, there comes a totally new first-time-in-my-life event: my mother gives birth to a baby girl. The baby arrives while my father and I and nearly everyone we know are taking part in a major international peace demonstration, advertised all over Paris on posters illustrated with Picasso's peace dove. That very same day, Picasso's daughter is born and is named Paloma—the dove. As for my sister, she is given the French version of the names of two of our aunts, Chana (who died in the Warsaw Ghetto), and Miriam (who died in Auschwitz). Baby Anne-Marie will be our bearer of the Old World into the New. What a triumphant way to leave Europe for America!

I WANT TO SHOW my sister everything. Since my parents are so busy, I get to take the baby for walks. I carry her in my arms all bundled up, as a baby should be. I'm taken for an unwed mother. But that's fine. I don't really mind. In fact, I indulge in some wild scenarios. Even though she doesn't understand anything, I want to carry her to all my important haunts. My parents, to honor her birth, have planted a rose bush in the garden of our Domont house, even though the house will soon cease to belong to us. So, although my own world will also cease to belong to me, I want to show it to Anne-Marie.

And here we are in the Buttes-Chaumont, my sister and I. Everything is so strange now that we'll be leaving! I'm dying to take in just one Guignol show, but at fourteen, I can't just sit there on a little bench with small children unless some of them are in my charge, and obviously a baby is too young to count as a spectator. My poor sister: she'll leave France before she can appreciate the Guignol and all the other pleasures of the park, the ones I knew in my childhood—a ride on a donkey, or a ferry ride across the lake between the Belgium waffle stand and the grottoes that lead up to the Temple of Meditation. I feel sorry for her. I can't imagine they will have as pretty a park in America. From all I hear, in America everything is on a huge scale—buildings, railroad tracks, national parks, the sky—as if the land had once been peopled by giants. Landscapes, buildings, and objects require a smaller scale, as in France, if they are to be endowed with exquisite charm, quaintness, or delicate beauty!

Each time we go for a walk, she and I, I take her somewhere else. She must like being walked, as she mostly sleeps in utter peacefulness. I want to take her to every place that's important to me. She won't remember any of it; but I will remember that I did the right thing by her, that I gave her the grand tour of my childhood world in the grand city of her birth, of my birth.

Going down our own street, I take her to Place de la République where I show her the statue of the Republic, a large and strong-willed woman of the people. She's the only monument in our neighborhood, but, like the Obelisk at Place de la Concorde, she's at the hub of all the circling cars. So which is it, really: am I showing the statue to the baby? or am I showing my little sister to the statue that has known me all my life?

On the way back home, we go up rue du Faubourg du Temple. I point out my favorite ice-cream store, and the movie theater across the street where I went so many times, first with my parents and later with my own friends—and even once, not long ago, with a boy. After the movie, we took a walk by the canal. I show Anne-Marie the canal; she opens her eyes. While I have her attention, I turn to the café where I had my first grown-up drink, when my mother was so thrilled at having found a cache of books that had survived the war by hiding. Resuming my walk, I show my sister the houses where Esther and I disturbed the concierges, and on and on till we get home, passing through the shabby Passage Jules Verne with the Public Baths, and across from it, that drab building. There, on the second floor to the right, is the leather gloves shop where Esther works. Nearer home, we pass the Burztyns' house. I go into the courtyard and point my sister's face up toward the attic where Léon came back to die in his own bed. He would have liked my baby sister! Before we enter our house, I make us walk the whole length of the square, so she can get a full view of the core of our daily life—on one side, the convent and its school, then the chain manufacturer; on the other side, a longer block starting near us with the Café de la Baleine, then the union workers' headquarters neighboring our pharmacy, a couple more stores and, at the corner, a bakery and pastry shop.

Finally, I get the courage to take my sister on the most important walk in my ritual farewell to Paris and my childhood—to my cousins' neighborhood, which I used to know almost as well as mine. After I realized what had happened to them, I lost heart. I went there less and less frequently until I stopped finding myself in those streets (unless totally by accident; at which point, I'd hurry away). The truth is, I don't now think of them very often, except for sure on my birthdays and if something extraordinary happens. Now something of that kind is happening: we are leaving France. Not to our deaths, as they did, but to a new life in a country with no war ruins. Since I haven't been in my cousins' neighborhood for a long time, I haven't kept up with all the changes. In some ways, I wish it would all change, that every store would be different from the way it was before the war, because when I do recognize a shoe-repair shop or a bakery, I can't stand it. I feel I'm going to cry or scream or fall unconscious. I want my dead back, walking in the street, alive, tickling my baby sister. I can't bear their absence; it's been too long an absence; they're just frozen into absence, eternal absence. I wish they had graves, seven of them, or one family grave for all of them—two parents and five children—a place of their own, an apartment of the soul, where I could pay a visit, bring fresh flowers, talk to them.

Again, and for the last time, I hurry away from the familiar streets and I walk to the nearby Cemetery of Père Lachaise. I go from grave to grave. I wish I could make believe that even just one of them belongs to my family, but I can't because there is always somebody else's name on the gravestone. Still, I walk up and down tree-lined allées that have street signs so people can look on a map and locate their dead. Eventually, I come to the monument to the memory of French Jews murdered by the Nazis. I pay my respects and say good-bye.

WE ARE MOVING closer to the end. My parents have found a buyer for the house. The new family won't know that the rose bush was planted in honor of my sister's birth, but the bush will bloom and grow. Now we'll have the money for our trip. To add to that, we're showing our apartment to prospective tenants. If they decide to move in, they'll pay the rent to the landlord and some "key money" to us, the old tenants. So it's important to keep the apartment spic and span, says my mother, who has become compulsive about picking up and cleaning up. I find it annoying; it's as if it's no longer our home, as if it already belongs to the new tenants, whoever they'll be.

To my surprise, people who come to look at the apartment are very critical of it. "There is only one window, and it's in the bedroom?" they complain. "You always need to have the lights on in the dining room and the kitchen?" "The kitchen is so small! The cupboards are falling apart. The sink is of greystone, not porcelain. Is that sanitary? Only one closet, and it's in the dining room! And one cupboard, and it's in the bedroom! And the wallpaper is peeling in many places!" and on, and on. I am crushed: the home I am so proud of! with a toilet of its own! What about that? They look, but they just aren't impressed. And what about the fact that it is on the first floor, just one flight of stairs? Doesn't that count for something?

The ultimate humiliation comes from the very people who end up renting the apartment. My parents generously throw in all our furniture: the round leaf table and chairs; the green sofa bed in the dining room; the kitchen cupboard; and, in the bedroom, their bed, my folding bed, the round wooden table held up by three lion legs, and the pot-bellied stove for winter.

After our offer is made, the future tenants consult briefly with each other and get back to us. They first complain that they will have to pay to have all our "junk" hauled away. If they had known this beforehand, they would have hesitated, but as they've now gone so far and have already set their minds on renting, they'll proceed anyway.

Now that it has been condemned, I wish I could salvage the furniture that shaped my childhood world, take it all with us to America and save it from destruction. But, no, there is nothing I can do; I simply have to let go. You don't take broken cupboards to the New Land.

There are some things, though, that are in my power to buy and put in my suitcase, things I might not find in the United States. Embroidery material, for instance, for many ambitious projects that should last me many years into my stay in America.

I don't have enough money to buy everything I want. Esther has an idea. I can sell those nice clothes from a family in Paradise, New Jersey, who sent me CARE packages soon after the Liberation: the red corduroy jumper, lengthened several times since, and all the outgrown skirts and blouses I won't be taking to America. There is the old-clothes merchant on Passage Jules Verne. We can go there. She'll help me pick all that look resellable. I think it's a great idea. We go to my home and sort the clothes. I keep offering her those in the best shape; they may fit her: she's shorter, thin and small-boned. No, no, she says. Those are the ones that will bring in the most money.

For the first time, we enter the intriguing shop we've passed so often.

Piles of tied bundles of clothes are everywhere; they crowd the dismal, barely lit shop. It's hard to distinguish a counter or a table. One object, however, is very clear: it's a large floor-size scale with a bundle still on it. The old man grumbles as if we've disturbed him. We open up my bundle for him, showing off the clothes from America: corduroy jumpers, jersey tops. He's not the least bit impressed; he's not even interested in looking at each piece of clothing. He throws it all back together into a pile and ties it up. Since he hasn't yet said a word, I figure he doesn't like my clothes any more than the new tenants liked our furniture, and that he is about to refuse to buy them from me. But no, I am wrong. He goes to the scale, pushes off the sitting bundle, replaces it with mine, which he weighs carefully, finally stating the result out loud and making his offer. Esther and I are shocked at how little it is. If my mother, eager to reduce our belongings, hadn't looked so happy to see me take the clothes away, I would protest that his offer is insulting, especially given the high quality of American clothing. But it is too late. I don't want to reappear at home with the old bundle, so I am forced to accept. Esther and I leave the store feeling depressed: we can't believe the clothes we admired have fetched so little money.

We then say our good-byes and might say them one more time if we get the chance. We promise to exchange long letters, full of detailed descriptions of life in America and life in Paris, so we can keep up with each other till we meet again in person—either when I return to Paris as an independent adult, or when she visits me in America, if she finds the money to do it, somehow, some time.

I FEEL TOTALLY DEJECTED. I've said goodbye to my best friend. I've been saying good-bye for months to all those people I've known—my parents' friends, relatives, acquaintances, my classmates, my buddies from the Jewish youth group, even neighbors and local merchants. I've said my good-byes to the Park of the Buttes-Chaumont, to the Père Lachaise Cemetery, good-bye to every monument, every museum, every open-air market, every bakery where I liked to buy a baba-au-rhum, every Métro station, every familiar bistro, every statue I thought I'd never see again. I've walked the banks of the Seine and the banks of the Canal. I've even finally had the courage to wander through my cousins' haunted neighborhood, to present my baby sister to my ghost family.

I feel dispossessed. Nearly everything I love is being taken away from me. And yet, strangely, it's all still around me, all still accessible. But I know soon it will be gone, all of it. The boat will have pulled me away from it forever, or at least till I'm grown up and make my own living and can pay the boat fare back to France and come and settle back in my country, no matter how sad I'll be to leave my parents and sister in Los Angeles. In the meantime, I feel as though I live in two dimensions at once—in the present with my treasures around me, and in the near future when I will have been permanently impoverished.

I feel like Cinderella at ten minutes after midnight: the furniture I loved turns out to be junk; my best clothes are worth only five skeins of embroidery thread.

All that peacock self-assurance that made me strut through my happiest year, all of it has just burst like a balloon. Now I can see that it was all borrowed—from Surrealism, from the Resistance, from atheism, from leftist politics, from the writings of others. All that—the thoughts and accomplishments of others—puffed my own self-confidence just because I had aligned myself with them; none of that was due to my own accomplishments. In fact, were I to stay in Paris any longer, I would be kicked out of school again as I was from Lycée Hélène Boucher. Given all that my parents have done for me, it is really shameful that I haven't done better.

Again, as I used to, I feel awkward, plain-looking, almost simpleminded, surely a disappointment to one and all, including myself. Who am I? What right have I to complain of all my losses?

I'm too wretched to go home. As I always do in such cases, I walk and walk obsessively, hypnotically, hoping either to feel better or to tire myself into a state of nonthinking, nonfeeling.

"*WHO AM I?*" I chant silently to myself. Over and over I repeat that question: "Who am I?" If everything is taken away from me, even that last identity I forged for myself this last year which seemed so satisfactory, fitted so well, if all, all can be taken away to trade for a passport to a new identity I don't yet know, whose language I don't yet understand, then what is it that's left of me? Who am I? Who am I?

As I chant those three words, they finally give out an echo: "Who I am will sooner or later appear etched by a diamond." What is that? Who said that? Have I read it somewhere? It must have caught my attention before if I remember it. Maybe I've read it several times over. Aside from poetry, the only book I've often re-read is André Breton's *Nadja*. So that's it: it's from *Nadja*! But why do I suddenly remember it?

I am so lost in thought that I haven't realized where I am until I face a familiar set of high double doors. Startled out of my reverie, I don't recognize them immediately, but there is something about those tall doors that urges me—with a fairy-tale authority—to stop and go no farther. So I stop. Trying to get my bearings, I see the word "concierge" to one side and instantly realize that the reference is not abstract. The concierges in question are Madame Marie and Monsieur Henri.

I stand outside a while, hesitating to go in. It has been so long since I last visited; how will I explain myself? In my year of depending on a full wardrobe of attractive identities to dress up in and walk tall, I have hardly thought of my self-assigned godmother, seamstress of all my early dresses, my concierge, my Madame Marie of the old rue d'Angoulême, my protector-in-chief who stayed in Paris and at the very same time also left invisibly for Vendée with me, passing as the Virgin Mary until I came back to Paris! How did I do without her this last year? And what shall I say now of my long absence?

I HAVEN'T YET rung the bell. I'm still sorting out my thoughts when one of the large double doors opens—to frame the large stature of Monsieur Henri. How did he know I am here? How uncanny of him to materialize unexpectedly at the very moment I need his hugely comforting and quiet presence—to rush me to the pharmacy when I got burned as a baby, to rush me away from a Paris roundup of Jews to the train that will take me to safety. And again, though we had returned to Paris two days late, for him to be there, waiting at our Métro station. And now that I feel so utterly lost, that I am indeed lost, Monsieur Henri, like a benevolent spirit assigned to guide lost travelers in a fairy-tale journey, stands quiet and sure and ushers me in.

A few words of greeting; then he explains he has some chores to attend to and will be joining me and Madame Marie in the loge in about an hour.

In this loge, a lace curtain on the glassed part of the door assures privacy. I ring the bell. Soon, the curtain is drawn and Madame Marie's round face appears. How stupid I've been to miss all those chances to see that wonderful face! And now I'm poised to cross a whole ocean then a whole country, while Madame Marie stays in Paris, so far, so horribly far from me! Aside from a couple of photographs, all I have is my yellow baby blanket, long stripped of its religious medals, which I'm smuggling into my new country, claiming that it's for my baby sister. I have no other trick. I'm no longer a child, so I won't be able to talk myself into hiding Madame Marie's spirit in a statue. She will simply not be there, not there at all.

HER SMILE HAS ushered me in. I look around to see what is new, what is the same as at my last visit. There is a feel of greater ease, less work, a slower pace. I notice, too, that she is treating me differently, as she would an adult. She actually pulls a chair for me, offers tea, sits at a little round table with me (though I can see she must have been at the sewing machine when I made my unannounced visit.) I don't know if it's because she realizes this may be a good-bye, or if, like others, she simply senses that I've grown up.

We catch up, both of us.

For the first time, I ask her about herself—how long the two of them plan on remaining concierges in this tool-and-die factory, and are they thinking of retiring to their cottage in the country? She is pleased that I've asked and for the first time tells me that their current job has been good for them; it's unpressured and they needed to slow down. But yes, they dream of moving to the cottage, gardening, getting a dog—but that will have to wait till the cottage becomes vacant.

Then it's my turn. I tell her what has happened to me. How, best of all, I'm no longer an only child: I have a beautiful baby sister. (She nods. She's seen the baby.) How wonderful also to have a best friend. How much better I learned to know Paris this last year. But how, of all that's good and wonderful, I can take along to America only my baby sister, my parents, and, from my father's side, my aunt, uncle, and girl cousin. But I can't take my best friend; I can't take Paris; I can't take all the people I love. I have to leave behind almost all I know and love. No one asked me if I wanted to go to America. Truth is, I don't. I have no desire to leave Paris, and the only other country I'd like to visit is Italy.

"You left Paris before. You came back," she says quietly, but as I'm about to elaborate on the legitimacy of my protest against my fate as an exile-to-be, she asks to be excused for just a few minutes: she needs to finish some sewing for a customer who is coming in an hour or so.

THE MINUTE Madame Marie is seated at her Singer machine, guiding the material with one hand, turning the wheel with the other and pedaling with one foot, she enters a thoughtful silence. And I enter that silence with her, as I used to do when I was a little girl, startled to have her stop chatting, although now that I'm older it occurs to me that the rhythm of her work must help order her thoughts, her feelings. It's a treat to watch her at the machine again! The world can be confusing, maddening, and a whole city, a whole country can vanish from one's life, but as long as Madame Marie sits at her sewing machine, everything can be made right again. As I sit in our common silence, I see her at all moments of my life—from my earliest memories to that dreadful day when I ditched school and, as punishment, had to sit still till I completed a thorough cleaning of my heart's apartment. Now it's been years since my last spring-cleaning; how messy it must be! I can see myself entering the apartment of my heart. When I turn on the light in the dining room, I see a clutter of books in precarious piles on the table, on chairs, on the floor; also clothing of all kinds, carelessly thrown on the sofa, the chairs, the piles of books on the floor, anywhere at all. I pick up the books, one by one, and stand them up against each other all along the wall, as there is no shelf space available. Then, I collect the clothes. Before I hang them neatly in the closet, I check the labels: Surrealism, Atheism, Communism, Womanhood, Art and Esthetics. There is even a yellow coat marked Juif, and here is a pair of wooden clogs from St. Fulgent. When I've put them all away, I realize someone is speaking to me and I awake from my reverie.

Madame Marie, with the authority of a chief concierge holding the full set of keys to Heaven and Earth and any residences in between, is reassuring me in simple imperatives: "You'll be all right! You'll keep Paris in your heart, and you'll always be French."

FIFTEEN

WORK, LIKE EVERYTHING else in America, had another face, another pace. And my parents had to adapt, like all immigrants before them. The Singer sewing machine in my father's Los Angeles garment shop looked the same as the one he had used in Paris but he swore it was ten times faster. Our name, too, took an American shortcut and became Miller. To keep from being depersonalized, to preserve his sense of self, my father went against the rules and smoked a pipe at work, bought Irish Sweepstakes tickets to fantasize freedom, and enjoyed every day of the slack season, when he could read and take walks to his heart's content. He was proud, though, that his work allowed my mother to stay home for a few years, taking care of my little sister and feeding us all good meals.

And that little sister grew up with immigrant parents and, briefly, with a much older sister who left home at seventeen. As Anne-Marie grew into an adult, she was neither fully American nor intrinsically European. But she drew her own complete individualism from her love of books—her family legacy. In her twenties she would begin her continuing career as a reference librarian.

When she returned to work, my mother had to change trades. Though she had been a skilled worker in the French knitting industry, she could no longer be a bobbin winder because American knitting machines were round. She became a low-paid finisher in a garment shop, sewing buttons and hems. She was paid by the piece, as was my father, so both of them had to work fast. Work days were long and stressful. But my mother enjoyed chatting and especially swapping recipes with Chicanas, Black Americans, and other immigrant Jewish women. My mother never ceased to wonder at the resourcefulness and ingenuity of poor women, and her cooking repertoire grew with every new minority represented by the workers in her shop. We enjoyed the diversity of American food inspired by poverty.

IN 1965 MY FATHER, prompted in part by the desire to find out what happened to Madame Marie and Monsieur Henri, is the first of our family to make a return trip to France.

He comes back with disturbing news: Madame Marie is in a convalescent home, unable to recognize anyone, and Monsieur Henri, now in a wheelchair, lives in Spartan conditions in a spare room of the otherwise comfortably furnished small-town merchant's house of one of his daughters.

The cottage (which Madame Marie had bought for Monsieur Henri's legal wife to occupy during her occasional interludes of partial sanity until her death, and which, after this first wife's death, she herself had at last been able to enjoy as the fully legal wife of Monsieur Henri) has been sold by his children—

and now, the elderly husband and wife have lost their home, their possessions, and each other's daily company . . . how unbearable a report!

My father describes what joy his visit brought Monsieur Henri, and how much Monsieur Henri wanted to talk about Madame Marie. We now have an address and of course we will write to him.

THE GRIM REPORT haunts me. I feel guilty and powerless: when I needed them, Madame Marie and Monsieur Henri were there for me, but when they were in need, I was not there.

Now all I can do is to write a long letter, send photos of my new family — my husband and two small children. Monsieur Henri answers with great warmth. He also corresponds with my parents. His "progress report" on Madame Marie is not encouraging. Not only does she no longer recognize him, but she who had been the soul of kindness now has fits of irrational meanness. Monsieur Henri feels helpless and terribly misses her as she used to be when she was his inseparable life companion. Finally, he announces that it's over: she has died without reverting back to her old self. Now he seldom leaves his daughter's home; there is no point in his going anywhere.

In November of 1967, he writes: *You can't imagine the pleasure it gave me to see your father again, it took me back to 30 years ago and it will be the same if, as you hope and as I also hope, I have the pleasure of seeing you again and of holding you in my arms before starting that great and ultimate journey that cannot be much longer delayed (since last July I entered my 89th year) So then??. . . .*

I think of Monsieur Henri a good part of each day. I wish I had the money to visit him.

Unexpectedly, luck is with me. I get a part-time teaching job, my first, teaching one French language class for which I will be paid $1000. Christmas vacation will more or less coincide with that of my graduate studies schedule. I long to go to Paris, then get on a train to visit Monsieur Henri. "Do it!" my husband urges me. "Use your teaching money; the children and I will manage. If you don't go, you'll regret it."

And so I go.

FROM PARIS, a train has taken me to Monsieur Henri, and my feet have brought me to the front door of a little house. It's the kind the French call "coquettish," meaning that the most has been made of a small-to-average space of undistinguished architecture which now radiates a smugly bourgeois sense of fullness and orderly well-being—quite a contrast to the loge that our concierges had occupied in my childhood!

What a solemn moment! I hold my breath, then knock at the wooden door. A gruff, familiar male voice invites me: "Come in, it's open!" I push the door: a few feet away, against the wall of the entry, Monsieur Henri rises from his wheelchair like Lazarus. I rush to embrace him before I can speak so I can hold him from falling or disappearing prematurely into ghosthood. Something of an invisible Roman pillar, of an ancient tree from the time of the Gauls grows in my arms and strengthens them, so we somehow hold each other up, the grieving widower and his prodigal spiritual daughter.

As I follow Monsieur Henri wheeling himself into the dining/living room filled with well-cushioned dark wooden furniture, I hear the ringing of a distinctive clock. It sets off an alarm through every artery of my heart, every vein in my brain. Dulled for decades into deep memory, an identical twin of that ring awakes my suddenly fully sensory body! Even before I look up to see Madame Marie's antique wall-clock, I know it to be that same loved and dreaded regulator of my childhood days. How terribly physical memory is! Somewhere in the regions of my heart and my stomach, I had stored the hushed ringing of that clock through eighteen years of living. Now it has popped up like a Swiss clock's wooden cuckoo forgotten between hours. Monsieur Henri noticed and was moved. "Yes, that's right," he sighed. "My poor Marie's clock! You remembered it."

We now had a couple of hours to ourselves before his daughter would come from the store to serve us lunch. He led me to his bedroom—something between a servant's quarters and a prisoner's cell. A cot covered by a plain beige blanket, a wooden chair, and a homely pine dresser were the only furnishings. Even the sole window was of modest size. It all looked uncomfortably anonymous, as if it had housed a long succession of polite boarders whose names and personalities got blurred in their landlord's memory.

Monsieur Henri first wheeled his chair to the dresser on the left, then reached to take down his only personal memento. He came back to hand me an old identification card of Madame Marie, complete with a photograph from her early fifties (just the way I remembered her!) "That's all I have left of her," he told me, "since my children divided up the proceeds of the sale of our cottage, as well as the furniture, the dishes, even the photograph albums." He sighed: "Luckily, though, no one could take away from us our most important possession: the double plot named "Briard-Chotel," in the Cemetery of St. Maur des Fossés near Paris. That was my wedding gift to her, just as she wanted it, with maintenance 'in perpetuity.' As soon as I lie by her side again, neither one of us will need anything else."

As he said that, my mind's eye went back to my childhood and stared at their big peasant bed which took up half their loge space. It was covered by a fluffy goose-feather comforter, itself covered by a crocheted multi-colored bedspread.

That bed, along with the Singer sewing machine, the antique wall-clock, and the small drop-leaf table, made up their home. However compact its nesting size, that home had managed to shelter others, especially in times of need.

Now, sitting across from that big-hearted burly man whom I loved like the grandfather I never knew, I took great comfort in looking at the small photograph of "my" Madame Marie. Her thick brown hair, pulled back but still covering half her ears, framed a fine oval-to-round face with piercing brown eyes under raised and curved eyebrows, a hint of a smile and of a double chin above a short neck adorned by a gold chain and a pendant. The half-circle collar of her dark print dress allowed her pendant exactly the display space it needed against her bare throat. Clever Madame Marie: she made everything work out, made everything fit! I couldn't stop looking at her I.D. photo: she was so beautiful; everything in her radiated kindness, clarity, and simple dignity.

Monsieur Henri talked and talked about her, so glad to talk of her. First, about the last terrible years. He needed to tell me everything, some of which I already knew from my father, but which I could hear again and again, however painful, because it evoked her struggle and I so wished I had been near her then.

Contrary to a fairy tale, this story started with: "At first they were happy," and ended with grief and separation.

Henri told how happy his Marie had been in the little cottage—with him staying home at all hours of the day, and her garden and her little dog to attend to and give her pleasure. She sewed to her heart's content, at last only for herself and her husband: curtains, tablecloths, pillow cases, dish towels, and, of course, all her dresses. The two of them would take pleasant walks together in the countryside. But after a few good years, trouble came. His legs remembered their old World War I injury, got weaker and weaker until they refused to hold him up any longer; he had to sit in a wheelchair; he could no longer help his wife in the house or the garden, and he could no longer run errands for her.

Trouble attracts trouble, so on their occasional visits, his daughters would squabble over the future division of the cottage's old furniture and painted porcelain dishes: the passage of time had turned those modest objects into valuable antiques. Marie would not say anything but Henri could tell she was upset. Even after the visits were over, she stayed despondent for days, though Henri and the dog did their best to cheer her up.

Finally, following those disturbing visits, Marie started on a strange new routine. She would take an empty suitcase and, without a word, would leave the house to start walking on the road. Henri could not follow her so he would call the sheriff's office. They would send someone to fetch her, someone who would be gentle about it.

The policeman would catch up with her on the road and politely ask: "Where are you going, Madame Marie?" No answer. After the question was repeated several times, she would finally answer: "I'm going." And she would keep on going. The policeman would follow, ask the same question, get the same answer. He would then warn her: it was dangerous for an older woman to walk by herself. No response; she kept going. The routine would end with one other question, which was kept in reserve till the others had been exhausted. After a while on the road, the policeman would finally ask: "And Monsieur Henri? Who will take care of Monsieur Henri, alone in the house?" At that, Marie would sigh, her pace would slow down, and without a word she'd turn around, walk back to the cottage, throw her suitcase on the bed, proceed to open it, probably in view of putting back its contents in the closet and the chest of drawers—but, to her astonishment, the suitcase was empty. With a start, she seemed to wake up from a somnambulist dream, and for a while she was herself again.

With time, though, the runaway episodes became more frequent, and Henri, more worried and frustrated. When his daughters understood what was going on, they put Madame Marie away in an institution. They pressured Henri to sell the cottage and move in with his eldest daughter, a suggestion he fought as long as he could, holding on to the hope that Marie would be able to come back. That was not to be. She simply got worse in the institution till she couldn't recognize him or anyone. She who had been so good-natured became sharp, even mean with nurses, thereby losing more and more of her already limited freedom until she was treated as a nuisance or, at best, when she was heavily sedated, as a human object sitting on a chair staring vacantly into space. It became sheer agony to visit her. At last she died on May 29, 1966, and she is now buried in their double plot.

He kept looking at the photo on her identification card. "She was a good woman; she didn't deserve such an end!" After a long silence, he said with a smile: "But she at least got a decent burial, and as soon as I join her, she'll never, for all eternity, be alone again." Then, as we were called in to lunch, he was about to put the I.D. card back on the dresser when he changed his mind and handed it to me: "Take it. This is all I have but it rightly belongs to you: you were her real daughter!"

I was vastly moved by this double blessing—baptized as her "real" daughter and offered her photo, but I couldn't bear the thought of depriving him of the only object of Madame Marie that actually belonged to him. I protested, but he refused to go back on his offer. I then thought of a compromise: I would take it, but as soon as I was back in the States, I would have the photo enlarged and reproduced and would send him a copy. That was all right with him: we had a deal. I took the photo and we went into the dining room for lunch, where much was made over him and we were served a delicious rabbit stew. The clock struck its half-hour, its hour, as it used to in the concierge's loge, and I eagerly tried to store its clear and joyous sound deep in the recesses of my memory underground, hoping I'd later be able to call it back at will.

ON MY RETURN to California, I immediately duplicate Madame Marie's photo. Now there are three copies: one on Monsieur Henri's dresser, one on mine and the third one just in case. . . . A rich correspondence establishes itself between Monsieur Henri and me whereby I learn more about Madame Marie's life, about Monsieur Henri's youth and his dreams of working at a job that requires wearing a uniform, which always elicits respect. He also describes attending Emile Zola's funeral, and witnessing the reinstatement of Captain Dreyfus, whose demotion as an alleged traitor to France by virtue of his Jewish birth had caused one of the most serious schisms in modern French society. I tell him more about myself, my poet-husband, the two children who fill out our lives, my Ph.D. dissertation on a little-known French woman poet of the early sixteenth century. — We love each other's letters and show them off.

In the summer of 1968, I have great news for him: my husband was awarded a poetry prize and has been granted a leave of absence for the following spring, which we will all spend in France. At last, Monsieur Henri will get to meet my family and we'll have a wonderful time together.

The answer to that letter is joyful but cautious: he hopes, oh how he hopes that he will last that long!

As the months pass, his letters get shorter, his handwriting more strained, harder to read; he complains of how long it takes him to write a letter. In my panic, I write longer letters, full of hope and encouragement: we'll see each other soon, soon. . . .

But in November, letters come with another handwriting, signed by his daughter and son-in-law. Henri is hospitalized, struggling to hang on to life. My parents and I write more frequently. His family's last letter to us, in that dreaded envelope bordered in black, informs us that he had our letters read to him to his very last day, that they were pleased and impressed with the strength of his overseas support, and that we are welcome to their home when next we come to France.

Our correspondence file is now complete.

EIGHTEEN YEARS LATER, in the summer of 1985, which is my sixth summer as a widow, I make my fifth return trip to France. I go on two pilgrimages: to my wartime village in Vendée, and to Madame Marie's native village in Lorraine.

On the first one, I am accompanied by my son, Daniel (whose middle name is Sergei, for his cousin). Alone in a train coach, we are seated across from each other for a four-hour ride to Nantes in Brittany, where we'll rent a car to drive to Vendée. He knows a few snatches caught on the run but has no overview of the whole story. I start telling him. He is fascinated, asks questions to clarify or unravel the complex knots of the narrative. Along the same route that took me, Cécile, Suzanne, and Paulette out of danger into a life of false identity, the now-strange story unfolds, taking all four hours of our train ride.

HERE WE ARE at last, parking our car in the back of
the church at Chavagnes-en-Paillers. I'm in a daze: just on the
other side, a block from the church entrance is that stone house
where, as a child, I exchanged one identity for another!

I would have loved to find Madame Raffin again, but no one
in my Paris circle has heard from her in two years and rumors
are that she died. Still, for old times' sake, I would like to see the
old house across from the seminary, a little way from an outdoor
Calvary Cross. Daniel is hungry. He'll go into a bakery behind
the church where I'll join him as soon as I've satisfied my urge
to look at the house on rue du Calvaire.

Long-stored memory takes over. My feet lead me to a familiar door. The top half is glassed and covered from the inside with
a lace curtain. I turn to the bell on the right; to my astonishment
its label says: Marie Raffin. Has the family not gotten around to
taking her name down after the funeral? or could it be, could it
really be that she is still alive and somewhere in the house?

As I peer through the lace curtain, an old lady with very
white hair hobbles to the door, a cane in each hand. No doubt
about it: that fine aristocratic face is that of Madame Raffin! But
oh dear what shall I say not to startle the frail old lady? She's
already at the door, opens it ajar, looks askance when . . . out
of my mouth come the most unlikely words I could utter to
someone I last saw when I was ten: "I come from far in time
and space." For the sake of better communication, I then add: "I
come from California and I lived here during the War." Without a second's hesitation, Madame Raffin opens the door wide,

cries: "Odette!" and welcomes me in. I point to my left and say: "Here used to be a table and on that table a round mirror tray and on that tray some glass swans frozen in their mirrored reflections . . . and here was a chair . . . and here. . . ." "Yes, that's what was there," said Madame Raffin. "But in the fifties we changed everything—put new wallpaper, moved the furniture upstairs, and turned the two front rooms into a grocery store, which we ran until we retired."

With an on-going comparative commentary on every detail we passed, we slowly crossed the house from the glassed front door to the back door, through which fumes from the cooking stove used to escape. I would say: "Here there used to be . . ." and Madame Raffin would proudly update me: "And then, we modernized the kitchen. . . ."

It was as if this reunion had been long planned and properly announced, as if we had each rehearsed our part of the catch-up dialogue, as if I had last been here just a couple of years ago instead of forty years earlier as a ten-year-old girl.

OUT THE BACK door, the view of the garden had barely changed. The narrow middle path that led to the dovecote was still the dividing line for beds of flowers and vegetables which arranged themselves neatly on either side of it. The well, though, now resembled a collector's item. It had been solidly covered and decorated with two oxcart wheels—silent witnesses to a long-gone rural past when empty buckets were lowered by pulley deep into the well and were lifted back to the surface filled with water, and slow oxen, pulling wooden carts, would find their way to the shop of Monsieur Raffin, carpenter and wheelwright.

As for the pigeons, Madame Raffin explained that they were really her oldest son Jacques's special love and that the dovecote had stayed empty during his entire army career, when he mostly lived abroad. Now that he had retired from the army and come back to Chavagnes, he had restocked it with pigeons and came every day to take care of them, and, at the same time, to pay her a visit.

After we had seen everything, we went back to sit at the table in the remodeled kitchen with its brown paisley-patterned wallpaper and its simple white and light-aqua storage cabinets, its electric stove and electric coffeemaker. The traditional oilcloth with its pictures of huge red roses on a cream-colored background made me continue to see double: this current décor was superimposed on the older, wartime one with its soldier photos of our fathers on the mantelpiece, Grandfather Raffin making miniature toys and furniture for us out of reeds and acorns, the grandmother warming her feet in the coal stove's open oven, and the six of us children running all over the house, inside and outside.

The next seven hours were pure bliss. When I told her that I had heard rumors she was no longer alive, Madame Raffin said she wasn't surprised: her health had been very precarious for the past few years, she had been in and out of the hospital, fearing each time she went in that she might not come out alive. And now, she had just returned from a particularly long stay in the hospital and was still very weak. But she couldn't believe her good luck, that I had come from so far to ring her doorbell, and here I was in her kitchen! I felt just as lucky.

After a short while of catching up on the last forty years, we settled into the past and reminisced about those critical months I had spent in her family. Again, our conversation was low-keyed and natural. Totally attuned to each other and our memories, it was as if we played a long, leisurely who-cares-who-wins ping-pong match. "Do you remember when . . . ?" one asked and, yes, the other remembered. Except for one incident: the time she made us crouch under the back door-frame as we watched a German plane fly so low and so near that our ears hurt and we covered them. What I remembered was that we feared a bomb would drop . . . but it didn't, and nothing happened. "Oh yes, Odette. Something did happen: a bomb fell in the lot behind our pigeons! You don't remember?" "No, I don't. Suzanne remembers, but no matter what I do, I can't."

When my son rang the bell, he was quite astonished to see me open the door and lead him into the kitchen where he met this very pretty and frail elderly lady, a live illustration of the story he had just fully heard during our train ride to Nantes. She was delighted to meet him, and he joined our endless talk at the kitchen table.

Throughout the afternoon, other relatives came in to check on her. Jacques appeared and was visibly moved to see me sitting at his mother's table. Later, Jean's wife and son came by. We talked, took photos. Finally, there were only four of us: Madame Raffin and I, my son, and her grandson, to whom an explanation had to be given as to who I was and what his grandmother's role in the life of four Jewish girls had been (at which revelation he was stunned into pride and admiration). Our young ones talked as we continued riding our stream-of-consciousness memories.

At one point, Madame Raffin reached out behind her on a counter for a box of loose photographs and startled me by finding without any hesitation several old photographs from those war years. All four of us girls in neat light-colored dresses, with wide bows of white ribbons in our hair. I was very moved. Yet I would be even more so after she commented on the photo: "I had two sons, and my sons had sons, but during the war God gave me four little girls!"

From Chavagnes-en-Paillers, where my memories were mostly sweet, I had to go to the town of St. Fulgent, where my life had been more turbulent, but where I had spent more time both with my mother and just on my own until more than two months after Paris was liberated.

ST. FULGENT! How incredible! Here I am facing the very church where I feared God the Father, worshipped my favorite and gentlest of saints—Little St. Theresa, St. Francis of Assisi, the Virgin Mary and her carpenter husband Joseph—and heard virulent anti-Semitic sermons!

The church plaza has barely changed. The hotel is at the site of the old café-bar where the men would hang out after church "in my days." The bus used to stop here with passengers and packages. This is where my mother, passing as a Parisian Catholic widow born in Prague and living in La Basse Clavelière with her illegitimate daughter, would periodically come to hand-deliver her mail to the bus driver. She would try to shield the name of the intended recipient of letters and occasional food packages to Germany—a certain George Melszpajz, at Stalag II-B, a prisoner-of-war camp in Hammerstein, Pomerania—but curious stares and gossip still prevailed. Given her apparent history of attraction to soldiers, it was generally believed that this "Melzpajz," with such an Alsatian or German name, must be a lover of Marie Petit, a single mother still in her thirties.

The City Hall still faces the church, but it has been rebuilt and is now part of a whole modern complex on a campuslike, manicured space that includes a supermarket, "low-rise" apartment houses, rows of tiny single houses separated from one another by little fenced yards, a children's playground, and cozy bench-and-trees areas for the older folks.

How strange to be actually, physically, walking in the double of my inner but clearly memorized town! Like a pilgrim, I make the rounds of the few streets and alleys as well as the City Hall, and a little farther, the public school. I go down the main street where I pass shops I remember: those of the jeweler, the pharmacist, the watchmaker whose window also displays formal photographs taken at celebrations of a Communion, a wedding, a baptism. Then there are some shops where my memory fails me: was there a grocery there? is that where we bought stationery? Did we buy stationery? We must have, as my mother was always writing letters and I had homework to do. Or did they give us notebooks at school?

As I've felt every time I've gone back to Paris, I don't mind seeing new buildings but I want to know exactly what has changed, what has remained the same, so my memory can make adjustments: that was then; this is now. The pain of exile is not knowing if what you remember still stands or if it's been replaced, and if so, by what.

To catch up, to get re-oriented, I go into City Hall and ask to see the mayor. To my surprise, the current mayor is an elegantly dressed woman with very genteel manners. When I explain that forty years ago I lived in La Basse Clavelière with my mother, she calls her aunt from a nearby office and asks her to join us.

Feeling like an object of curiosity, a relic of the past, I tell them that before I go back to the village, I'd like to know what happened to the villagers whom I remember vividly except for most of their names. The then-old ones, of course, have long died, so I ask about the then-children and their parents. I'm told that our landlords' family has fared very badly. Every kind of disaster seems to have hit them: fatal or crippling illnesses, accidents, birth defects, and other serious problems darkening the family history from generation to generation. Horrified at this litany of troubles, I remember that the family was connected by marriage to nearly every household in the village. I also remember that they believed my mother had put a curse on them because they had put our lives in danger when they suspected us of being Jewish. My mother, back in Paris, had simply laughed at such a show of superstition and went on with her life. She had probably not even bothered to answer the priest's plea to take away the curse. But what if, oh dear, what if the family took my mother's lack of response as a sign that the curse continued to be in effect?

When I finally have the courage to ask what happened to that boy who had led all the village children in an unsuccessful attempt to drown me, there is an awkward silence. The two women look at each other as if they suddenly have remembered something they would rather forget. "What happened to him?" I worry. "Oh," sighs the aunt, "there was the drowning." They both sigh. For a moment, I think I have forgotten how to breathe and will never again remember. "Drowning? What drowning?" I ask anxiously. The answer comes slowly, sadly: "Not long after you left, he was asked to watch a small boy, but instead he pushed him into the well and drowned him. He was never quite right in the head, you know!" Actually, I didn't know that then; he seemed like all the others. And what about his brother who lived with his parents behind us? "Oh, he's fine. He's become the keeper of the folkways of the village. You missed a wonderful exhibit done by a folklore group; we'll give you the catalogue of it. Your old neighbor was very helpful." "Does he have a family?" Again, a sad look. "No. Girls were afraid to marry him; in those days, people thought there was surely a curse on such a family."

I THANKED THEM and finally made my way to the village, past the low-walled cemetery. On either side of the paved road, where cultivated fields used to be, there were now little stucco houses, one after another, all equally uninteresting.

Finally, at the entrance to the village: an unfamiliar, new statue of the Virgin (to ward off the curse?). Behind her, to the right, is the way to "my house." The house has been remodeled, gaining modern, colorless uniformity at the expense of its old rural charm. But I see through it as one sees past the powdered and rouged, wrinkled middle-age face of an old friend one hasn't seen for years, all the way past to a youthful smile and lively eyes.

The village has lost its spatial and architectural integrity. The traditional plain-style Vendéen houses still left standing are those occupied only by the very old. In time, they too will inevitably be made to fit into the dominant suburban architecture, as generic and impersonal here as anywhere else.

The road was paved just a few years ago, I heard, and the forest recently pushed back from this new civilization.

La Basse Clavelière is no longer an integral peasant village, with the sound and smell of farm animals, the sight of vegetable gardens being attended, of children playing in the tobacco or wheat fields, hiding behind trees or climbing branches to the tops, screaming with excitement. Now it has an awkwardness because it is no longer that earthy village but it hasn't yet achieved what it seems to be aspiring toward: to become a residential annex to St. Fulgent, whose new prosperity depends no longer on agriculture but on a shoe factory.

Sign of an ideal marriage of the old and the new: towering over the village houses is an industrial-size silo with the name "Larrivé" in large letters, identifying a local native whose ancestors raised chickens and fed them on home-grown grain. I was told about him and how he has become an important manufacturer of chicken feed produced, milled, and packaged in the St. Fulgent area but exported far and wide. His workers, like those at the shoe factory, are very proud to have left farming behind, to have become salaried, with benefits and rights and supermarkets like city folks.

Startled by a voice asking my back: "You're Odette Petit, aren't you?" I turn to see a short man guarded by a tiny dog. "Yes, how did you recognize me?" "Well, the word got around that you were in town. And when I noticed a woman my age looking at your old house, I figured it must be you. Will you come in and have a drink?" Of course I would. I was delighted my old neighbor was so friendly.

As soon as I entered the house, I immediately recognized a handsome grandfather's clock with the maker's signature in clear old-fashioned handwriting on the lower part of the face. It filled me with joy to see it again, especially as I had forgotten it and so had not longed for it. When I admired it, my host stood on a chair to explain its mechanics, opened the glass case to the clock's face, and wound it up with a key.

He was terribly pleased: "Some years ago, antique dealers from the city started spreading like an epidemic around here, going from village to village, offering to buy any wooden furniture. The older it was, the higher the purchase price. I sold some of mine, like other people, but I stopped short at the grandfather's clock. I wouldn't part with it. No way. No matter how much they offered. After that, I started collecting the old stuff, whatever was left of it. Here, look, do you remember this? an oxen yoke? Do you remember the oxcarts?"

Did I ever remember! For the next few hours, we played a memory game: do you remember this? yes, and that? yes, and

then there were all those silver strips we collected once to decorate the Virgin's altar during the Month of Mary. Oh yes! I remember those!

He asks how my mother is—says she was a wonderful
woman, and I should be sure to send her his special greetings.
I tell him both my father and my mother are doing well. He is
startled: "I thought you didn't have a father!" I answer a quick
"I do" and move on to another subject—Madame Raffin, who
wants to visit the village where she grew up but which she hasn't
seen for years. "We'll be bringing her here by car in a couple
of days." "Oh, it will be good to see her again. Such a lady! You
come back with her, and I'll take you to my wine cellar for a
taste of my best home-made wines, better than anything you'd
buy in town."

All week long, in and around St. Fulgent, I retrace the steps
of my rural childhood—now all on paved roads, though my
feet remember on which of them it felt so good to be inside
slippers-lined wooden shoes with their pointed "prows" that so
effectively cut a path through slushy mud.

By arrangement of the mayor, I make my round of visits
to the town elders. They are proud of St. Fulgent having caught
up with modern times, though they feel the town has paid a
high social price for it. In the old rural days, they explain, farm
women were satisfied with their important role in the running
of the farm, the house, the family—but now that they leave
home every day to work in the factory and have a salary of their
own, they have become very demanding. They neglect their children, their husbands, their houses, and the church.

The elders obviously don't like to talk about the war years. They quickly dismiss it all with a brief: "Those were dark days indeed!" though, to my astonishment, the town librarian tries to "set the record straight." "To be fair," he says "we have to admit that our German soldiers, those who set up camp around here, were actually quite well-mannered."

W E   F U L F I L L our promise to Madame Raffin: we have a car; we will drive her anywhere she wishes. First, it's La Basse Clavelière, the *pays* where she grew up and where she is greeted with great respect and treated by my old neighbor to some extraordinary home-made wine.

Next, she leads us to the nearby village of La Rabatelière, where she met her husband at the local pilgrimage spot. It's a full-scale reproduction of a rococo tower overlooking statues of shepherds, a boy and a girl, kneeling in adoration to an apparition of the Virgin Mary. I suddenly remember going there with a Catholic youth group supervised by unusually joyful nuns. Madame Raffin giggles as she retells the story of meeting her husband. "We used to come here on Sundays after church, hoping to meet boys from other villages. And that Sunday, as a bunch of us girls climbed the narrow staircase to the top of the tower, a bunch of boys were coming down. There was no room for all of us, so we somehow tumbled to the bottom of the stairs together—and there he was, a handsome boy, as nice as could be, from another village. We just took one look at each other— and that was that." She giggled as she must have done then, as a very pretty young woman of marriageable age.

The meals in the St. Fulgent hotel dining room are rich and delicious, but we need to save money, so my son and I shop for picnic food in a little grocery store.

The owner is a cheerful woman about my age. As we are trying to decide what to buy, I notice her staring at me.

The second time we come into the store, she surprises me by saying, point-blank: "You look familiar. Aren't you my age? Weren't you in my class at the convent school?" Astonished, I tell her yes and my name is Odette Petit. Excited, she remembers me and immediately checks out my memories of teachers, classmates, events. She's pleased I indeed have some memories, even though I live so far away and this is my first return trip to Vendée, so she generously gives me back long-forgotten names. She also remembers that my mother pulled me out of the school when the nun punished me by locking me up in a dark closet all day—and that after that I went to the public school. "Too bad you missed an exhibit of St. Fulgent history put on by the Folklore Society, but if you go to the watchmaker up the block and tell him your story, he'll show you his collection of historical photographs of St. Fulgent. And there you'll see some school pictures taken in 1944; though maybe by then you were already in the public school. And do come back," she warmly insists. "I'll tell everybody you're here."

I do as she suggests, and in fact I am able to order a set of wartime photos of interest to me from the watchmaker/photographer.

Unfortunately, though, we are leaving the next day. My old classmate insists then that we come to her that very evening.

After the business day is over, she and her husband eat their dinner in a little back room. She invites us to come and join them.

A SUFFOCATING heaviness overtook me on that last day. I had introduced myself as the Odette Petit some of the townspeople and villagers still remembered. So again, forty years later, I was passing under my false identity as the Catholic illegitimate daughter of a woman who had migrated from Prague to Paris. After the initial sense of oddness, it had felt all right. The common memories suddenly shared with my peers brought us the joyous gift of a free, barefoot childhood mutually remembered. But as I was about to leave, I could not stand the thought of leaving as Odette Petit; I wanted, needed, to disclose my true identity. I knew I could not, literally could not, leave St. Fulgent without telling at least someone the truth about us. I finally determined that, no matter what, that evening I would tell the grocers.

On this last afternoon in St. Fulgent, it seems appropriate to conclude my visit by going to the cemetery.

The dead describe themselves with few words: their name, date of birth, date of death. The living who still remember them add plaques, stating the dead's relationship to themselves: mother, brother, husband, niece. Some of the graves have flowers —fresh ones for the newly dead, artificial ones for those buried long ago.

Here, the names repeat themselves with slight variations: some are of my time, some are of classmates already dead, some

I don't remember at all. Lording it over the entire cemetery of mostly small-to-medium-size tombs is one of those sepulchral chapels, like the ones that heavily populate Paris's Père Lachaise Cemetery. It is the family sepulcher of Comte Paul Constant Legras de Grandcourt, that fine and upright mayor of St. Fulgent who had saved us from the Gestapo. He died in 1945. I stop to pay my respects.

As in fairy tales, during my time of greatest danger I had three rescuers. Two were poor women of illegitimate birth — Marie Chotel of Lorraine and Moïsette-Marie Raffin of Vendée. One was an enlightened man of the old aristocracy — the Comte de Grandcourt. The fact that at ten I was still alive and was able to return to Paris with my mother and that both of us were home when my father returned from five years in captivity, that miracle was due to those three people: Marie Chotel, Moïsette-Marie Raffin and Comte Paul de Grandcourt — all three growing up in solid French farm country. How does one repay a debt of life granted beyond early childhood?

OUR LAST EVENING has come. We're leaving early the next morning. I've run out of time: my Vendée pilgrimage is done for the time being, except for the dinner at the grocers.

There, we are received with great hospitality. The back room is pleasantly cozy, the modest meal delicious, and the local wine exquisite. At the end of a lovely evening of catching up with forty years of one another's lives, I finally say: "I can't leave St. Fulgent without telling somebody the truth. You've been so good to us, so I'll tell you." I catch my breath and plunge into the truth: "My mother and I were living here on false identity so the Germans wouldn't send us to concentration camps as Jews. And my mother was not an unwed mother; she was married to my father, who was a prisoner of war in Germany and came back after the war."

A brief silence. Then my hostess said very warmly: "You were not the only one. We found out a few years ago that there was another Jewish girl in St. Fulgent and others in other burgs. They've recently come back and told us, like you. But you know, St. Fulgent has changed a great deal in forty years, and people are sorry for the anti-Semitism of those days!"

Astonished I ask: "What happened? What caused people to have a change of heart?" She says: "Television." "Television?! How?" I ask. "Well," she answers, "we saw those grim documentaries on concentration camps and also a televised production of Anne Frank's *Diary*." She thinks it over a moment, then sighs, as if in her turn she is unloading a heavy regret: "We didn't know THEN that what we said against Jews could lead to THAT!"

What a comforting way to leave Vendée!

I THANK MY SON for having helped me revisit my past and assure him I can now go on my own for the second part of my pilgrimage. He goes his way, and I go off to Lorraine. I will see for myself the sites of Madame Marie's past: her birthplace of Vanifosse, and the nearby towns of St. Dié and Epinal, where she married and worked before moving to Paris to become a concierge and live with Monsieur Henri.

I take up headquarters in Nancy, the capital of Lorraine (and of Art Nouveau!). I've come with a notebook and some copies of Monsieur Henri's letters in which he mentions Madame Marie's native village of Vanifosse.

I've never been here before and I know no one, but for some reason, I'm not worried; I'm sure everything will work out just right.

The modest hotel I find quite by chance is run by a family. At my first breakfast, the owners engage me in a conversation, discover the subject of my quest, and immediately are eager to cooperate. They bring out their most detailed map of the area with a view of pinpointing Vanifosse. To their surprise, it is not on the map, so they suggest I go to the Musée Lorrain or, across the street from it, to the Librairie Lorraine, the scholarly bookstore on the region's history and culture. There they should have the most complete maps of Lorraine.

I go first to the bookstore, tell my story, and ask if they can help me locate Vanifosse. Of the several Lorraine specialists present, none has ever heard of Vanifosse. In true scholarly style, old books are consulted, and finally the bookseller reports that in 1714 the village of Vanifosse had a population of "9 inhabitants and 1 boy" and officially belonged to the "commune" of Pair-et-Grandrupt in the district of St. Dié in the Vosges Mountains region. We consult the map and, although no mention is made of Vanifosse, there is at least Pair-et-Grandrupt!

The bookseller, about to close his shop for lunch, tells me that his wife has always dreamed of visiting California, especially San Francisco. Would I accept a lunch invitation at their home? Yes, of course.

On the way to lunch, I learn that my host's brother is a local priest who arranges outings to the Church of Domrémy for his parish's children. It turns out that he got his training in the Chavagnes-en-Paillers seminary. "Across the window from where I slept!" I exclaim, astonished at the sequence of coincidences.

To my added surprise, lunch with the bookseller's family takes place in a dining room furnished with that distinctive dark and heavy Vendéen wooden furniture of plain but comforting simplicity. We talk of San Francisco, American culture, and my quest for Madame Marie's past. Animated, opinionated, and very warm, they give me a crash course in Lorraine history and culture.

Was it a pilgrimage I was making, or was I again living out a fairy tale?

My notebook was filling up with names and addresses, invitations, book titles, and general advice from people I had just met and who were most eager to help. My last entries were made during my visit to the small Jewish Community Center of Nancy.

There I learned that, during the war, when the Nancy police were given the order to round up the Jews the following morning, they instead knocked at their doors in the middle of the night to warn them of the danger and urge them to hide. The only Jews who were taken that day were those who hadn't believed the policemen. I wonder what it means: were the Lorrains free of anti-Semitism or were they particularly hostile to the Germans who were obsessed with annexing them?

I have a stake in understanding the Lorrains, since they are Marie Chotel's people! I spend a great deal of time studying them in books, in the streets, in all public places. From all these sources, I learn the same thing: the Lorrains have a strong sense of being naturally connected to their family, their animals, their land, their community but, like all peasants and especially mountain folk, they value independent thinking, cleverness, resourcefulness. In the past, traditional Lorraine village houses combined a family area (three rooms and a kitchen) with partitioned spaces for the farm animals (a horse stable, a cow barn, or a sheep pen), all within the same set of exterior walls. Together, those houses faced the street with its gathering place at the well and the adjoining washing trough. At their backs extended a row of gardens, separated by very low walls and guarded by chicken and rabbits, an occasional cat or dog.

No wonder regional history has had so many stories of local communities sticking together, like their houses! A sign, too, of living in constant danger, so close to the mountainous frontier.

Among other reminders of military presence: numerous statues of Joan of Arc in full armor, on her horse, holding a banner, leading her troops to liberate the French kingdom from the English.

This is Joan's country: Joan the warrior, Joan the clever maid, Joan the pious, Joan the defender of France, the pride of Lorraine. Between Joan and the Virgin Mary, the country will be protected. Mary, though, doesn't go off to battle; she stays put, assuring protection of the home ground.

Doors to Madame Marie

ST. MARY IS very fond of heights. In the countryside, from her special niches above the houses' main entrances, true Queen of Heaven, she most courteously receives prayers and gives blessings of domestic peace. She stands on church steeples for a privileged view of approaching danger or of festive processions in her honor. Framed on museum walls, palms down in a gentle gesture, Our Lady of Lorraine, opening her blue coat like a hen her wings, draws into divine protection groups of small-scale assorted Christians whose clothing befits their particular centuries.

My hotel keepers, eager to help guarantee the success of my quest, take me to the most potent of all protective statues of Mary: that of the Virgin of the Hill of Zion. As are other such statues of the Virgin in this region, it is located on the hilltop, on the very spot where a banished pagan goddess was once worshipped.

We park the car and start to climb the hill. Everywhere, groups of people are bent over, gathering something, as if they are harvesting or gleaning. I'm told we are about to do the same: to find and collect tiny but sparkling stones spread on the Hill of Zion. My guides let me wonder for a moment, the better to startle me with the explanation: every night, jewels from the Virgin's crown fall and scatter on the hill; they will bring good luck to those who pick them up. I am handed a little tin box in which to collect my "jewels." I carefully select those that look the most like slivers of diamond. My good helpers add their catch to mine.

Later, I place my well-stocked tin can of crown jewels in

my purse with Madame Marie's photo: with this double protection, the last leg of my quest should be easy.

AS IN A FAIRY TALE, helpers appear along the road,
each with a specific task.

The rabbi at the Jewish Center insisted I contact an amateur historian of the Jewish Resistance in World War II, a retired
businessman who knew everybody. In a fairy tale, you follow
every instruction without question.

Entering the ex-partisan's study, I'm startled, no, more than
that, I'm slapped in the chest of memory by the prominent display of a familiar object: a cotton-cloth yellow star bearing the
word Juif. We talk. I tell my war story and about the Madame
Marie connection. He proudly tells me of his participation with
the Resistance in Lyon and shows me original material, posters,
newsletters—when again, I'm startled by what I see: a familiar signature—"Gleb"—affixed to a couple of powerful drawings
of a partisan caught by the Germans. Gleb: my father's painter
friend! Ah yes, I remember, he too was in Lyon! I ask if I may
have some Xerox copies made, to give to Gleb when I return to
Paris. "Of course, we'll arrange that, no trouble!" says my jovial
host. "You've asked the right person. I can arrange anything!"
This gives me the courage to ask if he can help me figure out
how I can get to the village of Vanifosse of the commune of Pair
et-Grandrupt in the district of St. Dié. "No problem! It will take
one phone call. I have a buddy who owns a men's clothing shop
in Epinal. He'll take time off to drive you." I have trouble believing that this will happen, but after he issues a very brief set of

orders—"You have to take this Californian lady to her rescuer's village"—he hands me the phone to hear his buddy's invitation: "My friend said I should drive you to your rescuer's village. Come by train to Epinal on Wednesday so you're at the store at one o'clock in the afternoon. I'll drive you."

I'm given the address and sent off with many astonishing stories, good cheers, and copies of Gleb's wartime drawings.

I *APPEAR* at the men's clothing shop at the appointed hour, and without hesitation I recognize Mr. Broda who was never described to me. I feel like a partisan on a special mission. He introduces me to his family as the "Californian lady looking for her rescuer's village," and we're off.

During our eighty kilometers on a main road, in between bouts of intense and futile efforts to visualize Vanifosse, I hear detailed descriptions of battles in Italy where somehow my driver ended up joining the Allies. I'm getting anxious about Vanifosse, especially as there is no sign predicting its imminent appearance.

When we feel we should be getting close to the commune of Pair et Granrupt, we stop to inquire. No, nobody knows of either the commune or the village. We go on, stopping at every village with the same inquiry, which elicits the same response. Finally, we see an elderly woman in front of a farm. Elders must know, we figure; we stop and ask, and yes, she does know Vanifosse: it's the second village from here. We have to be alert, though, she warns us, as villages don't show from the main road; they're hidden in the hills; all that can be seen of the village from the main road is its café. But we're in luck: the Vanifosse café,

in a renovated farmhouse, doubles as a gas station and so is easy
to spot.

Here it is! The café/gas-station near a couple of traditional
farmhouses. This is it! At least it is the visible part of Marie Chotel's native village which, in 1714, had boasted a population of "9
inhabitants and 1 boy." Surrounding the café, a serene and generous setting of dark green fields is broken up here and there by
a house and, in the distance, by bits of wooded areas. Behind the
café, gentle hills, and far behind them, gently sloped mountains.

To ascertain that the café area is indeed Vanifosse, we approach a woman in her mid-sixties, standing in her garden in
front of a huge farmhouse typical of the old-time architecture
of Lorraine. We explain our presence at her gate, ask if this is
Vanifosse. Yes, she says. Did she ever know the family of a Marie
Chotel? With a smile, she sets us straight: She can't be of any
use to us; as she isn't a native of Vanifosse, she wouldn't know.
She was young when her mother moved here from a nearby village as a widow with five children. Yes, the house is hers now.
She smiles again: Hard work, you know; had to pay off all the
brothers and sisters. She herself has two children. One of them,
a daughter, lives across the road with her own son, who is a railroad worker in Nancy.

When I tell the farmhouse proprietor that Marie Chotel
had saved Jews, she looks sadly into the distance and softly says:
"I saw Jews taken away in wagons. They were being treated like
animals. I cried to see that. They evacuated us, took everything.
Burned St. Dié . . ." But no, so sorry, she doesn't know any Chotels; good luck to us anyway. If we go in the café, they might be
able to help us. (I was later to learn that she herself was indeed

born a Chotel; but she didn't let on, of course, in a first conversation with strangers!)

We go into the café. The indoor décor is simple. A couple of men, one woman are at the counter; some others are sitting at plain, square tables. There is a lot of warm, good-humored talk, laughter. These people have always known one another, that's sure. We explain what we're looking for. The owner, a man in his thirties, fetches his mother from a back room. As she enters, I hear her say to her son: "A woman from America? Maybe it's my wartime godmother! She lives in Florida, but we haven't heard from her in a good thirty years." But as soon as she sees me, she realizes that, no, I'm not her American godmother from World War I. In that case, who am I and what do I want? Her son makes her understand. She then apologizes that her husband, the mayor of the commune, is bedridden with a serious illness. She and her son decide that I should come back the next day, between two and three, when I can catch the vice-mayor in City Hall.

By then, one of the men at the counter has gotten involved. "Marie Chotel," he muses. There is a Marie Chotel in the next village; she's seventy-eight. In fact, he continues, he's always heard his mother talk about Chotels. There are quite a few of them in the area. In the meantime, before we return to Epinal, we should come along and visit his mother and his aunt. We agree. He gets into his car, we get into ours, and we follow him up a road behind the café—a gentle, slight mountain road along which the village slowly unrolls against a cheerful, gentle, Edenlike landscape. So, that's how it goes. Just as we've been told: a café and a few farms down below; the rest of the village, its very core, hidden in the hills. As we go higher, houses are more modern, though still simple and solid; we see young people working in fields and gardens here and there; some children playing; cars at every house. It seems as though the whole hill is one family estate and that whoever passes on the village road is known to everyone.

Finally, we park in front of a plain house. A couple of small, tan dogs come barking. A few pups stare from their home-made kennel, near which we can see a variety of tools, old and relatively new.

An old man comes out, wearing an apron. We're asked to excuse the apron: he's preparing a soup. We tell him of Marie Chotel, he gets very interested, quickly summarizes the facts so he can think about it. (I'll continue to be struck by the quick intelligence of all the people I'll meet.) My "native guide" is very excited, eager to help me meet someone who could tell me about my Marie Chotel. Suddenly, he looks behind trees down the road and cheerfully announces: "Here is my mother!" Riding a motorcycle comes a middle-age woman in a plain raincoat.

Her husband, the man in the apron, goes into the kitchen to quickly check the soup—and rushes back to the conversation. Not a second's astonishment or hesitation in any of those people. The young man's mother gets right with it. Off her motorcycle, with many gestures: "Mais . . . la Yvonne! la Marie! la Toussaint! . . ." she thinks out loud. "Of course, they should know . . . they're Chotels! Well, let's see, your Chotel would be 102, and she left the region in 1919; had no children; last visit in 1935. . . ." She thinks for a moment and then quickly nears despair and just as quickly retreats from it: "Why didn't you come before? Some of the old ones who surely knew have died by now. . . . But still, everyone knows things from their parents. Someone would have to remember something . . ." She's obviously determined that, within the next five minutes, she'll figure it out. Her sister comes out and joins the problem-solving discussion: who is of what age? who has moved away from the village? who would be most likely to know?

While the two sisters talk to me with animated gestures, the aproned man tells my Jewish guide how in the last war he was made prisoner and the Germans thought he was Jewish because of his German-sounding name. They made him undress and eat lard. He passed both tests and came out Christian. Time is hurrying on and my Epinal clothier is getting itchy to get back to his business. It's hard to leave; everyone is so eager and warm, but I will see them the next day when I come to see the vice-mayor.

THE NEXT DAY, I come alone. From the train station at St. Dié, I take a taxi. The driver explains he was born in St. Dié of an Alsatian father who moved into the French Vosges to avoid being drafted into the German army. Many Alsatian men did the same. To this day, when he goes into Alsatian territory (a few kilometers away) he is called "the Frenchman," and this part of Lorraine is referred to as "France." He doesn't like it because it forces him to be denied his Alsatian ancestry.

At the café, I'm greeted like an old-timer. Customers are drinking draught beer or Mirabelle (a local plum vodka). My young friend isn't there to drive me back to his parents' home but has left word for the café owner to drive me to his farm, and from there, he'll take me back to his folks and later to the mayor's office. As we get to his farm, an old-fashioned one, looking into splendid landscapes in either direction, down into the valley and up into the mountains, we see him coming down a path with another couple of men and a child while a young woman, probably his wife, comes out of the house with a couple of adults and one child. No one seems to be alone around here! I get out of the café owner's car into the farmer's car and, as we go up the mountain village road, we chat as if we had known each other a very long time.

Here we are again! Dogs, pups, tools, a little girl, a bigger boy are outside. We go in—through a kind of storage garage, then a narrow door to a very small room crowded with furniture. Against the wall, in a bed: an old man dressed but lying under a blanket (he's very ill, they say; still he insists on sitting up to greet me; they let him do so and then persuade him to lie down again). On the table, a scale with two skinned and dressed rabbits, waiting to be weighed.

THE TWO SISTERS are fussing over me, agitated over how to give me good leads about the Chotels. I keep trying to say they mustn't regret if I can't find someone who knew her personally; I don't expect that. I just want to see the place and tell the village somehow what a good person Marie Chotel was. And maybe talk to the elders about how things were in the old days. "Oh, they were very different! And people didn't marry far, you know. . . . But as to that Marie Chotel, there's Valentine and Marie, and Bernadette, they should know; even if they were too young, they must have heard something. Forget Yvonne, though.

There's no point in asking her. She doesn't remember anything." And again she despairs: "Oh, why didn't you come earlier?" I feel guilty. "She's doing her best," says my driver. "Oh, my God, yes," the sisters agree. "And all the way from California! Have you eaten?" I'll get to that later, I explain, as I have to go to the mayor's office." The two sisters fuss. "Would you eat duck eggs? It will be quick and you'll be on time for your appointment." Before I can answer, they set to work together and in no time lunch is ready: two very sunny-side-up huge duck eggs, accompanied by freshly picked lettuce with vinaigrette, homemade bread, homemade cheese, good local red wine. And a coffee.

They have me describe my California town. I leave my address: if anyone from the village ever comes my way, please have them call on me. They shake their heads dreamily, no one ever goes that far and, even if they did, they would feel too uprooted, so far from home. I reassure them: French people really like the Bay Area. "It has pretty houses, gardens, cafés; even French bakeries, cheese stores, charcuteries, a French school, French restaurants and good wine." I tell them that quiche is popular. They're impressed by that, but mostly by the availability of French bread, good cheeses, good wine—all the way in California!

Time to go to the mayor. The mother kisses me good-bye. "You come back now!" I promise. The aunt kisses me. They treat me as if I've come to my mother's village.

On the way to City Hall, I tell my driver: "Coming from Vanifosse, no wonder Madame Marie was a remarkable person!"

He is very proud. He loves his village. "Farming doesn't pay anymore," he tells me. "But the young people have either stayed or
come back. They do whatever work they find in the area — in for-
estry, paper manufacturing, furniture factory — and they live in
their family houses or in new ones they've built for themselves.
It's a good life: no one's rich but we all have what we need. We
all know each other. And there's lots of space. And forests. And
rivers to fish in." Then, to answer my question, he puts Vanifosse
in its regional context: of the nine villages in the Commune of
Pair-et-Grandrupt, Vanifosse is the largest. It spreads over several
kilometers and with its 200 inhabitants, it accounts for half the
commune's population.

THE CITY HALL, like other local structures, occupies
one section of a larger whole — here a plain one-storey building
with a bare courtyard. The room on the left is the mayor's office.
The one on the right is the elementary school, for children up to
age eleven (older than that, they get driven or bused to St. Dié).

By the entrance, symmetrically arranged on either side of
the front door, are two plaques honoring the Vanifosse war dead.
On the left: 1914–1918; on the right: 1939–1945. The latter plaque
includes a category for the deported: three names, two of them,
"Lanzman" (an Alsatian name); then a list of the dead in battle
and of those shot in enemy reprisals.

We go in. A couple of other "clients" are lined up to get
documents. One man is walking away; he has just registered a
new child and answers someone in line that the mother is fine,
thank you, and back from the hospital after a week.

There are two officials. The one behind the desk is the city clerk as well as the schoolteacher. The other man, sitting on a chair near the desk is the vice-mayor and a local high school teacher. I make my request: are there any documents about a Marie Chotel born in the early 1880s? Without a word, the city clerk leaves the desk, goes behind me to access a shelf from which he pulls out a regular-size hard-cover notebook. As he walks back to the desk, he begins to read out loud, with slow and clear enunciation, the following words and dates that reso-nate in the sudden silence that greets them:

Marie Gabrielle Chotel, born July 24, 1883.

-mother:	Julie Chotel, 34, farm hand
-father:	unknown
-grandfather:	Jean-François Chotel, 87
-grandmother:	Marie Barbe Martin, 81
-married:	Feb. 7, 1903, at St. Dié
	to Henri Gonzales
-married:	April 30, 1913 at Epinal
	to Stanilas Henri Joseph Durant
-married:	Sept. 2, 1957 at St. Maur des Fossés (Marne)
	to Henri François Briard
-deceased:	May 29, 1966 at Neuilly sur Marnes

All present are quick to comment on oddities of the entry. One says: "She married for the third time at seventy-four? "Marie was born to a thirty-four-year-old unwed mother!" "Maybe the 'unknown father' was Julie's boss!" "Imagine: Julie's mother was forty-seven when she had her!" "No indication of Marie's divorce. Maybe her first two husbands died?" "No children?" As for me, all this matched the biographical information Monsieur Henri had given me in his letter, except for one important point: he had mentioned only one previous marriage, effectively merging the first two (out of ignorance or forgetfulness?).

My host is very pleased that my quest was successful: "You see, your trip wasn't for nothing!"

Later at the café, I tell the owner what we found at City Hall. He smiles dreamily, like the others. Mysteries of the past! Part of their village's past, and I've helped them regain a bit of it. In exchange, they've made me feel welcome in my godmother's village, and I will always love them for it.

I take rolls of film with pictures of Marie's school, her church, and her grandparents' tombstone in the adjoining cemetery; the hills, the mountains, and the main road of her childhood.

THE NEXT DAY, researching archives in Epinal, I come across the official certificate of Madame Marie's second marriage. It is dated April 30, 1913, and elucidates the question of her remarriage as a possible widow. Here it is:

April 30, 1913

Marriage certificate of Marie Chotel and Stanislas Durand,
City Hall of Epinal, Lorraine

Marie Gabrielle Chotel, divorced spouse of Henri Gonzales.
Cook. Officially registered as a resident of Besançon
and living in Epinal, 54 Quai des bons enfants; born
July 24, 1883, in Vanifosse

and

Stanislas Henri Joseph Durand; Café waiter. Officially
registered as a resident of Besançon and living in
Epinal, 54 Quai des bons enfants; born May 15, 1881,
at La Gaubretière (Vendée). Father: Amédée Durant,
died at La Gaubretière. Mother: Marie Brossard, no
profession, widowed, residing at La Gaubretière.
[witness for the bride: Virginie Chotel, her aunt, residing
at Neuvillers sur Fave.]

• divorced June 25, 1919, at the City Hall of Epinal.
• marriage dissolved by the court, June 26, 1920.

Now I've moved from a fairy tale to a detective story! Besides being astonished at her Vendéen connection by marriage
(La Gaubretière is near Chavagnes-en-Paillers!), I'm curious to

check her Epinal address. I decide to try my luck and soon find myself at 54 Quai des enfants.

On a quai indeed, I'm now facing a modest-looking hostelry, the Azur Hotel. I enter and ask the young receptionist if she knows the history of the hotel. No, she doesn't, but the owner of the photography shop next door is elderly and knows a lot of the local history. I go to see her and explain why I would like to know what this hotel was like in 1913. To my immense good luck, she does know and describes something I will later find confirmed in period guide books of the St. Dié archives: this used to be a wagon stop inn for horse-drawn public carriages. Here the horses could rest and be fed while passengers who were continuing on the trip could eat and even stay overnight in the hotel rooms. The lobby served as the waiting room for passengers. The café and the dining room were used by both overnight hotel guests and passengers waiting for the carriage.

I am giddy with excitement. It all falls into place: Madame Marie and her husband had an official address in Besançon but lived in this Epinal inn, where Marie was a cook and Stanislas was a waiter.

Now I remember other stories, those my mother had told me: that Stanislas (the waiter, who suddenly has a name) drank too much and when drunk was violent, that eventually, at the end of World War I, Madame Marie volunteered as a nurse for wounded French soldiers in the local hospital and there she met that large and wonderful man, Henri Briard, married with children, whose wife was in an insane asylum. They fell in love and, contrary to his advice, she arrived in Paris carrying a suitcase, knocked at his door, and moved in with him for the rest of her life. In June 1919, Stanislas must have registered for a divorce, the marriage to be formally dissolved by the court one year later. Marie would then live "in sin" with a married man from 1919 until 1957, when Henri's legal wife died and Marie became his second wife.

IT WAS EXHILARATING to be learning about Madame Marie's life! I could now visualize my godmother as a young girl going to her school, to her church, climbing the hill of her village to visit a friend. I could feel the excitement of the decisive moments of her youth: at fifteen leaving Vanifosse village to start adult life by entering domestic service in a wealthy St. Dié house, then marrying at nineteen (another domestic from the same household? the gardener for instance? someone from another house?), then. . . . (Here is a great blank where I can't follow her—a full ten years before she will remarry. Who was this Henri Gonzales? A strange name for this area. How long were they married? Why didn't the marriage work? If she had children, they would be listed on her birth certificate. Since none is mentioned, does it mean she never got pregnant, or that she did, and then decided it would be best for all concerned if the child weren't born?)

The birth certificate, the certificate of her second marriage, Monsieur Henri's letters which I kept consulting, everything I saw and heard from her people in her village—all of it gave me a tantalizing but incomplete story of her time before she ended up, to my infinite luck, as our concierge in Paris. So, although I now had some tangible documentation for her early years, she still remained an enigma. There was no way I could ever fill in all the blank spaces, no way I could ever know her fully. As I surely would have, I felt, had I grown into adulthood in France, where I could have gotten to know her as much as any grandmotherly godmother would let herself be known. At least my questions about how it was in the old days back on the farm would likely have been answered, with that selection of favorite stories old people like to tell. Now, despite all the wonders of my trip, with its qualities borrowed from the genres of the fairy tale, the quest, the detective story, and despite some wonderful new knowledge, photos, illustrated books, a full cache of memories and ideas—I would still return to my land of exile without sufficient material to write an "authoritative" biography of Madame Marie.

So then, how to write her story? Would it be more honest, as a writer friend had advised, to write a memoir of my childhood, where Madame Marie could be seen in the context I had known her?

HALF ASLEEP in the train rolling back to Paris, I hosted images from all the places seen on my trip. From Nancy: an exuberance of fanciful Art-Nouveau stained glass windows in cafés, restaurants. From Epinal: the Azur Hotel with its phantom horse-drawn public carriages unloading weary travelers eager to eat Marie's cooking. And also the museum of imagery, with its framed collection of popular eighteenth-century posters, those early one-page comic books on large sheets with crude colors, green, reds, blues, and yellows, depicting fairy tales with morals, history with morals, practical science with morals. The moral was basically always the same: the hard-working, pious, kind, and modest youth would overcome all adversity and would triumph over evil, thereby eventually also becoming rich and famous. From Vanifosse came the Chotels' tombstone in the church cemetery, and the fine-looking elderly woman who wouldn't admit to being a Chotel herself. As I became more sleepy, anarchy set in, and images came tumbling in from everywhere at once with varying degrees of completeness and clarity.

Finally, it all focused on a remembered photograph of a typical Lorraine farm from Madame Marie's days. It was so comforting to slip into the heart of the house by the coal stove, with the warm smell of cows on the other side of the wall, and to watch two kittens, an old dog, a few children all gathered around the stove smelling the hot oxtail soup about to be served to all the human folk within the hearing circle of the mother's dinner call. . . . The steam soothed and hypnotized: as in freezing weather, when you bring all clothing closer to your skin, piling up sweaters, coats, woolen scarves, woolen gloves, the better to stay warm in a hostile world, so I now felt that all around me had turned as soft as velvet and angora and I was pulling it all toward myself to keep me warm and cozy: all the human and animal smells mixed in with the steaming soup, the exterior walls and beyond, the streets with the well, the backyards with the chickens. . . . . At last I felt very warm, insulated, protected. . . . I would stay this way forever, totally safe. . . .

Odette Meyers. Photograph by Gerda S. Mathan

With my husband, Bert Meyers. Los Angeles, California. 1961
Photograph by Seymour Linden

With our children, Daniel and Anat Meyers.
Claremont, California. 1967. Photograph by Seymour Linden

With Madame Raffin. Chavagnes-en-Paillers. 1985

The reunion. In Madame Raffin's kitchen with her son,
Jacques, and with Jean's son, Yann. 1985

The tomb of Marie Chotel's grandparents. Vanifosse (Lorraine). 1985

At Pair-et-Grandrupt, the City Hall and a one-room school share this building. Since 1986, a Yad Vashem medal honoring Righteous Gentiles Marie Chotel and Henri Briard has been displayed in the entry hallway, where it is read by the townspeople and schoolchildren.

Marie Chotel

EPILOGUE

AFTER MY PILGRIMAGE to Vendée and Lorraine, I was more motivated than ever to write my childhood memoir. In its pages, Madame Marie would take her rightful seat (by the sewing machine) as my godmother whose heart offered me a warm and soothing refuge, where I could sit on her guest rocking chair and, through every crisis in my life, rock all my griefs to sleep.

In the process, though, I had to dwell in my House of Memory longer than I wished, longer than I could bear. My book depended almost solely on memories, so I had to invite them all, hold open house for them in my half-private, half-public living room. I sent out a call. Some came on their own. First among them: the good memories with happy stories to tell. Others, with darker stories, had to be coaxed, bribed, while more stubborn ones continued to hide. Those had long ago been put away for safekeeping (or forgetting)—in dusty corners of the basement, in the attic's discarded dresser's middle drawer, or elsewhere in the house, in an overstuffed closet, a bag of old toys, an album of faded photographs—I needed everyone to come, to answer the roll call, to help me do my work, but I was plagued with interruptions brought on by job, overdue bills, or depressing newspaper headlines. Those enemies of Memory caused me frequently to lose or misplace all sorts of innocent objects the outside world had put in my path: glasses, papers, books, names, airplane tickets — and while I looked for those lost objects, just-gathered memories of my past would slip, disappear and then, at the first chance, the first moment the world would turn its back on me, I'd rush to seek them out again and bring them back home.

Finally, when my manuscript was nearly done, the Holocaust Memorial Museum opened its doors to the public in Washington, D. C., April 1993. That summer, since I was on the East Coast, I went to visit the museum accompanied by two old friends.

The admirably intelligent architecture of this museum aesthetically invites its visitors without hiding its major function: to make public the most coherently presented documentation of all aspects of the Holocaust.

STANDING IN LINE, I feel apprehensive. I, who am of so little courage, shielding my eyes at the movies the instant a scene of violence begins, how will I get through three floors of a comprehensive exhibit of the most monstrous state-approved serial murder in history?

But once inside, I trust the museum and follow the crowd through a series of congested rooms. Slowly, panel by panel, with photos, text, film footage, interactive videos, period artifacts, the journey unfolds, rationally, inexorably leading us, step by step, as it did in life, to the brink of the catastrophe, at which point the power ride takes on dizzying speed, racing to crash into a ravine filled with the stench of millions of corpses — criss-crossed skeletal arms and legs interspersed by skulls with carved eye-pits. We follow and follow, room by room, remembering and relearning or suddenly at last realizing how a particular piece fits into the multimillion death puzzle.

We're caught up; we've entered into a classical Greek tragedy, knowing from the first that Fate will not stray from its awesome path, that almost all the people being rounded up in the photographs will soon be killed and we cannot stop this from happening. Yet we want to follow their every move, guess their thoughts, their feelings. We want to reclaim them as our individual and collective brothers and sisters, parents, ancestors. Though we feel small and blessed with the immense luck of having been spared death, we grow large with our desperate wish for them to get the visa, board the boat, cross the frontier, escape from the ghetto, smuggle into Palestine. We want to increase the numbers of those who escaped, who were rescued, but History will not let us. History of the Shoah is a Greek tragedy: it will stir up all our feelings yet prove all our hopes wrong. It is best experienced in a live crowd, awed by the enormity, the solemnity of the event, striving to learn something of major importance to its survival, watching every detail of every act, trying to catch the moment, the gesture, the word missed that would have, if expressed, stayed the murderous hand.

I merge with the crowd in the museum, but also with those larger crowds in which my cousins, my aunts and uncles, my grandfather, my family friends, all "disappeared" into oblivion—But I must at all times have at least one of my two friends clearly in view. I'm embarrassed to realize that, ever since we entered the museum, I've kept careful track of them.

Suddenly, the crowd is such that I can't spot either one of my friends and to my shame I'm paralyzed with panic. I can't move. I can't breathe. I won't survive the separation. My mind can't believe what my psyche feels. Luckily, the crowd has cleared enough to show the familiar back of one friend, then of the other. Again I can move, I can breathe, I can forget my shame and go on.

On with the tragedy, scene after scene leading to the mass madness that gripped our century at its half point, cutting it in two.

Ah but wait! Here is a good story at last: the Danes' rescue of their Jews! Here on display is the very boat—how small, how beautiful!—in which Jews were smuggled into the safety of Sweden. I want to touch the wood; I want to kiss this giant mezuzah!

Up on a video screen to the left is a short film showing an actual rescue episode. It runs continuously and so I stay to watch it twice before I go on. I check on my friends; they're both reasonably near by. Soon they too will get to see the holy Danish boat.

And now what is that wall over there, covered with names? It reminds me of the outdoor Vietnam War Memorial I've seen just the night before. I cried along the whole length of the black mirrored wall. But this indoor wall is white and matte. On closer look, I see it's the Wall of the Righteous Gentiles, where they are listed alphabetically, by country. I go immediately to the heading FRANCE, and instantly I read *Henri Briard* and, a few entries down, *Marie Chotel*. I can't contain my joy! I rush to my friends to come and see: "Quick, quick, come!" They rush back with me. I point to the list as to a holy scroll, toward French names starting with a B, a C . . . and then I can't help it: I shatter the reverent silence of the crowd by saying the names out loud: "Marie Chotel," "Henri Briard." My friends are thrilled. Strangers look at me in surprise. "Those are my rescuers," I proudly explain.

M A D A M E   M A R I E crossed my life into history. After she died, I sent her name to Jerusalem, to have her story recorded in "the good book" at Yad VaShem, which in turn sent her name to Washington, D.C. Along with that of Monsieur Henri and of all the others on that white wall, her name is now a protective medal for all of us, and the Wall of Righteous Gentiles who rescued Jews is a fitting end to the museum's representation of the tragedy of the Holocaust. Had there been more such people, more such names—hundreds of thousands, millions of them —the tragedy would have been curtailed, or would not have happened.

As we now approach a new century, with our deathstained suitcases heavy with ashes, what restrictions are written on our passports, what kinds of visas do we have, what will they allow us to do, and for how long, and can we even enter?

As always when I am given to doubt, Madame Marie appears to me—and I hope to you now as well. I feel that if we petition her politely, she'll put her signature on our passports and let us in through the doors of the new apartment house of the next century, telling us how to be good tenants: "Just be courteous, considerate, helpful, and enjoy yourselves! And don't forget to keep your own apartments tidy—dust and neaten every day, have food and drink to offer guests, and keep a vase of flowers on your tables."

Doors to Madame Marie

Odette Meyers. Berkeley, California. 1996
Photograph by Lynda Koolish

APPENDIX
The Melczak Family

JULY 9, 1939 was a happy day for my mother and her family. In Paris, her sister Miriam had a new daughter, Henriette, and in Buenos Aires, on the very same day, her brother David welcomed his first child, Rosita. In Warsaw, the patriarch of the family would soon receive photographs of his two newest granddaughters.

I met my Argentinian cousin Rosita for the first time in early July of 1995, when she came to Berkeley, California, for my mother's ninetieth birthday celebration. Rosita was then turning fifty-six. Lively, very pretty, she showed us pictures of her children and grandchildren, her nieces and nephews, as well as some of the many cousins we share, most still living in Argentina, some in Israel, and two in the United States. Four of my mother's brothers, including Rosita's father, migrated from Poland to Argentina in the 1920s and were therefore spared the war. The brothers worked hard in the garment trades. Their children became professionals: teachers, doctors, and psychiatrists.

Rosita and I, so glad finally to meet, struggled to communicate with each other in English mixed with Spanish, French, and Yiddish words. We filled the conversation gaps with many smiles. It was stunning to look at her and to think that our cousin Henriette would also be turning fifty-six had she not instead — and forever — turned into a picture of a little girl with curls, not quite three years old, sitting uneasily in a photographer's studio.

I wondered if our grandfather had a copy of that photograph in the Warsaw Ghetto, where he died of "extermination disease." Dead also from the same cause: four of his five daughters, nine of his ten grandchildren, and numerous other relatives then living in Nazi-occupied Europe.

Henriette had just turned three when she was deported to Auschwitz in the summer of 1942, the very summer our grandfather was expected to visit us in Paris. Third Reich fate canceled that visit.

The Melczak family had no rescuers, no protectors — neither individuals nor government — to guard them against the Final Solution to the Jewish Problem. To the Nazis and their anti-Semitic European collaborators, the problem was that Jews existed. The solution was to systematically exterminate all Jews, including the children. The Melczak family was part of that solution. The two eldest sons each sought to ally themselves with armed protest — Maurice, at eighteen, who died in battle just before his twentieth birthday, and Charles, at sixteen, who was immediately betrayed and caught, then sent to the Pithiviers detention camp, where he and his family were soon deported to Auschwitz.

But for the courage of my three rescuers — Madame Marie, Madame Raffin, and the Comte de Grandcourt — I too would have been packed into a cattle car, riding the train against my will, from France to Poland, with my mother or separated from her.

Here and now, privileged with having lived a full life, I would like to construct within these pages a memorial chapel, representative of those stone chapels, each devoted to a single family, which I so venerated in the Père Lachaise Cemetery. Above its doors, this one will bear the inscription: The Melc-zak Family. When it is complete, it will be ornamented with the memories and photographs that appear throughout the text of this book, and with the love of their family.

To build it, though, I must use what few materials I have, however painful the source. As is fitting for this kind of shelter for the dead, I must account for the death of each member of that family. Except in the case of Maurice, there are no civilian death certificates, only the deportation lists on which their names are noted, together with the dates and places of their births. Maurice's name is on the list of Jews shot by the Germans in France, and on the tombstone erected and attended by the villagers saved by his actions. And so, I describe here the convoy lists, and I include as well a note, written by my cousin Charles and thrown from the cattle train in July of 1942. Out of those wagons, a voice.

Such are the stones with which I must build. I know how the colonized Africans felt when the only language they could use to effect their liberation was the language of their colonizers. But even though I must use documentation created by the murderers of my family, my chapel is situated in a friendly, welcoming space; its doors are open to anyone. These pages are its doors.

On her Sunday outings to the Père Lachaise Cemetery, Madame Marie used to open the doors of a stranger's chapel and enter to dust, straighten a photograph, pay her respects, because she was exiled from her own family's grave in her native village. I welcome any readers who, feeling exiled from your individual or collective dead at memorials for the six million, would like to step into this chapel dedicated to the memory of one family consisting of two parents and five children. Stay a moment, then just begin to try to multiply that number until you get to six million. If it's too hard, take a break, count to seven, then try to resume your count to six million. . . .

The Convoy Lists

The fate of my five Melczak cousins and of my aunt Miriam and uncle Motl is spelled out in archival documents, now faded and crumbling, housed in the Centre de Documentation Juive Contemporaine at the Memorial du Martyr Juif Inconnu, 17 rue Geoffrey l'Asnier, Paris 4th arrondissement. These documents have been published in France and the United States, largely through the efforts of Serge Klarsfeld. I am grateful to New York University Press for permission to use material included in their 1996 publication, *French Children of the Holocaust: A Memorial*, by Serge Klarsfeld, and I would refer readers also to *Memorial to the Jews Deported from France, 1942–1944; Documentation of the deportation of the victims of the Final Solution in France*, by Serge Klarsfeld (New York: Beate Klarsfeld Foundation, 1983).

During World War II, beginning in March of 1942 and continuing until the day of liberation in August 1944, more than 75,000 Jews living in France, including 11,000 children—most of them French-born, with French first-names proudly given to them by their immigrant parents—were arrested by the French police on orders of the Vichy government and turned over to the Germans for deportation.

Only a handful of children survived the death camps. My Melczak cousins did not. From the round-up of July 16, every child perished. Sarah, Serge, and Henriette were separated from their parents and older brother at Pithiviers. They were detained briefly at Drancy and were then deported to Auschwitz in Convoy 21 on August 19, 1942. Upon arriving in Auschwitz, all the children from Convoy 21, all of them French-born, were immediately gassed.

My cousin Charles and my uncle Motl were together in Convoy 13 on July 31, but my aunt Miriam, in Convoy 16 on August 7, had none of her family with her at the end.

My cousin Maurice, born in May 1924 in Warsaw, was away on the day of the round-up. When he found out about it, he vowed to avenge his family and joined the underground Resistance fighters (the Maquisards). He died a hero's death on April 8, 1944, in a battle in the Corrèze (Brive-la-Gaillarde) against German soldiers who were aided by French militia armed with tanks and a plane. His name and the date and place of his death are documented in the Gestapo lists of Jews Shot or Summarily Executed in France (Klarsfeld 1983).

The following information on Convoys 13, 16, and 21 is based on documentation published in Klarsfeld (1983, 1996) and on my notes translated from the French edition of Klarsfeld.

Archival material related to Convoys 13 and 14 (August 3) includes these memoranda (XXVb-112), here translated from the original German:

Excerpt of a note from SS Commandant Hagen, August 1:

"Re conversation with Bousquet, secretary general of police, on July 29, 1942, regarding the Jewish question. Brought up subject of executing the agreed-upon delivery of stateless Jews from the unoccupied territory to IV J. Bousquet confirmed once more, referring to the meeting between Leguay and IV J, that 3,000 Jews, as agreed, would be handed over no later than August 10th."

Excerpt of a memo from Gestapo Chief Dannecker, August 3: Dannecker enumerates for General Oberg the issues he would take up with Laval, in particular the delivery of Jews from the unoccupied zone:

"To President Laval, who was complaining at the time of his last interview, during dinner at the "Paris, Paris" [restaurant], of the large number of Jews streaming into the unoccupied zone, we can now say that, thanks to the measures proposed above, most Jews will no longer have any desire to leave for the unoccupied zone."

CONVOY 13, JULY 31, 1942

A telex, dated July 31 and signed by Heinz Rothke, head of the anti-Jewish section of the Gestapo in France, was sent to Eichmann's office in Berlin, the Inspector of Concentration Camps in Oranienberg, and the Commandant of Auschwitz, confirming that at 6:15 a.m. a convoy of 1,049 Jews left the Pithiviers train station for Auschwitz escorted by Lieutenant Kleinschmidt.

There were 690 men and 359 women, including 131 adolescents between the ages of 15 and 20. Most were Polish and Russian by birth nationality. The list, dated and signed by the commandant of the Pithiviers camp, is organized by Pithiviers barracks, but not in alphabetical order. It must today be read with the help of a magnifying glass and includes many spelling errors, having been typed by French camp guards. Listed here are Moradko [Motl] Melsczack, born in 1896 in Mordy, Poland, and Charles Mlezak, born March 20, 1926, in Warsaw.

On their arrival in Auschwitz on August 2, the men were registered as numbers 55083 through 55775 (3 more than listed) and the women were assigned numbers 14156 through 14514. Archival documents relating to this convoy are dated July 23 (XXVb-91), July 27 (XXVb-95), July 29 (XXVb-103), and July 30 (XXVb-108).

In 1945 there were 13 survivors from this convoy. My uncle and my cousin were not among them.

CONVOY 16, AUGUST 7, 1942

Telexes, dated August 7, were sent to Berlin, Oranienburg, and Auschwitz, stating that at 6:45 a.m. a convoy of 1,069 internees from Pithiviers and Beaune-la-Rolande left the train station at Pithiviers for Auschwitz escorted by Staff-Sergeant Hoffman.

The list of names includes that of Marja [Miriam] Melczack,

born in 1899 in Bryzon. The convoy was composed of 198 males and 871 females. Among these were children (124 girls and 135 boys) ages 13 to 15. After their arrival in Auschwitz on August 9, only 63 of the males (those over age 18) were left alive. The 211 women who were spared received numbers 15961 through 16171; the men received numbers 57720 through 57782. The rest—almost 800 people, including all the children—were immediately gassed. Archival documents relating to this convoy include (XXVb-120) and (XLIX-36).

In 1945 there were 7 survivors from this convoy. My aunt was not among them.

CONVOY 21, AUGUST 19, 1942

The usual telexes, signed by Rothke, were sent to Berlin, Oranienburg, and Auschwitz, stating that a convoy of 1,000 Jews left on this date from the Bourget/Drancy train station for Auschwitz, escorted by Sergeant-Major Weise.

Deportees in this group were from 4 separate French detention camps and were listed accordingly on 4 sublists. The 487 who had been transferred from Pithiviers to Drancy were apparently loaded randomly onto the 20-car cattle train, along with others from different camps. Car 2 held 7 adults and 51 children from the Pithiviers list, including the three Mleczack [Melczak] children: Sarah, born in Paris on April 6, 1928; Serge, born September 29, 1929; and Henriette, born July 9, 1939.

The lists show that a number of brothers and sisters were together, traveling in the same car, and sometimes their mother or father was with them. This renders all the more stark those records showing separation from family. Car 4 lists only one child from the Pithiviers camp, traveling alone—Robert Goldberg, three years old.

Upon their arrival at Auschwitz, 138 men were given numbers 60471 through 60609. Forty-five women were given numbers 17875 through 17919. The other 817 people, including all the children, were immediately gassed. All of these children were of French nationality.

In 1945 there were 5 survivors from this convoy. Not one of my younger Melczak cousins was among them.

A Note from Charles Melczak

Dear Aunt Berthe

I arrived at Pithiviers where I found the whole family. But unfortunately I had to go away again and I am at present in a cattle train with Dad and hundreds of men and women; we think that our first stop will be Metz. Mom is in Pithievers [sic] with the children. She has written you several letters but as of today the 30th [July] she has not yet received any letter or package from you. We are sure that you have done everything necessary because the food is insufficient. We now have three days' worth of food left. We hope that at least you will not be bothered [hassled]. You are the only person we have left in Paris to help your sister and the children. Have the suitcase that is at attorney Derville picked up and keep it at your place. It is possible that Mom will also be sent away, and that they [the children] will be handed over to the Red Cross to be placed with whatever remaining family they have. Aunt Brauch is still at Pithiviers with her daughter. Aside from that the morale is good and we hope it is the same with you. Take care of the correspondence with Maurice. Good bye and I'll see you soon. [My translation.]

A note from my cousin, Charles Melczak, born in Warsaw
in March 1926 and deported from Paris in July 1942. The note,
written in pencil on both sides of a half-sheet from a writing tablet,
was thrown from the cattle train on July 30, 1942.

Nous avons actuellement trois
jours de vivre. Nous espérons
qu'au moins tu ne seras pas
embêté. C'est toi seul qui
nous reste à Paris pour
aider ta sœur et les enfants.
Fait enlever la valise qui est
chez Mr Derville et garde la
chez toi. Il se peut qu'on
envoie maman aussi, et que
l'on confient à la croix rouge pour
les placer chez leur famille qui
reste. La tante Brauch est
à Pithiviers encore avec sa
fille. A part ça le moral est
bon et nous espérons qu'il en est
de même chez toi. Occupe toi
de la correspondance de Maurice
tu verras et a Bientôt

Charles's note has long been in my possession. I took it from my mother with the intention of placing it in the Paris archives during one of my trips back, but never could make myself part with it. Then I agonized, when the Washington, D.C., Holocaust Museum was built, as to whether I should place it there. And again, I couldn't part with it. So it's still with me.

It got to my mother, hand-delivered, in an envelope she destroyed because it was addressed to her in Paris. She was with the Resistance, and had to take great precautions that her whereabouts not be known to the police. French railroad workers (cheminots) were very anti-Vichy and anti-Nazi. They had a feeling something ominous was happening with their trains. And so, sidestepping the government mail service, they picked up and hand-delivered all the missives thrown out of the cattle cars. They did so through a network of trains, buses, taxis, bicycles, and foot-messengers.

We learned, years later, that my mother's parcel had been misdelivered to another Melczak family, also relatives, and was therefore never received by her sister.

On July 16, Charles had managed to escape the round-up of his family and, eventually, to reach the Spanish border and pay a *passeur* to get him to the other side where he planned, like Maurice, to join Resistance fighters. The *passeur*, however, took his money and left him stranded. Charles was caught and sent to Pithiviers, where, as he says, he found his family (minus Maurice, who was by then with the Maquisards). On July 30, Charles and his father were deported to Auschwitz.

And so, Charles's note reached my distraught mother.

Another, briefer note, written in the margin of a newspaper by her sister Miriam and also thrown from a cattle train, said: "Take good care of the children. We're being sent to Poland." And before that, a letter from Serge, which I re-read so often after the war that my mother hid it from me. In it, he asked her to send food for Henriette, who was crying all the time for her mother and for food other than the thin camp "soup." And, although short in stature, Serge was always conscious of how he dressed. So now, there was something he wanted for himself: a beret to cover his shaved head. Also, echoing Charles's note, he told of the "good news" that, if they could produce the addresses of relatives living anywhere in France, they would be released to their care. But, as my mother was painfully aware, this was no more than a trick to catch those relatives and pull them into the camp as well. (Correspondence between detention camp inmates and their endangered relatives was handled through Jewish organizations that would not give out addresses to the authorities.)

How then do you set about writing a letter (likely to be censored anyway) explaining that kind of deception to children dreaming of food, warmth, and loving care?

Heavy doors of the cattle trains would close in on the Melczak family . . .

Doors of the gas chamber would open, close, let out only smoke. . . .

Such are the materials with which my chapel is built. Add to it, though, to turn it into a sacred space, the content of every day lived by every one of that family, separately and together, and the lifelong remembrance and sorrow felt by their surviving relatives.

Now, I can dust the shelves, rearrange the photographs, put fresh flowers in glass vases . . . then close the doors.